REMOTE PILOT FAA PART 107 STUDY GUIDE IN FULL-COLOR: THE COMPLETE UAG TEST PREP WITH 3 FULL PRACTICE EXAMS

ALL-IN-ONE PREP BOOK INCLUDES:

FULL SUMMARIZATION OF ALL SECTIONS

FULL-COLOR SECTIONAL CHARTS & DIAGRAMS

300+ PRACTICE QUESTIONS

BOLTON ☘ PREP

Copyright © 2026 by Foundry Direct LLC

ALL RIGHTS RESERVED. By purchase of this book, you have been licensed one copy for personal use only. No part of this work may be reproduced, redistributed, or used in any form or by any means without prior written permission of the publisher and copyright owner.

Foundry Direct LLC is not affiliated with or endorsed by any testing organization and does not own or claim ownership of any trademarks. All test names (and their acronyms) are trademarks of their respective owners. This preparation book is for general information and does not claim endorsement by any third party.

This publication is designed to provide accurate and authoritative information regarding the subject matter covered. It is distributed with the understanding that the publisher, authors, or editors are not engaged in rendering legal or another professional service. If legal advice or other expert assistance is required, the services of a competent professional should be sought.

Foundry Direct LLC is not legally liable for any mistakes, omissions, or inaccuracies in the content of this publication. Foundry Direct LLC does not guarantee that the user of this publication will pass the exam or achieve a level of performance. Individual performance on the exam depends on many factors, including but not limited to the level of preparation, aptitude, and individual performance on test day.

Printed in the United States of America.

TABLE OF CONTENTS

Introduction i

I. Regulations 1

Task A. General 1

Task B. Operating Rules 8

Task C. Remote Pilot Certification with an sUAS Rating 24

Task D. Waivers 27

Task E. Operations Over People 29

Task F. Remote Identification (RID) 42

Answer Key for I. Regulations 47

II. Airspace Classification & Operating Requirements 51

Task A. Airspace Classification 51

Task B. Airspace Operational Requirements 60

Answer Key for II. Airspace Classification & Operating Requirements .. 73

III. Weather 75

Task A. Sources of Weather 75

Task B. Effects of Weather on Performance 82

Answer Key for III. Weather 90

IV. Loading & Performance 91

Task A. Loading and Performance 91

Answer Key for IV. Loading & Performance 96

V. Operations 97

Task A. Radio Communications Procedures 97

Task B. Airport Operations 101

Task C. Emergency Procedures 111

Task D. Aeronautical Decision-Making 118

Task E. Physiology 123

Task F. Maintenance and Inspection Procedures 129

Answer Key for V. Operations 134

Practice Tests 137

Practice Test 1: Answer Sheet 138

Practice Test 1: Questions 139

Practice Test 1: Answer Key 152

Practice Test 2: Answer Sheet 157

Practice Test 2: Questions 158

Practice Test 2: Answer Key 172

Practice Test 3: Answer Sheet 177

Practice Test 3: Questions 178

Practice Test 3: Answer Key 192

Appendix 197

Certification Knowledge Test, Eligibility, and Test Center 197

Test-Taking Strategies 199

Test Day Rules and Materials 201

Certification Process After Passing Your Exam 202

Abbreviations and Acronyms 204

INTRODUCTION

Congratulations on taking the next step toward becoming an FAA-certified Remote Pilot. The FAA Part 107 Remote Pilot Certificate allows individuals to operate small unmanned aircraft systems for commercial purposes, including aerial photography, real estate, mapping, agriculture, public safety support, and many other professional applications.

Before earning the certificate, you must pass the FAA Unmanned Aircraft General, or UAG, knowledge exam. This exam evaluates your understanding of the rules, procedures, airspace concepts, weather information, aircraft performance considerations, and operational decision-making required to conduct safe and legal drone operations.

This study guide is designed to help you prepare for the exam in a clear, structured, and practical way. The material is organized around the FAA's official Airman Certification Standards, commonly referred to as the ACS, which define the knowledge areas and tasks applicants are expected to understand before becoming certificated remote pilots.

Throughout this guide, you will study the major subject areas tested on the exam, including:
- **Regulations**: Part 107 operating rules, remote pilot responsibilities, waivers, limitations, and accident reporting requirements.
- **Airspace**: Class B, C, D, E, and G airspace, controlled airport environments, sectional chart interpretation, and authorization requirements.
- **Weather**: Basic weather theory, aviation weather products, METARs, TAFs, and how weather conditions affect small unmanned aircraft operations.
- **Loading and Performance**: Weight, balance, density altitude, battery performance, environmental factors, and other conditions that can affect aircraft performance.
- **Operations**: Airport operations, radio communication procedures, emergency procedures, crew management, risk management, and aeronautical decision-making.

Each chapter is designed to build your knowledge step by step. Key concepts are explained in plain language, followed by review questions that help reinforce what you have learned. At the end of the guide, you will find three full-length, 60-question practice exams to help become comfortable with the style and structure of exam questions.

This book is based on official FAA materials and is intended to help you study efficiently, understand the reasoning behind the rules, and apply that knowledge to real-world remote pilot operations. Use this guide carefully, work through the practice questions, review any areas where you feel uncertain, and approach the exam with confidence.

I. REGULATIONS

TASK A. GENERAL

Applicability of 14 CFR Part 107

Title 14 of the Code of Federal Regulations (14 CFR Part 107), is the primary set of federal rules governing the operation of most civil small unmanned aircraft systems (sUAS) within the U.S. National Airspace System (NAS). It establishes requirements for drone registration, remote pilot certification, and the operational limitations that apply to commercial and other non-recreational sUAS operations.

However, Part 107 does not apply to certain specific types of operations. Understanding these exceptions is important for determining which rules govern a particular flight.

> **Important Concept:** Scope of Part 107
> If you are flying a drone that weighs less than 55 pounds for any purpose other than pure recreation, you are almost certainly operating under Part 107.

Part 107 does not apply to:
- Limited recreational operations (which are governed by 49 U.S.C. § 44809)
- Operations conducted outside the United States
- Amateur rockets
- Moored balloons, unmanned free balloons, and kites
- Public aircraft operations (e.g., government or law enforcement)
- Air carrier operations

Key Definitions for Part 107

Understanding the specific terminology used in Part 107 is essential for correctly interpreting the regulations. The FAA defines several key roles, components, and concepts that form the foundation of the rules.

Key Definitions
- **Small Unmanned Aircraft (sUA):** An unmanned aircraft weighing less than 55 pounds on takeoff, including everything that is on board or attached to the aircraft.

- **Small Unmanned Aircraft System (sUAS):** The sUA itself plus all its associated elements required for safe operation, such as the control station, communication links, and components.
- **Control Station (CS):** The interface (e.g., a remote controller) used by the remote pilot or person manipulating the controls to fly the sUA.
- **Remote Pilot in Command (Remote PIC):** A person holding an FAA Remote Pilot Certificate who has the final authority and responsibility for the operation and safety of a flight conducted under Part 107.
- **Person Manipulating the Controls:** A person other than the Remote PIC who is flying the sUA under the direct supervision of the Remote PIC.
- **Visual Observer (VO):** A crewmember designated by the Remote PIC to assist in seeing and avoiding other air traffic or ground-based objects.
- **Corrective Lenses:** Standard eyeglasses or contact lenses.

Falsification, Reproduction, or Alteration of Records

Under 14 CFR §107.5, integrity in all required documentation is mandatory. The FAA prohibits any fraudulent or intentionally false statements on records and reports used to show compliance with Part 107. This includes altering or reproducing any certificate, rating, or authorization for a fraudulent purpose.

Violating this rule can lead to significant consequences, as the FAA relies on the accuracy of these documents to ensure safety in the National Airspace System.

> **Important Concept:** Integrity of Documentation
> Any act of dishonesty involving official FAA paperwork is a serious offense.

Consequences of Falsification:
- Denial of an application for a remote pilot certificate or waiver.
- Suspension or revocation of any certificate, waiver, or other authorization you already hold.
- Imposition of civil penalties (fines).

Accident Reporting

A Remote PIC is required to report an sUAS accident to the FAA within **10 calendar days** if it meets specific injury or property damage thresholds. This requirement ensures the FAA can track sUAS incidents, identify safety trends, and investigate when necessary.

FAA Reporting Thresholds:
- **Serious Injury:** Any injury to a person that is classified as Level 3 or higher on the Abbreviated Injury Scale (AIS). This includes any loss of consciousness, a broken bone, a head trauma, or a laceration that requires sutures (stitches).
- **Property Damage:** Damage to any property, other than the sUAS itself, where the cost to repair or replace the item (whichever is lower) exceeds **$500**.

> **Exam Tip:** Memorize the Reporting Triggers
> For the Part 107 exam, you must know the three key components of the FAA accident reporting rule:
> **1. Serious injury** to any person.
> 2. Property damage **greater than $500** (excluding the drone).
> 3. The report must be filed within **10 days**.

The report should be made to the appropriate FAA Regional Operations Center (ROC) or the local Flight Standards District Office (FSDO).

NTSB Reporting Distinction
Certain sUAS accidents must also be reported immediately to the National Transportation Safety Board (NTSB). The NTSB has different criteria, which include any accident involving a death, serious injury, or "substantial damage" to an unmanned aircraft with a maximum gross takeoff weight of **300 pounds or greater**. For Part 107 operators (sUAS under 55 lbs), NTSB reporting is primarily relevant in cases of serious injury or death.

Inspection, Testing, and Demonstration of Compliance

Under 14 CFR §107.7, a Remote PIC, sUAS owner, or person manipulating the controls must be able to demonstrate compliance with FAA regulations at any time during an operation. This means having required documentation available and cooperating with any authorized inspections or tests.

Documentation Requirements:
- The Remote PIC must have their **Remote Pilot Certificate** and a valid form of **identification** (e.g., driver's license, passport) in their physical possession and readily accessible while flying.

Who Can Request an Inspection?
You must present your certificate, ID, and any required records to any of the following individuals upon request:
- An authorized representative of the FAA (Administrator).

- An authorized representative of the NTSB.
- Any Federal, State, or local law enforcement officer.
- An authorized representative of the TSA.

System Inspection and Testing:
In addition to document checks, the FAA has the authority to test or inspect the sUAS, the Remote PIC, the person manipulating the controls, and the Visual Observer to ensure they are complying with Part 107 rules. A Visual Observer is a designated crewmember who assists the Remote PIC by maintaining visual line of sight and providing traffic and hazard awareness during the operation.

Operating Multiple Unmanned Aircraft

The regulation under 14 CFR §107.35 is direct and absolute: one person cannot operate more than one unmanned aircraft at the same time. This rule applies to every member of the flight crew.

The rule is designed to ensure that the crew's full attention is dedicated to a single sUAS operation, preventing the division of focus that could lead to a loss of situational awareness.
- A Remote PIC cannot command more than one sUAS simultaneously.
- A person manipulating the controls cannot fly more than one sUAS simultaneously.
- A Visual Observer cannot be responsible for watching more than one sUAS simultaneously.

Record Retention for Operations Over People

For manufacturers, designers, or modifiers of sUAS intended for operations over people (Category 2 or 3), specific record-keeping requirements apply. These rules ensure that the FAA can verify that an sUAS meets the necessary safety standards defined in its Declaration of Compliance (DOC) or Means of Compliance (MOC).

The length of time records must be kept depends on your role in the sUAS's creation.
- **Producers/Manufacturers:** Must retain supporting information for a DOC for two years after production of that sUAS model ceases.
- **Designers/Modifiers:** Must retain supporting information for a DOC for two years after submitting the DOC to the FAA.
- **MOC:** The detailed description of an MOC must be retained for as long as the MOC remains accepted by the FAA.

These records must be made available to the FAA upon request.

Remote Identification (Remote ID) Compliance

Effective since March 16, 2024, all sUAS operating in the National Airspace System must be equipped with Remote ID. This technology broadcasts identification and location information, enhancing safety and security by allowing the FAA, law enforcement, and other agencies to distinguish compliant drones from potential threats.

For sUAS that were not manufactured with built-in Remote ID (Standard Remote ID), there are two primary ways to comply with the rule.

Compliance Options for sUAS without Standard Remote ID:
1. Use a Remote ID Broadcast Module:
- This is a separate device attached to the sUAS that broadcasts the required message elements (e.g., drone's serial number, location, altitude, and takeoff point).
- The serial number of the broadcast module must be listed on the sUAS's Certificate of Aircraft Registration.
- A module can be moved between different aircraft, but the registration for each aircraft must be updated with the module's serial number before it is flown.
- Operations with a broadcast module must be conducted within VLOS.

2. Operate within an FAA-Recognized Identification Area (FRIA):
- A FRIA is a specific geographic area where sUAS without Remote ID capabilities can be legally flown.
- These areas are approved by the FAA and are typically established for educational institutions or community-based organizations.
- Operations within a FRIA must also be conducted within VLOS.

Task A. General – Practice Questions

✓ The answer key is located at the end of this chapter on Page 47

1. Which of the following operations is subject to the requirements of 14 CFR Part 107?

   A. Flying a kite to collect weather data.
   B. Operating an sUAS for a fire department under public aircraft operation rules.
   C. Using a 10-pound drone to take commercial real estate photos.

2. According to 14 CFR Part 107, who is ultimately responsible for the safe operation of the sUAS?

   A. Flying The Visual Observer.
   B. The Remote PIC.
   C. The person manipulating the controls.

3. A remote pilot intentionally falsifies a maintenance record for their sUAS. This act could be a basis for

   A. a mandatory flight review.
   B. suspension or revocation of their remote pilot certificate.
   C. a warning notice from the NTSB.

4. During an operation, an sUAS collides with a building, causing $750 worth of damage to the building's window. The drone itself is completely destroyed. When must the Remote PIC report this accident to the FAA?

   A. Within 10 calendar days.
   B. Within 24 hours.
   C. A report is not required.

5. A remote pilot is approached by a local law enforcement officer who asks to see their pilot certification. The remote pilot must

   A. refer the officer to the local FAA FSDO.
   B. only comply if an FAA inspector is also present.
   C. present their remote pilot certificate and identification for inspection.

6. According to 14 CFR Part 107, is it permissible for a single Remote PIC to operate two sUAS at the same time if they are both within visual line of sight?

   A. Yes, if a visual observer is assigned to each aircraft.
   B. No, a person may not act as a remote pilot for more than one unmanned aircraft at the same time.
   C. Yes, if the operation is conducted in a sparsely populated area.

7. A person modifies an existing sUAS and submits a Declaration of Compliance to the FAA for Category 3 operations. For what period must they retain the supporting documentation?

A. For two years after the date the Declaration of Compliance was submitted.
B. For one year after the last flight of the modified sUAS.
C. For five years from the date of the modification.

8. A remote pilot owns two drones and one Remote ID broadcast module. If the pilot moves the module from the first drone to the second, what must be done before flying the second drone?

A. The Certificate of Aircraft Registration for the second drone must be updated with the module's serial number.
B. A new pre-flight inspection checklist must be created for the drone-module combination.
C. The pilot must notify the local FSDO of the equipment change.

TASK B. OPERATING RULES

sUAS Registration and Marking

Before any operation under Part 107, a small unmanned aircraft must be registered with the FAA. The primary method for this is through the streamlined online system established by 14 CFR Part 48, which is designed for sUAS operated within the United States. Registration ensures accountability and traceability of all unmanned aircraft operating in the National Airspace System.

Registration Requirements
- **Who Must Register:** The owner of any sUAS that will be operated under Part 107 must register it. The only exception is for aircraft weighing 0.55 pounds or less that are flown exclusively for recreational purposes.
- **Eligibility:** The owner must be a U.S. citizen, a legal resident alien, or a specific type of U.S.-based corporation.
- **Minimum Age:** The person registering the sUAS must be at least 13 years of age. If the owner is younger than 13, a person who is at least 13 must register it on their behalf.
- **Where to Register:** Registration is completed online through the FAA's DroneZone website.

> **Important Concept:** Part 107 vs. Recreational Registration
> - Part 107 (Commercial): Registration is per-aircraft. Each drone gets its own unique registration number.
> - Recreational: Registration is per-owner. A recreational flyer receives one registration number that can be used on all the drones they own.

Certificate of Registration Details
- **Cost:** The fee for issuing or renewing a registration is $5.
- **Validity:** A Certificate of Aircraft Registration is valid for **3 years**.
- **Information Updates:** If any of the information provided during registration changes (e.g., address, email, or if the drone is sold or destroyed), the owner must update the information in the DroneZone system within **14 calendar days**.
- **Invalidation:** Registration becomes invalid if the aircraft is sold, destroyed, registered in a foreign country, or the owner loses their U.S. citizenship or resident alien status.

Aircraft Marking Requirements

After registering, the unique identifier (registration number) issued by the FAA must be physically displayed on the aircraft.

- **Location:** The number must be on an external surface of the sUAS.
- **Visibility:** It must be legible and maintained in a readable condition.
- **Durability:** The marking must be affixed to the aircraft in a way that ensures it will remain attached for the duration of each operation.

Condition for Safe Operation

Under 14 CFR §107.15, the Remote PIC is responsible for ensuring the sUAS is safe to fly. This is a continuous responsibility that begins before takeoff and lasts until the operation is complete.

- **Preflight Check:** Before every flight, the Remote PIC must conduct a check of the sUAS to verify that it is in a condition for safe operation. This includes inspecting the aircraft, control station, and any other necessary components.
- **Ongoing Assessment:** The duty to ensure safety does not end after takeoff. If the Remote PIC knows or has reason to know that the sUAS is no longer in a condition for safe operation, they must terminate the flight.

Medical Condition

The fitness of the flight crew is just as critical as the mechanical condition of the aircraft. Under 14 CFR §107.17, no person may act as a Remote PIC, person manipulating the controls, or Visual Observer if they have a physical or mental condition that could interfere with the safe operation of the sUAS.

While a formal FAA medical certificate is not required for a Remote Pilot Certificate, a self-assessment of fitness for flight is mandatory for all crew members.

Understanding Your Medical Responsibility

Although you do not need to visit an Aviation Medical Examiner, you are still legally prohibited from flying if you are medically unfit. This includes temporary conditions like illness, fatigue, or the effects of medication. Examples of conditions that could interfere with safe operation:

- Taking any medication that warns against operating heavy machinery.
- Illness causing symptoms like blurred vision, dizziness, or severe pain.
- A temporary or permanent loss of dexterity needed to operate the control station.

- An impairment that prevents effective communication among the crew, unless an alternative method (like sign language) is used.

Responsibility and Authority of the Remote PIC

The Remote PIC is the key figure in any Part 107 operation. As defined in 14 CFR §107.19, the Remote PIC is the final authority as to the operation of the sUAS. Their decisions regarding safety and regulatory compliance are paramount and cannot be overruled by a client, employer, or other crewmember.

Core Responsibilities of the Remote PIC:
- Must be designated before or during the flight.
- Is directly responsible for, and is the final authority as to, the operation.
- Must ensure the sUAS will pose no undue hazard to people, aircraft, or property in the event of a loss of control.
- Must ensure the entire operation complies with all applicable Part 107 regulations.
- Must have the ability to direct the sUAS to ensure compliance with all rules.

In-Flight Emergencies

Safety is the highest priority in aviation. 14 CFR §107.21 grants the Remote PIC the authority to deviate from the rules of Part 107 during an in-flight emergency.

- **Authority to Deviate:** In an emergency requiring immediate action, the Remote PIC may deviate from any Part 107 rule to the extent necessary to safely resolve the situation. For example, the PIC could fly over people or beyond visual line of sight if it is the safest course of action to avoid a mid-air collision.
- **Reporting Requirement:** After deviating from a rule during an emergency, the Remote PIC is only required to send a written report of the deviation to the FAA if requested to do so by the Administrator.

> **Exam Tip**
> The requirement to file a report after an emergency deviation is not automatic. Pay close attention to questions on the exam; a report is only mandatory if the FAA asks for one.

Hazardous Operations

14 CFR §107.23 establishes broad safety rules that prohibit operating an sUAS in a manner that creates an unnecessary risk to others.

Careless or Reckless Operation

No person may operate an sUAS in a careless or reckless manner so as to endanger the life or property of another. This is a general safety regulation that prohibits flying in a way that demonstrates a disregard for the safety of others. Examples could include flying aggressively close to people, vehicles, or buildings without a clear operational need.

Dropping Objects

A person may not allow an object to be dropped from a small unmanned aircraft in a manner that creates an undue hazard to persons or property. This rule does not prohibit dropping objects entirely. It means that if an operation involves dropping items (e.g., for agriculture, rescue, or delivery), it must be done in a way that ensures the safety of people and property on the ground. The Remote PIC is responsible for assessing the risk and ensuring the operation is safe.

Operating from a Moving Aircraft or Vehicle

14 CFR §107.25 places strict limitations on operating an sUAS from a moving platform to ensure the Remote PIC can maintain situational awareness and control.

Platform	Rule	Conditions / Restrictions
Moving Aircraft	**Prohibited**	It is never permissible to operate an sUAS from a moving airplane, helicopter, or any other type of manned aircraft.
Moving Land or Water Vehicle	**Permitted**	The operation must be conducted over a **sparsely populated area**, AND the sUAS is not transporting another person's property for compensation or hire.

Alcohol and Drugs

Part 107 incorporates the same strict rules regarding alcohol and drug use that apply to pilots of manned aircraft under 14 CFR Part 91. These regulations apply to every crewmember, including the Remote PIC, the person manipulating the controls, and the Visual Observer.

Prohibitions on Use (§91.17):
No person may act as a crewmember of an sUAS:
- Within **8 hours** after consuming any alcoholic beverage ("8 hours bottle to throttle").

- While under the influence of alcohol.
- While having a blood alcohol concentration (BAC) of **0.04%** or greater.
- While using any drug that affects their faculties in any way contrary to safety.

Testing and Enforcement:
- **Implied Consent:** As a certificate holder, you must submit to a blood or breath test upon the request of a law enforcement officer who has reason to suspect a violation.
- **FAA Request:** The FAA can also request that you furnish the results of any alcohol or drug tests taken within 4 hours of an operation.

Consequences of Violations:
Violating these rules, being convicted of a federal or state drug/alcohol statute, or refusing to submit to a test can result in severe penalties.
- **Refusal to Test:** Refusing to submit to a required alcohol test is grounds for the denial of an application for a Remote Pilot Certificate, or the suspension or revocation of a certificate you already hold.
- **Drug/Alcohol Offenses:** A conviction related to narcotic drugs, marijuana, or other controlled substances is also grounds for denial, suspension, or revocation of your certificate.

Daylight, Twilight, and Night Operations

While sUAS operations are permitted at any time of day, flying during periods of low light (civil twilight and night) requires the Remote PIC to meet specific training requirements and the sUAS to have special equipment.

Key Definitions
- **Daylight:** The period from official sunrise to official sunset.
- **Civil Twilight:** The period 30 minutes before official sunrise and 30 minutes after official sunset.
- **Night:** The period between the end of evening civil twilight and the beginning of morning civil twilight.

Requirements for Twilight and Night Operations:
To operate an sUAS during civil twilight or at night, two conditions must be met:
- **Pilot Training:** The Remote PIC must have completed the updated initial knowledge test or recurrent training after April 6, 2021, which includes questions on night operations.
- The sUAS must be equipped with anti-collision lighting that is:

- o Visible for at least **3 statute miles**.
- o Has a flash rate sufficient to avoid a collision.

The Remote PIC may reduce the intensity of the anti-collision lights if they determine it is in the interest of safety (e.g., to reduce glare), but they **may not extinguish** them.

Time of Operation	Anti-Collision Lights Required?
Daylight	No
Civil Twilight	Yes (Visible for 3 statute miles)
Night	Yes (Visible for 3 statute miles)

Visual Line of Sight (VLOS) Operations

The cornerstone of sUAS safety under Part 107 is the requirement to maintain VLOS. This rule ensures that the flight crew can see the aircraft at all times, allowing them to monitor its position, avoid other air traffic, and ensure it does not pose a hazard.

- **Who must see the aircraft:** The Remote PIC, the person manipulating the controls, and the Visual Observer (if used).
- **How they must see it:** With vision that is unaided by any device other than corrective lenses (eyeglasses or contact lenses). Binoculars, telescopes, or first-person view (FPV) cameras do not satisfy the VLOS requirement, though they can be used momentarily to enhance situational awareness.
- **Why VLOS is required:** To know the sUAS's location, determine its attitude and direction, observe the airspace for hazards, and ensure it does not endanger life or property.

> **Important Concept:** The See-and-Avoid Doctrine
> VLOS is the sUAS pilot's primary method of complying with the fundamental aviation principle of "see and avoid." At any point during the flight, either the Remote PIC or a designated Visual Observer must be able to see the aircraft and scan the surrounding airspace.

Using a Visual Observer (VO)

A Visual Observer (VO) is an optional but highly valuable crewmember who can be designated by the Remote PIC to assist with maintaining VLOS and situational awareness. While not required for a standard Part 107 operation, using a VO is a key risk mitigation strategy, especially in complex or high-traffic environments.

When a VO is used, specific requirements must be met to ensure the crew operates as a cohesive team.
- **Effective Communication:** The Remote PIC, person manipulating the controls, and the VO must maintain effective, direct communication with each other at all times. This can be achieved through speech, radio, or other reliable methods.
- **VO's Line of Sight:** The Remote PIC must ensure the VO is positioned to be able to see the sUAS and scan the surrounding airspace effectively, meeting all the standard VLOS requirements.
- **Coordination:** The entire crew must coordinate their duties, scanning the airspace for potential collision hazards and maintaining awareness of the sUAS's position through direct visual observation.

Prohibition on Carrying Hazardous Material

Under 14 CFR §107.36, a small unmanned aircraft is **prohibited from carrying hazardous material (HAZMAT)**. This is a strict limitation to prevent the risks associated with transporting dangerous goods via sUAS under Part 107.

Hazardous Material: A substance or material that the Secretary of Transportation has determined is capable of posing an unreasonable risk to health, safety, and property when transported. The official definition and list of materials are found in the Department of Transportation regulations (49 CFR 171.8).

It is important to note that the sUAS's own lithium-ion battery is not considered hazardous material in this context; the rule applies to the transportation of hazardous materials as cargo. Operations intending to carry HAZMAT, such as certain agricultural chemicals, require specific exemptions or certifications outside the scope of Part 107.

Right-of-Way Rules and See-and-Avoid

In the National Airspace System (NAS), sUAS are at the bottom of the right-of-way hierarchy. Under 14 CFR §107.37, the Remote PIC has an absolute responsibility to see and avoid other aircraft and to yield the right of way to all other airborne vehicles.

> **Important Concept:** Yield the Right of Way
> "Yielding" means the sUAS must give way to the other aircraft and is prohibited from passing over, under, or ahead of it unless well clear. The fundamental goal is to ensure the other aircraft does not need to take any evasive action. The sUAS pilot is always responsible for preventing a collision hazard.

This see-and-avoid responsibility requires the Remote PIC to be aware of the sUAS's location and flight path at all times and to actively scan the airspace for any potential conflicts.

Operations Over Human Beings

Flying an sUAS directly over people is generally prohibited under 14 CFR §107.39 due to the risk of injury from a falling aircraft. However, the rule provides specific exceptions that permit this type of operation under controlled conditions.

An sUAS may be operated over a human being ONLY if one of the following conditions is met:
- The person is **directly participating** in the operation (e.g., the Remote PIC, person manipulating controls, or Visual Observer).
- The person is located under a **covered structure** or inside a **stationary vehicle** that provides reasonable protection from a falling sUAS.
- The operation meets the specific safety requirements of one of the four operational categories defined in **14 CFR Part 107, Subpart D**. (These categories involve specific aircraft designs, weight limits, and impact energy thresholds.)

Operations in Controlled Airspace

To ensure safety and prevent conflicts with manned aircraft, sUAS operations within most classes of controlled airspace require prior authorization from Air Traffic Control (ATC).

Under 14 CFR §107.41, a remote pilot must obtain ATC authorization before operating in the following airspace classes:
- Class B
- Class C
- Class D
- The surface area of Class E airspace designated for an airport.

> **Exam Tip**
> Not all Class E airspace requires authorization. The rule specifically applies to the Class E airspace that begins at the surface around an airport (often depicted by a dashed magenta line on a sectional chart). Authorization for controlled airspace is most commonly obtained through the FAA's Low Altitude Authorization and Notification Capability (LAANC) system.

Operating in the Vicinity of Airports

Beyond the specific rules for controlled airspace, 14 CFR §107.43 establishes a general safety requirement for all sUAS operations near airports. This rule applies regardless of the airspace class, including at non-towered airports in Class G airspace.

The Rule: No person may operate an sUAS in a manner that interferes with operations and traffic patterns at any airport, heliport, or seaplane base.

This requires the Remote PIC to maintain awareness of airport operations and be prepared to land or maneuver their sUAS to stay clear of any approaching or departing aircraft.

Operating in Prohibited or Restricted Areas

The FAA designates certain areas of the NAS as Prohibited or Restricted to protect national security or to contain activities that are hazardous to non-participating aircraft (e.g., military exercises).

- **Prohibited Areas (P-###):** Flight of aircraft is **prohibited** at all times. These areas are established for security or other reasons associated with national welfare. Operating an sUAS in a Prohibited Area is not allowed.
- **Restricted Areas (R-###):** Flight is not entirely prohibited but is subject to restrictions. These areas contain invisible hazards to aircraft, such as artillery firing or aerial gunnery. To operate an sUAS within a Restricted Area, the remote pilot must have **permission from the using or controlling agency**.

Temporary Flight Restrictions (TFRs)

A Remote PIC must comply with all flight restrictions established by the FAA. Many of these are temporary and are communicated to pilots through a **Notice to Airmen (NOTAM)**. It is the PIC's responsibility to check for NOTAMs before every flight to ensure no Temporary Flight Restrictions (TFRs) are active in their planned area of operation.

Key Definitions
- **Notice to Airmen (NOTAM):** A notice containing information essential to personnel concerned with flight operations but not known far enough in advance to be publicized by other means. It concerns the establishment, condition, or change in any aeronautical facility, service, procedure, or hazard.
- **Temporary Flight Restriction (TFR):** A type of NOTAM that defines an area of airspace where air travel is limited for a specific period.

TFRs are issued for various reasons to ensure safety and security. Remote pilots must be aware of the most common types:
- **Disaster/Hazard Areas:** Issued over locations like wildfires, hurricanes, or chemical spills to protect persons and property on the surface and to provide a safe environment for disaster relief aircraft. No sUAS may operate within this area unless participating in the official relief activities.
- **Presidential and VIP Movement:** TFRs are established to protect the President, Vice President, and other public figures. Flight is strictly prohibited in these areas.
- **Major Sporting Events:** The FAA routinely issues TFRs over major sporting events like NFL games, MLB games, and major college football games. These TFRs typically restrict flight within a **3 nautical mile radius** of the stadium, up to **3,000 feet AGL**, starting one hour before the event and ending one hour after.
- **Aerial Demonstrations:** TFRs are established for airshows (e.g., Blue Angels, Thunderbirds) to ensure the safety of spectators and participants.

> **Exam Tip**
> Always check for NOTAMs and TFRs as a standard part of your preflight planning. The FAA expects remote pilots to be aware of all airspace restrictions affecting their operation. Failure to comply with a TFR can result in significant penalties.

Preflight Assessment and Actions

Under 14 CFR §107.49, the Remote PIC must perform a thorough preflight assessment before every flight. This is a mandatory safety procedure to ensure the pilot, crew, and aircraft are ready for the specific conditions of the planned operation.

The preflight assessment must include:
1. **Operating Environment:**
   - Check **local weather conditions** (wind, visibility, precipitation).
   - Assess the **local airspace** and check for any flight restrictions (like TFRs).
   - Identify the location of **persons and property** on the surface.

- Note any other **ground hazards** (e.g., wires, towers, trees).
2. **Crew Briefing:**
    - Ensure all direct participants are briefed on operating conditions, emergency procedures, roles, and potential hazards.
3. **Aircraft System Checks:**
    - Verify that all **control links** between the control station and the sUAS are working properly.
    - Ensure there is sufficient **power** (battery life) for the entire planned operation.
    - Confirm that any attached **payload or object** is secure and does not negatively affect the aircraft's controllability.

sUAS Operating Limitations

14 CFR §107.51 establishes the standard "rules of the sky" for sUAS operations under Part 107. These limitations are designed to keep sUAS separated from manned aircraft and to ensure operations are conducted in safe weather conditions. These rules set limitations on groundspeed, altitude, visibility, and distance from clouds.

Limitation	Rule	Exception / Detail
Maximum Groundspeed	**100 mph** (87 knots)	---
Maximum Altitude	**400 feet AGL** (Above Ground Level)	When inspecting a structure, you may fly up to 400 feet *above the structure's uppermost limit*, as long as you remain within a 400-foot radius of it.
Minimum Visibility	**3 statute miles**	As observed from the location of the control station.
Cloud Clearance	**500 feet below** clouds and **2,000 feet horizontally** from clouds.	---

Automated Operations

Part 107 permits automated operations where the sUAS flies a pre-programmed route. However, the use of automation does not relieve the Remote PIC of their responsibilities.

- **Ability to Intervene:** Even during an automated flight, the Remote PIC must retain the ability to immediately take control of the aircraft. This includes being able to change its routing, alter its altitude, or command it to land to avoid a hazard or yield the right of way.
- **One Pilot, One Drone:** The use of automation does not allow a person to operate more than one sUAS at the same time.

Transportation of Property

Part 107 permits the transportation of property for compensation or hire, but this type of operation is subject to several key limitations.
- **Weight Limit:** The total weight of the sUAS, including the property being transported, must be less than **55 pounds**.
- **Intrastate Only:** The transport must occur within the boundaries of a single state.
- **VLOS Required:** The operation must be conducted within the VLOS of the remote pilot. This requirement cannot be waived for property transport operations.
- **No Moving Vehicles:** An sUAS transporting property for compensation or hire cannot be operated from a moving vehicle. This limitation also cannot be waived.

Transponder and ADS-B Out Prohibition

To prevent interference with the air traffic control system used by manned aircraft, Part 107 prohibits the use of certain electronic surveillance equipment on sUAS unless specifically authorized by the FAA.
- **Transponder:** A person may not operate an sUAS with a transponder turned on.
- **ADS-B Out:** A person may not operate an sUAS with Automatic Dependent Surveillance-Broadcast (ADS-B) Out equipment in transmit mode.

These devices broadcast an aircraft's position to ATC and other aircraft. Because sUAS operate at very low altitudes, their signals could clutter ATC radar scopes and create confusion for manned aircraft pilots. This rule does not prohibit the use of **ADS-B In** equipment, which only receives signals and can enhance situational awareness.

Task B. Operating Rules - Practice Questions

✓ The answer key is located at the end of this chapter on Page 47

9. A Certificate of Aircraft Registration issued for an sUAS under Part 107 is valid for what period of time before renewal is required?

A. 24 months.
B. 3 years.
C. For the life of the aircraft.

10. Which of the following conditions would be considered disqualifying for a remote pilot to fly?

    A. A hearing impairment that is mitigated by the use of text messaging between the pilot and VO.
    B. A severe migraine headache that impairs concentration and vision.
    C. Wearing corrective lenses (glasses or contacts) to achieve 20/20 vision.

11. During a flight, the Remote PIC notices a crack developing on one of the propellers. What action must the pilot take?

    A. Continue the flight as long as the aircraft remains controllable.
    B. Immediately notify the FAA of the equipment malfunction.
    C. Terminate the flight as the sUAS is no longer in a condition for safe operation.

12. Who is directly responsible for and the final authority as to the operation of an sUAS?

    A. The owner of the sUAS.
    B. The person manipulating the controls.
    C. The Remote PIC.

13. During an in-flight emergency, a Remote PIC deviates from Part 107 rules to ensure the safety of the operation. What must the PIC do after the flight?

    A. Submit a detailed report to the NTSB within 48 hours.
    B. Suspend all flight operations for 7 days pending an investigation.
    C. Upon request from the FAA, send a written report of the deviation.

14. According to 14 CFR Part 107, may an object be dropped from an sUAS?

    A. Yes, provided it does not create an undue hazard to persons or property.
    B. Yes, but only with a specific waiver from the FAA.
    C. No, dropping any object from an sUAS is strictly prohibited.

15. Under what condition is it permissible to operate an sUAS from a moving land vehicle?

A. The operation must take place over a sparsely populated area.
B. The vehicle must not exceed 25 miles per hour.
C. The Remote PIC must have a Visual Observer present.

16. A person may not act as a crewmember of an sUAS operation if their blood alcohol concentration is

A. 0.08% or greater.
B. 0.04% or greater.
C. detectable in any amount.

17. To operate an sUAS during civil twilight, the aircraft must be equipped with anti-collision lights that are visible for at least

A. 1 statute mile.
B. 3 statute miles.
C. 5 nautical miles.

18. A remote pilot uses binoculars to get a better view of their sUAS, which is now too far away to be seen with their naked eye. Is this operation in compliance with Part 107?

A. Yes, as long as the pilot can still determine the aircraft's attitude and direction.
B. Yes, binoculars are considered a tool for enhancing situational awareness.
C. No, vision must be unaided by any device other than corrective lenses.

19. When a Visual Observer is used, what is a critical requirement for the flight crew?

A. The VO must hold a Remote Pilot Certificate.
B. The Remote PIC, person manipulating the controls, and VO must maintain effective communication.
C. The VO must be positioned within 10 feet of the Remote PIC.

20. Which crewmember is permitted to be responsible for more than one unmanned aircraft at the same time?

A. The Remote PIC.
B. The Visual Observer.
C. None of the above.

21. What is the regulation regarding the carriage of hazardous materials by a small unmanned aircraft under Part 107?

A. It is permitted if the material is properly packaged and labeled.
   B. It is prohibited.
   C. It is allowed with a waiver from the FAA.

22. An sUAS is operating in the vicinity of a manned helicopter. Which aircraft has the right of way?

   A. The aircraft that is lower in altitude.
   B. The sUAS, if it is not flying over people.
   C. The helicopter.

23. Under which circumstance may a remote pilot operate an sUAS over a person?

   A. The person is a spectator at a sporting event.
   B. The person is inside a stationary automobile.
   C. The person has provided verbal consent to be flown over.

24. Authorization from ATC is required to operate an sUAS in which of the following airspace classes?

   A. Class G and Class E.
   B. Class B, Class C, and Class D.
   C. All airspace below 1,200 feet AGL.

25. While operating near a hospital, a remote pilot observes a medical helicopter on final approach to a rooftop heliport. The remote pilot must

   A. ensure their sUAS does not interfere with the helicopter's flight path.
   B. ascend to 400 feet AGL to remain clear of the helicopter.
   C. continue the operation as planned, as helicopters have different traffic patterns.

26. To operate an sUAS within a Restricted Area, what is required?

   A. A waiver from the FAA.
   B. Prior authorization from Air Traffic Control.
   C. Permission from the using or controlling agency.

27. A remote pilot is planning to fly in the vicinity of a major sporting event. Where should the pilot find information about any potential flight restrictions?

A. In the Aeronautical Information Manual (AIM).
B. By checking for any active Notices to Airmen (NOTAMs).
C. In the Chart Supplement U.S.

28. Which of the following is a mandatory preflight action for the Remote PIC?

    A. Ensure there is enough available power to conduct the flight for the intended operational time.
    B. Calibrate the sUAS compass before every flight.
    C. Log the planned flight time with the FAA.

29. What is the maximum legal altitude for an sUAS operation?

    A. 400 feet above the ground or, if flying over a structure, 400 feet above the structure.
    B. 1,200 feet above ground level to align with Class G airspace limits.
    C. 500 feet above ground level to match cloud clearance rules.

30. Does the use of automation allow a single Remote PIC to operate multiple sUAS simultaneously?

    A. Yes, if the flights are fully pre-programmed.
    B. No, a person may not operate more than one small unmanned aircraft at the same time.
    C. Yes, but only if a Visual Observer is assigned to each aircraft.

31. To operate an sUAS during civil twilight, what is required?

    A. A waiver for night operations from the FAA.
    B. Anti-collision lighting visible for at least 3 statute miles.
    C. Two Visual Observers to scan the airspace.

32. Unless otherwise authorized by the FAA, a person may not operate an sUAS

    A. with a transponder on.
    B. equipped with ADS-B In.
    C. using a GPS for navigation.

TASK C. REMOTE PILOT CERTIFICATION WITH AN sUAS RATING

Offenses Involving Alcohol or Drugs

Under 14 CFR §107.57, the FAA holds remote pilots to a high standard of conduct regarding alcohol and drugs. Offenses can impact your ability to obtain or keep a Remote Pilot Certificate, even if the offense was not directly related to flying an sUAS.

The FAA considers two main types of offenses as grounds for action against a pilot's certificate:
- **Drug-Related Convictions:** A conviction for violating any Federal or State statute related to the growing, processing, manufacturing, sale, possession, or transportation of narcotic drugs, marijuana, or other controlled substances.
- **Prohibited Acts:** Committing an act prohibited by aviation regulations, such as operating an sUAS within 8 hours of consuming alcohol, having a BAC of 0.04% or higher, or flying while under the influence of any drug that affects safety.

Consequences of these offenses include:
- Denial of an application for a remote pilot certificate for up to 1 year.
- Suspension or revocation of an existing remote pilot certificate.

Refusal to Submit to an Alcohol or Drug Test

As a certified airman, a remote pilot is expected to cooperate with law enforcement and the FAA regarding alcohol and drug testing. Under 14 CFR §107.59, refusing to submit to a required test is a serious offense with significant consequences for your pilot certificate.

This rule is based on the principle of "implied consent." By accepting a Remote Pilot Certificate, you consent to these tests when requested under the proper circumstances.

Refusing a test is grounds for:
- **Denial of an application** for a Remote Pilot Certificate for a period of up to 1 year after the date of refusal.
- **Suspension or revocation** of a Remote Pilot Certificate you already hold.

This applies to refusing a test requested by a law enforcement officer or refusing to furnish test results to the FAA when requested.

Eligibility Requirements for a Remote Pilot Certificate

To be eligible to earn a Remote Pilot Certificate with a small UAS rating under 14 CFR Part 107, an applicant must meet four specific requirements. These standards ensure that all certified remote pilots possess the minimum age, language proficiency, medical fitness, and aeronautical knowledge to operate safely in the National Airspace System.

The four eligibility requirements are:
- **Age:** Be at least 16 years of age.
- **Language:** Be able to read, speak, write, and understand the **English language**.
- **Physical and Mental Condition:** Be in a physical and mental condition that allows for the safe operation of an sUAS.
- **Aeronautical Knowledge:** Demonstrate aeronautical knowledge by either:
    - Passing the initial **Unmanned Aircraft General - Small (UAG) knowledge test**; or
    - For existing Part 61 pilot certificate holders (non-student pilots), completing the appropriate **online training course**.

Aeronautical Knowledge Recency

Holding a Remote Pilot Certificate is not a one-time event. To legally exercise the privileges of a Remote PIC, you must ensure your aeronautical knowledge is current. Under 14 CFR §107.65, this means you must have passed an initial knowledge test or completed recurrent training within the preceding **24 calendar months**.

This requirement ensures that remote pilots remain up-to-date with regulations and best practices, which can change over time.

> **Important Concept:** 24 Calendar Months
> The recency period runs to the end of the 24th month. For example, if you pass your recurrent training on June 10, 2026, your privileges are valid until June 30, 2028.

How to Maintain Knowledge Recency:
To remain current, a remote pilot must accomplish one of the following within the previous 24 calendar months:
- Pass the initial **Unmanned Aircraft General - Small (UAG)** knowledge test again.
- Complete the FAA's **recurrent online training course**.
- For pilots who also hold a Part 61 pilot certificate (e.g., for airplanes or helicopters), complete the specific online training designed for them.

The most common method for Part 107 pilots to maintain currency is by completing the free online recurrent training course offered by the FAA.

Task C. Remote Pilot Certification with an sUAS Rating - Practice Questions

✓ The answer key is located at the end of this chapter on Page 47

33. A conviction for the violation of a state statute relating to the possession of marijuana is grounds for

    A. a mandatory recurrent knowledge test.
    B. suspension or revocation of a remote pilot certificate.
    C. a 30-day waiting period before reapplying.

34. A remote pilot is requested by a law enforcement officer to submit to a blood alcohol test. What is a potential consequence of refusing?

    A. The pilot must surrender their sUAS to law enforcement.
    B. The pilot's remote pilot certificate may be suspended or revoked.
    C. The pilot will only be subject to state-level penalties.

35. What is the minimum age requirement to be eligible for a Remote Pilot Certificate with an sUAS rating?

    A. 16
    B. 17
    C. 18

36. A remote pilot who holds a Part 61 certificate for airplanes wants to ensure they maintain their Remote PIC privileges. In addition to the standard options, what specific pathway is available to them?

    A. Submitting their manned aircraft flight log to the FAA as proof of recent experience.
    B. They are automatically considered current as long as their Part 61 certificate is active.
    C. Completing a specific online training course designed for pilots who also hold a Part 61 certificate.

TASK D. WAIVERS

Certificate of Waiver

The FAA recognizes that some sUAS operations may require deviation from the standard rules of Part 107. A Certificate of Waiver is an official document issued by the FAA that authorizes a remote pilot to deviate from certain specific regulations, provided the applicant can demonstrate that their proposed operation can be conducted safely.

The Waiver Application Process
To obtain a waiver, a person must submit a request to the FAA through the DroneZone portal.
- **Safety Justification:** The applicant must provide a complete description of the proposed operation and a thorough justification that establishes how they will mitigate risks to ensure the flight can be conducted as safely as an operation that follows the standard rules.
- **Responsible Party:** The application must designate a "Responsible Party," who is the official holder of the waiver and is accountable for the safe conduct of the operation and compliance with the waiver's terms. This person is not required to be the Remote PIC but must have ongoing knowledge of the operations.
- **Compliance:** If a waiver is granted, the holder must comply with all conditions and limitations specified in the certificate of waiver.

Regulations Subject to Waiver

Under 14 CFR §107.205, the FAA may issue waivers for the following specific regulations:
- §107.25: Operation from a moving vehicle or aircraft.
- §107.29: Anti-collision lighting requirement for night and twilight operations.
- §107.31: VLOS aircraft operation.
- §107.33: Visual observer requirements.
- §107.35: Operation of multiple small unmanned aircraft.
- §107.39: Operation over human beings.
- §107.51: Operating limitations (maximum groundspeed, altitude, minimum visibility, and cloud clearance requirements).
- §107.145: Operations over moving vehicles.

> **Important Concept:** Limitations on Waivers
> While many rules are waiverable, there are critical exceptions related to the transportation of property for compensation or hire. A waiver will not be issued to allow:
> - Operation from a moving vehicle or aircraft while carrying another's property for hire.
> - Beyond visual line of sight (BVLOS) operation while carrying another's property for hire.

Task D. Waivers - Practice Questions

✓ The answer key is located at the end of this chapter on Page 47

37. A remote pilot wishes to conduct a package delivery service that would require flying beyond visual line of sight (BVLOS). According to the regulations, can this operation be approved with a waiver?

    A. No, a waiver for §107.31 (VLOS) will not be issued to allow the carriage of property for compensation or hire.
    B. Yes, any regulation in Part 107 can be waived with a sufficient safety case.
    C. Yes, but only if the operation is conducted in a sparsely populated area.

38. A remote pilot has submitted a request for a Certificate of Waiver. What must their justification establish to the FAA?

    A. That the proposed operation can be safely conducted under the terms of the waiver.
    B. That the operation has a significant economic benefit.
    C. That the current regulation is outdated for their specific model of sUAS.

TASK E. OPERATIONS OVER PEOPLE

Remote Pilot Responsibilities for Operations Over People

When conducting operations over people, the Remote PIC assumes additional responsibilities beyond the standard preflight checks. The primary duty is to ensure the flight is conducted using an sUAS that is eligible for the intended category of operation.

The Remote PIC is responsible for:
Determining the correct operational category (1, 2, 3, or 4) for the planned flight.
Verifying that the sUAS is properly listed on an FAA-accepted Declaration of Compliance (DOC), if required for the category.
Visually inspecting the aircraft to ensure it has the correct category label affixed, if required.

These tasks are a mandatory part of the preflight assessment, in addition to all other requirements under §107.49.

Operations Over People at Night

The rules and categories for conducting sUAS operations over people are the same for both day and night operations. The performance-based safety requirements (e.g., weight, impact energy limits) do not change based on the time of day.

However, a remote pilot conducting an operation over people at night must still comply with all standard night operation rules under §107.29. This includes having completed the required updated training and ensuring the sUAS is equipped with anti-collision lighting visible for at least 3 statute miles. Manufacturers seeking a Declaration of Compliance for Category 2 or 3 must account for the weight of this anti-collision lighting in their safety analysis.

Categories for Operations Over People

Category 1
Category 1 provides a pathway for operating very small sUAS over people with minimal regulatory requirements. This category is based on the principle that a very light aircraft poses a low risk of injury.

Requirements for Category 1:
- **Weight:** The sUAS must weigh **0.55 pounds or less**, including everything on board or attached.

- **Construction:** The sUAS must **not contain any exposed rotating parts** that could lacerate human skin on impact.
- **Documentation:** No FAA-accepted Declaration of Compliance (DOC) is required.
- **Operations:** Sustained flight over open-air assemblies is prohibited unless the operation is compliant with Remote ID rules.

The Remote PIC is solely responsible for verifying that their sUAS meets the weight and construction requirements before every flight.

Category 2
Category 2 allows for operations over people with sUAS that weigh more than 0.55 pounds, provided they meet specific safety thresholds related to the kinetic energy they could transfer upon impact.

Requirements for Category 2:
- **Performance:** The sUAS must not cause injury to a human being equivalent to or greater than the severity of injury caused by a transfer of **11 foot-pounds of kinetic energy**. It also must not have any exposed rotating parts that could lacerate skin.
- **Documentation:** The sUAS must be listed on an **FAA-accepted Declaration of Compliance (DOC)**.
- **Marking:** The sUAS must have a **label affixed** indicating it is eligible for Category 2 operations.
- **Operations:** Sustained flight over open-air assemblies is prohibited unless the operation is compliant with Remote ID rules.

The Remote PIC must verify the aircraft's DOC status online and visually confirm the presence of the Category 2 label before flight.

Category 3
Category 3 allows for operations over people with sUAS that have a higher potential impact energy than Category 2, but it imposes significant operational restrictions to ensure safety.

Requirements for Category 3:
- **Performance:** The sUAS must not cause injury to a human being equivalent to or greater than the severity of injury caused by a transfer of 25 foot-pounds of kinetic energy. It also must not have any exposed rotating parts that could lacerate skin.
- **Documentation & Marking:** The sUAS must be listed on an **FAA-accepted DOC** and have a **Category 3 label** affixed.
- **Strict Operational Limitations:**

- The operation must be within a **closed or restricted-access** site where all people within the site have been notified.
- **OR**, if not in a closed site, the sUAS may **not maintain sustained flight over any person** unless that person is directly participating in the operation, under a covered structure, or inside a stationary vehicle.
- Operations over **open-air assemblies are prohibited**.

Category 4

Category 4 is reserved for sUAS that have been certified by the FAA in a manner similar to manned aircraft. This category requires the highest level of safety assurance.

Requirements for Category 4:

- **Certification:** The sUAS must have an **FAA-issued airworthiness certificate** under 14 CFR Part 21.
- **Operating Limitations:** The sUAS must be operated in accordance with the operating limitations specified in the FAA-approved Flight Manual.
- **Maintenance:** The aircraft must be maintained and inspected according to the manufacturer's instructions, and records of all maintenance must be kept. The owner or operator is responsible for this.
- **Operations:** Sustained flight over open-air assemblies is prohibited unless the operation is compliant with Remote ID rules.

Selecting an Operational Area

Part of the remote pilot's preflight risk assessment involves a careful evaluation of the operational area. This includes considering all factors that could affect the safety of the flight, particularly in relation to people and property on the ground.

When selecting an area, the pilot should assess:
- The location and potential movement of people, vehicles, and vessels.
- Terrain features and structures that could pose a hazard or affect flight characteristics.
- Any other conditions that could impact the safe maneuvering of the sUAS.

Minimum Distances from a Person

14 CFR Part 107 does not establish a specific, mandatory stand-off distance that an sUAS must maintain from people on the ground. Instead, the regulation places the responsibility on the Remote PIC to determine and maintain a safe distance.

To determine an appropriate stand-off distance, the pilot should evaluate several factors and be prepared to adjust the distance as conditions change.

Factors to Consider for Safe Distance:
- The sUAS's performance and maneuverability.
- Environmental conditions, especially wind and gusts.
- The density and movement of people in the operational area.
- The pilot's own familiarity and skill with the specific sUAS.
- The potential for failures and the ability to perform emergency maneuvers.

Operations Over Moving Vehicles

Part 107 permits sUAS operations over people inside moving vehicles, provided the sUAS meets the requirements for one of the four operational categories. However, the rules for these operations depend on the location.

Operations Within a Closed or Restricted-Access Site
When operating over moving vehicles within a site that is closed to public access (e.g., a movie set, construction site, or private racetrack), the rules are more permissive.
- **Notification is Key:** For Categories 1, 2, and 3, any person inside a moving vehicle within the site must be on notice that an sUAS may fly over them.
- **Category 4:** Operations are permitted as long as they are not prohibited by the operating limitations in the aircraft's FAA-approved Flight Manual.

Operations NOT Within a Closed or Restricted-Access Site
When operating in an area open to the public, the rules are more restrictive to protect unsuspecting motorists.
- **Transit Only:** For Categories 1, 2, and 3, the sUAS may briefly pass over a moving vehicle, but it **may not maintain sustained** flight over it. This allows for crossing a road but prohibits following a car down the street.
- **Category 4:** As with closed sites, operations are permitted if not prohibited by the aircraft's specific operating limitations.

Modifications to an sUAS for Operations Over People

Modifying an sUAS that has been declared eligible for Category 2 or 3 operations can render it ineligible to fly over people. The manufacturer's remote pilot operating instructions are the primary source for determining what modifications are allowed.

- **Allowed Modifications:** If a modification (e.g., replacing propellers with an approved type) is listed as permissible in the operating instructions, the sUAS remains eligible.
- **Unapproved Modifications:** Any modification not allowed by the operating instructions will render the aircraft's Declaration of Compliance (DOC) invalid for operations over people.
- **Becoming an Applicant:** A person who performs an unapproved modification and still wishes to fly over people must assume the role of an "applicant." They are then responsible for conducting the necessary safety analysis and submitting a new DOC to the FAA for the modified aircraft.

Closed and Restricted-Access Sites

A closed or restricted-access site is a location where the operator can control entry and ensure that anyone present is aware of the sUAS operation. This is a key risk mitigation strategy required for certain Category 3 operations.
- **Controlling Access:** The remote pilot is responsible for ensuring no unauthorized persons enter the site. This can be achieved with physical barriers (fences, barricades) or monitoring personnel. Natural features like cliffs or rivers can also serve as effective barriers.
- **Notification:** Everyone within the site must be on notice that an sUAS may fly over them. They should also be advised of any safety precautions to take.
- **Open-Air Assemblies:** Even on a closed site, operations over open-air assemblies (dense gatherings of people) are still prohibited for Category 3.

Remote Pilot Operating Instructions

For an sUAS to be eligible for Category 2 or 3 operations, the manufacturer or applicant must provide remote pilot operating instructions. They inform the pilot how to operate the aircraft in compliance with the rules for flying over people.
- **Content:** The instructions must provide enough detail for a pilot to understand how to configure and operate the sUAS to meet the specific category requirements. This includes information on required components, allowable modifications, and any operational limitations.
- **Availability:** The applicant can provide the instructions in any format (e.g., in the packaging, online) but must ensure they are kept up-to-date.
- **Pilot's Responsibility:** While the instructions provide guidance, the Remote PIC is ultimately responsible for ensuring the safe operation of the aircraft.

Required and Optional Components

The remote pilot operating instructions must specify the required configuration for the sUAS to meet its declared category. This includes listing any optional components or payloads that can be attached without invalidating the Declaration of Compliance (DOC). Required Components: The instructions will detail the standard, required configuration of the sUAS.

- **Optional Components:** If the manufacturer has tested and approved certain optional components (e.g., a specific alternative camera or payload), they will be listed in the instructions. Attaching a non-listed component would be considered an unapproved modification.
- **Secure Attachment:** Any permissible payload must be securely attached for the duration of the flight.

Failure to adhere to these configuration requirements will render the sUAS ineligible for its declared category of operations over people.

Applicant Responsibilities for sUAS Operations Over People

An "applicant" is any person or entity who produces, designs, or modifies an sUAS intended for operations over people under Category 2 or 3. This role comes with specific responsibilities for ensuring and declaring the safety of the aircraft.

Who is an Applicant?
- A manufacturer who **produces** an sUAS.
- A person who **designs** an sUAS.
- A person who assembles an sUAS from a **kit** or from **separate parts**.
- A person who **modifies** an existing sUAS in a way that affects its eligibility for operations over people (i.e., a modification not permitted by the original operating instructions).

Key Applicant Responsibility:
The primary duty of an applicant is to use an FAA-accepted MOC to verify that the sUAS meets the performance-based safety requirements for its intended category and then submit a **Declaration of Compliance (DOC)** to the FAA.

Declaration of Compliance (DOC)

A DOC is a formal statement submitted by an sUAS applicant (designer, producer, or modifier) to the FAA. It certifies that an sUAS meets the required performance-based safety standards for either Category 2 or Category 3 operations over people. This declaration is a prerequisite for any sUAS in these categories to be legally flown over people.

When submitting a DOC, the applicant declares that they have:
- Used an FAA-accepted MOC to demonstrate the sUAS meets the safety requirements.
- Established a process to notify owners and the FAA of any unsafe conditions that arise.
- Verified the sUA does not contain any safety defects.
- Agreed to allow the FAA to inspect facilities, records, and witness tests to verify compliance.

Remote pilots must verify that their sUAS is listed on an FAA-accepted DOC before conducting Category 2 or 3 operations. This can be checked on the FAA's public DOC website.

Maintenance for Operations Over People (Category 4)

While standard Part 107 operations do not have the stringent maintenance and record-keeping rules of manned aviation (14 CFR Parts 43 and 91), Category 4 operations are different. Because Category 4 aircraft have an FAA-issued airworthiness certificate, they are subject to specific maintenance requirements to ensure they remain safe to fly over people.
- **Part 107 Maintenance Rules Apply:** Even with an airworthiness certificate, a Category 4 sUAS operated under Part 107 follows the maintenance rules specified in Part 107, not the more complex rules of Part 43 and 91.
- **Flexibility for Dual Operations:** An owner who may want to operate the same sUAS under both Part 107 and Part 91 can elect to comply with the more stringent maintenance and record-keeping requirements of Parts 43 and 91. This makes it easier to demonstrate compliance if they switch between operating rules.

Means of Compliance (MOC)

A MOC is the specific method—comprising tests, analysis, or inspections—that an applicant uses to demonstrate that their sUAS meets the safety requirements for Category 2 or

Category 3 operations. The FAA must review and formally accept an MOC before it can be used to support a Declaration of Compliance (DOC).

Key Aspects of an MOC:
- **Purpose:** To prove an sUAS does not exceed the injury severity limits (impact kinetic energy), has no exposed rotating parts that could lacerate skin, and is free of safety defects.
- **Who Can Develop an MOC:** Anyone, including an individual, a manufacturer, or a standards body (like ASTM), can develop and submit an MOC to the FAA for acceptance.
- **FAA Acceptance:** Once the FAA accepts an MOC, it becomes a standardized method that any applicant can use to certify their aircraft.
- **Ongoing Review:** The FAA continuously reviews accepted MOCs and can rescind acceptance if a method is found to be no longer valid.

Impact Kinetic Energy

For Category 2 and 3 operations, the primary safety metric is the amount of kinetic energy the sUAS would transfer to a person upon impact. The FAA has established specific thresholds for each category.
- **Category 2 Threshold:** Must not cause injury equivalent to or greater than the transfer of **11 foot-pounds (ft-lbs)** of kinetic energy.
- **Category 3 Threshold:** Must not cause injury equivalent to or greater than the transfer of **25 foot-pounds (ft-lbs)** of kinetic energy.

To provide a straightforward path for compliance, the FAA has developed a pre-accepted MOC based on a simple calculation. This MOC determines the maximum kinetic energy based on the sUAS's weight and its maximum possible impact speed, which is derived from its top forward speed and its terminal velocity in a free-fall.

The formula for kinetic energy is **$KE = 0.0155 \times w \times v^2$**, where w is the weight of the small unmanned aircraft (lbs) and v is the maximum impact speed measured in feet per second (ft/s).

> **Exam Tip**
> You are not expected to perform complex physics calculations on the exam. However, you should understand the concept that kinetic energy is a function of weight and speed. The tables provided in the source material show that for a given weight, a higher maximum speed will result in a higher kinetic energy value.

Maximum Impact Speeds (**ft/sec**) for a Given Weight and Impact Kinetic Energy Under FAA-Provided MOC

Weight (lbs)	Category 2 (11 ft-lbs)	Category 3 (25 ft-lbs)
1.0	26	40
1.5	22	33
2.0	19	28
2.5	17	25
3.0	15	23

Maximum Impact Speeds (**mph**) for a Given Weight and Impact Kinetic Energy Under FAA-Provided MOC

Weight (lbs)	Category 2 (11 ft-lbs)	Category 3 (25 ft-lbs)
1.0	18	27
1.5	15	22
2.0	13	19
2.5	11	17
3.0	10	16

Exposed Rotating Parts

A critical safety requirement for Category 1, 2, and 3 operations is that the sUAS must not have any exposed rotating parts that could lacerate human skin upon impact. This is designed to prevent cutting injuries, which can be severe even from a low-energy impact.

An MOC must demonstrate compliance with this requirement.
- **Compliance Method:** The simplest way to comply is to design the sUAS with no exposed rotating parts, such as by using ducted fans where the propellers are enclosed within the aircraft's frame.
- **Impact Considerations:** If parts are not normally exposed, testing or analysis may be needed to show they would not become exposed during a typical impact. If an impact is likely to break the frame and expose the propellers, the design would not satisfy the requirement.

Task E. Operations Over People - Practice Questions

✓ The answer key is located at the end of this chapter on Page 47

39. Prior to conducting an operation over people, what is the Remote PIC's primary responsibility regarding the aircraft's eligibility?

   A. To ensure the aircraft has a freshly charged battery.
   B. To determine the aircraft is in the appropriate category for the operation.
   C. To verify the aircraft's firmware is the latest version.

40. How do the category requirements for operating an sUAS over people change for a night operation?

   A. The sUAS must be in a more restrictive category at night.
   B. The sUAS must be at least one pound lighter to account for lights.
   C. The categories and their respective restrictions do not change.

41. To be eligible for Category 1 operations over people, a small unmanned aircraft must weigh:

   A. less than 55 pounds.
   B. more than 0.55 pounds but less than 5 pounds.
   C. 0.55 pounds or less.

42. Before conducting a Category 2 operation, the Remote PIC must verify that the sUAS:

   A. has its original propellers installed.
   B. is listed on an FAA-accepted DOC and has a Category 2 label.
   C. has an operational flight time of at least 30 minutes.

43. Which of the following is a requirement for conducting a Category 3 operation over people?

   A. The operation must take place over a closed or restricted-access site where people have been notified.
   B. The remote pilot must hold a specific Category 3 endorsement.
   C. A minimum of two Visual Observers must be used.

44. What is the primary requirement for a small unmanned aircraft to be eligible for Category 4 operations over people?

   A. It must weigh less than 10 pounds.
   B. It must have an airworthiness certificate issued by the FAA under Part 21.
   C. It must be operated by a pilot who also holds a Part 61 certificate.

45. When assessing an operational area, a remote pilot should consider:

   A. only the weather conditions at the time of flight.
   B. the location of persons and property on the surface and other ground hazards.
   C. the availability of Wi-Fi for the control station.

46. What is the minimum distance that a small unmanned aircraft must maintain from a person on the ground according to Part 107?

   A. 25 feet horizontally.
   B. 50 feet in any direction.
   C. Part 107 does not impose a specific stand-off distance.

47. A remote pilot is using a Category 2 sUAS to film a car commercial on a public road. Which of the following actions is permissible?

   A. Following the car down the road to get a tracking shot.
   B. Briefly transiting over the car to get from one side of the road to the other.
   C. Hovering over the car while it is stopped at a traffic light.

48. A remote pilot replaces the camera on their Category 2 sUAS with a new, heavier model that is not listed as an approved modification in the operating instructions. What is the status of the aircraft for operations over people?

   A. It is no longer eligible for Category 2 operations over people until a new DOC is submitted.

B. It remains eligible as long as the total weight is under 55 pounds.
C. It is automatically re-classified as a Category 3 aircraft.

49. What is a key requirement for establishing a closed- or restricted-access site for a Category 3 operation?

A. The remote pilot must ensure no inadvertent or unauthorized access to the site occurs.
B. The site must be located in Class G airspace.
C. The site must be no larger than one square mile.

50. For which categories of operations over people are remote pilot operating instructions required?

A. Category 1 only.
B. Category 2 and Category 3.
C. All four categories.

51. A remote pilot wants to attach a new payload to their Category 3 sUAS. How can they determine if this is permissible without invalidating the aircraft's eligibility?

A. By ensuring the total weight remains under 55 pounds.
B. By obtaining verbal permission from the manufacturer.
C. By checking if the payload is listed as a pre-approved optional component in the remote pilot operating instructions.

52. A person buys separate components and builds a custom sUAS with the intention of flying it over people under Category 2 rules. In this scenario, that person is considered

A. a hobbyist operator.
B. an applicant.
C. a public aircraft operator.

53. For which categories of operations over people is a Declaration of Compliance (DOC) required?

A. Category 1 only.
B. Category 2 and Category 3.
C. All four categories.

54. A remote pilot operates a Category 4 sUAS exclusively under Part 107. Are they required

to follow the maintenance regulations of 14 CFR Part 43?

   A. Yes, all aircraft with an airworthiness certificate must follow Part 43.
   B. No, the maintenance requirements of Part 107 apply.
   C. Only if the aircraft weighs more than 25 pounds.

55. What is the purpose of a Means of Compliance (MOC)?

   A. To provide a standardized flight training syllabus for remote pilots.
   B. To act as an alternative to aircraft registration for small drones.
   C. To serve as the method for showing that an sUAS meets the safety requirements for Category 2 or 3.

56. To be eligible for Category 2 operations, an sUAS must be shown not to transfer more than what amount of kinetic energy upon impact?

   A. 11 ft-lbs.
   B. 25 ft-lbs.
   C. 55 ft-lbs.

57. Which of the following sUAS designs would most likely satisfy the requirement regarding exposed rotating parts?

   A. A quadcopter with standard, open propellers.
   B. An sUAS with a ducted fan configuration, where the propellers are internal to the frame.
   C. A fixed-wing sUAS with a propeller mounted on the nose.

TASK F. REMOTE IDENTIFICATION (RID)

Standard Remote Identification

A Standard Remote ID unmanned aircraft is one that has the Remote ID broadcast capabilities built-in by the manufacturer. This integrated system broadcasts a specific set of message elements, providing situational awareness to the FAA, law enforcement, and other airspace users.

Broadcast Message Elements:
A Standard Remote ID sUAS broadcasts the location of both the aircraft and the Control Station.
- **Identity:** The sUAS serial number or a temporary session ID.
- **Control Station Location:** Latitude, longitude, and geometric altitude.
- **Aircraft Location:** Latitude, longitude, and geometric altitude.
- **Aircraft Status:** Velocity (speed and direction), a time mark, and an emergency status code.

Operational Requirements:
- The Remote ID system must be functional and broadcasting from takeoff to shutdown.
- If the system stops broadcasting during flight, the pilot must land the aircraft as **soon as practicable**.
- The aircraft's serial number must be listed on its FAA Certificate of Aircraft Registration.

Alternative Remote Identification

For sUAS that were not manufactured with Standard Remote ID, there are two alternative methods to comply with the Remote ID rule. Both of these alternative methods require the operation to be conducted entirely within the VLOS of the person manipulating the controls.

1. Remote ID Broadcast Module:
- This is a separate device attached to the sUAS. It broadcasts its own serial number and the location of the sUAS and its takeoff point (it does not broadcast the control station's location in real-time).
- The module's serial number must be listed on the sUAS's Certificate of Aircraft Registration.
- If the module stops broadcasting, the pilot must land as **soon as practicable**.

2. **FAA-Recognized Identification Area (FRIA):**
   - A FRIA is a specific geographic area where sUAS without any Remote ID equipment can be legally flown.
   - These areas are typically sponsored by educational institutions or community-based organizations.
   - The sUAS must remain within the defined boundaries of the FRIA for the entire duration of the flight.

Aeronautical Research and ADS-B Prohibition

The FAA has established specific rules regarding exemptions for aeronautical research and the use of other tracking technologies for Remote ID compliance.
- **Aeronautical Research (§89.120):** The FAA Administrator may authorize specific operations to be conducted without Remote ID if the flight is solely for the purpose of aeronautical research or to demonstrate compliance with regulations. This is a specific, limited exception not available for general Part 107 operations.
- **ADS-B Out Prohibition (§89.125):** Automatic Dependent Surveillance-Broadcast (ADS-B) Out equipment, which is used by manned aircraft to broadcast their position to air traffic control, **cannot be used** to meet the Remote ID requirements for an sUAS.

Confirmation of Identification for Foreign Aircraft

Foreign-registered civil sUAS are not registered in the FAA's system in the same way as U.S. aircraft. To operate a foreign-registered sUAS with Remote ID in the United States, the operator must first submit a **notice of identification** to the FAA.
- **Process:** The operator provides information such as their name, address, aircraft details, and country of registration to the FAA.
- **Issuance:** Upon successful submission, the FAA issues a **Confirmation of Identification**. This document is not a U.S. aircraft registration but serves as proof that the required notification has been made.
- **Requirement:** The operator must maintain the Confirmation of Identification at the control station during all operations and present it upon request to the FAA or law enforcement.

Remote ID Message Elements

The specific information broadcast by a Remote ID system differs slightly between a Standard Remote ID sUAS and a broadcast module.

Message Element	Standard Remote ID	Broadcast Module
Aircraft Serial Number / Session ID	✓	✓
Aircraft Location (Lat, Lon, Alt)	✓	✓
Aircraft Velocity	✓	✓
Time Mark	✓	✓
Control Station Location	✓	
Takeoff Location		✓
Emergency Status	✓	

> **Exam Tip**
> The key difference to remember for the test is what location data is broadcast. Standard Remote ID broadcasts the **Control Station's live location**. A Broadcast Module broadcasts the **aircraft's static takeoff location**.

Product Labeling for Remote ID

To help pilots and officials easily identify compliant equipment, manufacturers are required to label their products.

- **Standard Remote ID sUAS:** The aircraft itself must have a label that is legible, prominent, and permanently affixed, indicating that it meets the Remote ID requirements.
- **Remote ID Broadcast Module:** The module must have a label that is legible, prominent, and permanently affixed, indicating that the module meets the Remote ID requirements.

This labeling allows a remote pilot to quickly verify that the equipment they are using has been declared compliant by the manufacturer.

Task F. Remote Identification (RID) - Practice Questions

✓ The answer key is located at the end of this chapter on Page 47

58. A key feature of a Standard Remote ID unmanned aircraft is that it broadcasts the location of

   A. the aircraft only.
   B. both the aircraft and its control station.
   C. the nearest airport.

59. A remote pilot attaches a broadcast module to their non-Standard Remote ID drone. What information must be updated before flying?

   A. The pilot's contact information in the DroneZone profile.
   B. The sUAS's Certificate of Aircraft Registration must include the serial number of the broadcast module.
   C. The sUAS must be relabeled as a "Standard Remote ID" aircraft.

60. Under what circumstance may an sUAS be operated without Remote ID?

   A. If the flight is solely for aeronautical research and has been authorized by the Administrator.
   B. If the operation is for recreational use only.
   C. If the sUAS is operating in Class G airspace.

61. What must the operator of a foreign-registered sUAS obtain before operating in the United States under the Remote ID rules?

   A. A U.S. Certificate of Aircraft Registration.
   B. A temporary airworthiness certificate.
   C. A Confirmation of Identification from the FAA.

62. Which of the following message elements is broadcast by a Standard Remote ID sUAS but NOT by a broadcast module?

   A. The geometric altitude of the unmanned aircraft.
   B. The velocity of the unmanned aircraft.
   C. The location of the control station.

63. How must a manufacturer indicate that a broadcast module is compliant with Remote ID requirements?

   A. By including a statement in the user manual.
   B. By displaying a label on the module that is legible, prominent, and permanently affixed.
   C. By registering the module's serial number on a public website.

ANSWER KEY FOR I. REGULATIONS

1. C. - Commercial photography with an sUAS weighing less than 55 pounds is a civil operation that falls directly under the applicability of Part 107.
2. B. - The Remote PIC holds final authority and responsibility for the operation and safety of the sUAS flight.
3. B. - The commission of a fraudulent or intentionally false record is a basis for suspension or revocation of any certificate issued by the FAA.
4. A. - The accident must be reported to the FAA within 10 calendar days because the property damage exceeded the $500 threshold.
5. C. - A remote pilot must present their certificate and identification for inspection upon request from any federal, state, or local law enforcement officer.
6. B. - The regulations strictly prohibit a person from acting as a Remote PIC, person manipulating the controls, or visual observer for more than one unmanned aircraft at a time.
7. A. - A person who modifies a small unmanned aircraft must retain the required records for two years after submitting the Declaration of Compliance.
8. A. - The serial number of the Remote ID broadcast module must be listed on the Certificate of Aircraft Registration for the specific aircraft being operated.
9. B. - A Certificate of Aircraft Registration issued under Part 48 expires 3 years after the date of issue.
10. B. - A debilitating physical condition, such as a severe migraine, would render a remote pilot unable to safely perform their duties.
11. C. - A remote pilot may not continue a flight when they know or have reason to know the sUAS is no longer safe to operate.
12. C. - The Remote PIC is directly responsible for and is the final authority as to the operation of the sUAS.
13. C. - A written report of a deviation made during an emergency is only required if the FAA requests it.
14. A. - The regulation allows objects to be dropped as long as the operation is conducted in a manner that does not create an undue hazard.
15. A. - Operation from a moving land or water-borne vehicle is only allowed over a sparsely populated area, and provided no property is being transported for hire.
16. B. - The blood alcohol concentration limit for any sUAS crewmember is 0.04% or greater.

17. B. - For operations during civil twilight or at night, the sUAS must have anti-collision lighting visible for at least 3 statute miles.
18. C. - The VLOS requirement states that the sUAS must be visible with vision that is unaided, with the only exception being corrective lenses.
19. B. - The regulations require all crew members to maintain effective communication with each other at all times during the operation.
20. C. - No person, regardless of their crewmember role, may operate or be responsible for more than one unmanned aircraft simultaneously.
21. B. - Part 107 explicitly states that a small unmanned aircraft may not carry hazardous material.
22. C. - The small unmanned aircraft must yield the right of way to all other aircraft, including helicopters.
23. B. - A person located inside a stationary vehicle that can provide reasonable protection from a falling sUAS is one of the exceptions to the rule.
24. B. - Operations in Class B, C, and D airspace (as well as the surface area of Class E) require prior authorization from ATC.
25. A. - The regulations prohibit interfering with operations at any airport, heliport, or seaplane base.
26. C. - No person may operate in a restricted area without permission from the using or controlling agency.
27. B. - Temporary Flight Restrictions, such as those for major sporting events, are issued via Notice to Airmen (NOTAM).
28. A. - The Remote PIC must ensure the sUAS has enough power to operate safely for the duration of the intended flight.
29. A. - The standard altitude limit is 400 feet AGL, with an exception allowing flight up to 400 feet above the immediate uppermost limit of a structure.
30. B. - The one-person, one-drone rule applies to all operations, including automated ones.
31. B. - For any operation during civil twilight or at night, the sUAS must be equipped with anti-collision lighting visible for at least 3 statute miles.
32. A. - The regulations prohibit operating an sUAS with an active transponder unless specifically authorized.
33. B. - A conviction related to drugs, including marijuana, is grounds for the denial, suspension, or revocation of a remote pilot certificate.
34. B. - Refusing to submit to a test requested by a law enforcement officer is grounds for the suspension or revocation of a remote pilot certificate.

35. A. - A person must be at least 16 years of age to be eligible for a remote pilot certificate.
36. C. - The regulations provide a dedicated training option for those who are current under Part 61.
37. A. - The regulations explicitly prohibit the issuance of a VLOS waiver for operations involving the transportation of property for compensation or hire.
38. A. - The primary finding the FAA must make before issuing a waiver is that the proposed operation can be conducted safely with the provided risk mitigations.
39. B. - The remote pilot is responsible for determining that they are operating an sUAS in the appropriate category for the type of operation they will conduct.
40. C. - The categories and their respective restrictions for operations over people do not change due to conditions of night.
41. C. - Category 1 is established for small unmanned aircraft that weigh 0.55 pounds or less on takeoff.
42. B. - It is the remote pilot's responsibility to ensure that the sUAS is listed on an FAA-accepted DOC and is labeled as eligible to conduct Category 2 operations.
43. A. - Category 3 operations are only allowed over a closed/restricted-access site where people are on notice, or under other very limited conditions.
44. B. - Eligible Category 4 small unmanned aircraft must have an airworthiness certificate issued by the FAA.
45. B. - The preflight assessment must include the location of persons and property on the surface and other ground hazards.
46. C. - Part 107 does not impose a specific stand-off distance requirement from people when operating a small unmanned aircraft.
47. B. - When not in a closed-access site, an sUAS may not maintain sustained flight over a moving vehicle.
48. A. - A modification not allowed by the remote pilot operating instructions may render the small unmanned aircraft ineligible for operations over people.
49. A. - Remote pilots are responsible for ensuring no unauthorized access to the site occurs, which can be done through barriers or monitoring personnel.
50. B. - The FAA requires applicants to provide remote pilot operating instructions for a small unmanned aircraft eligible to conduct Category 2 or Category 3 operations.
51. C. - A pilot may not affix any payload to the sUAS unless it is listed in the remote pilot operating instructions.
52. B. - Someone who builds a small unmanned aircraft from separate components and parts is considered an applicant and is required to submit a DOC for Category 2 or 3

operations.
53. B. - For a small unmanned aircraft to be eligible to conduct Category 2 or 3 operations, the applicant must submit a Declaration of Compliance.
54. B. - When a remote pilot operates an sUAS with an airworthiness certificate under Part 107, the maintenance requirements of Part 107 apply, not those of Part 43.
55. C. - An MOC is a method to show that a small unmanned aircraft meets the performance-based safety requirements for operations over people.
56. A. - The impact kinetic energy threshold for Category 2 is 11 foot-pounds.
57. B. - If the propellers are internal to the unmanned aircraft, such as in a ducted fan configuration, and would not make contact with a person during a typical impact, the parts would not be considered exposed.
58. B. - A Standard Remote ID unmanned aircraft must broadcast the latitude, longitude, and geometric altitude of both the control station and the unmanned aircraft.
59. B. - The Certificate of Aircraft Registration for the sUAS must include the serial number of the Remote ID broadcast module being used.
60. A. - The regulations allow the Administrator to authorize operations without remote identification for the purpose of aeronautical research.
61. C. - A person operating a foreign-registered civil unmanned aircraft with remote identification must obtain a Confirmation of Identification from the FAA prior to operating in the U.S.
62. C. - Only a Standard Remote ID unmanned aircraft is required to broadcast the location of its control station.
63. B. - A person may not produce a remote identification broadcast module unless it displays a label indicating it meets the requirements of the part.

II. AIRSPACE CLASSIFICATION & OPERATING REQUIREMENTS

TASK A. AIRSPACE CLASSIFICATION

Airspace Authorization for sUAS Operations

Under 14 CFR §107.41, the fundamental rule for sUAS pilots is that you must receive prior authorization from Air Traffic Control (ATC) before operating in most types of controlled airspace. This is to ensure that all air traffic, both manned and unmanned, can be safely integrated.

> **Important Concept:** Controlled Airspace Authorization
> Prior ATC authorization is required for an sUAS to operate in Class B airspace, Class C airspace, Class D airspace, and the **surface area of Class E** airspace designated for an airport.

Authorization is most commonly obtained through the Low Altitude Authorization and Notification Capability (LAANC) system.

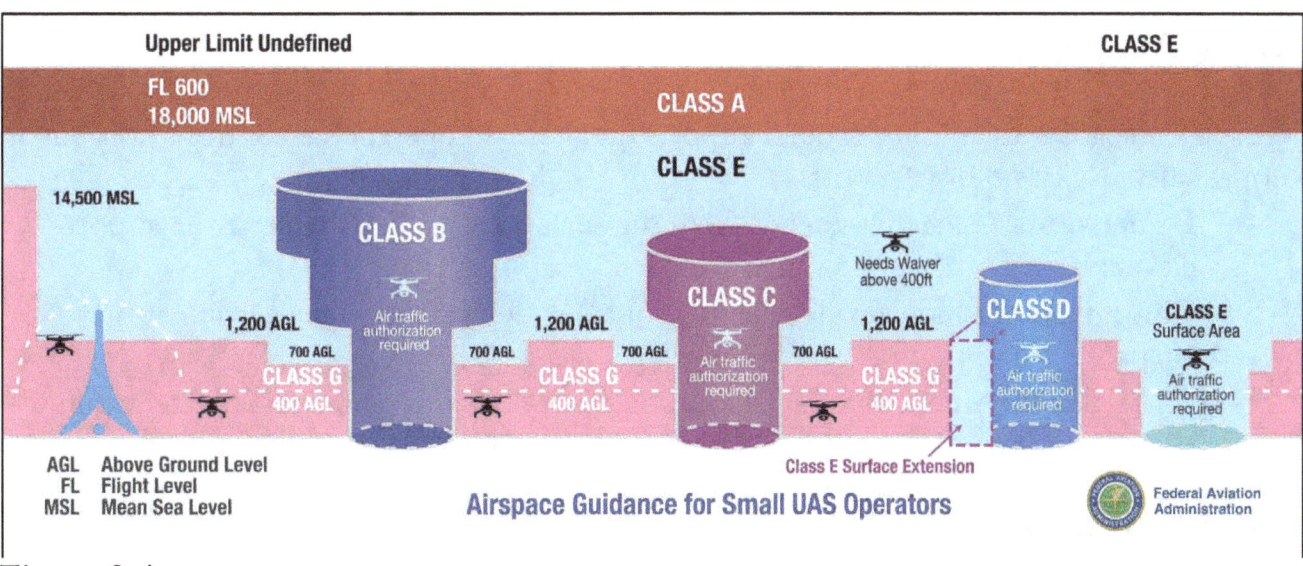

Figure 2-A.

Class B Airspace

Class B airspace is established around the nation's busiest airports. It is designed to contain all instrument procedures for aircraft arriving at and departing from these airports. Due to the high volume and complexity of traffic, it is the most restrictive type of airspace.
- **Dimensions:** Generally extends from the surface to **10,000 feet MSL**.
- **Configuration:** Individually tailored for each airport, but typically resembles an "upside-down wedding cake," with layers of airspace that increase in diameter at higher altitudes.
- **sUAS Requirement:** Prior authorization from ATC is required to operate within Class B airspace.

Class C Airspace

Class C airspace is found around airports that have an operational control tower and are serviced by radar approach control, but are less busy than Class B airports.
- **Dimensions:** Generally extends from the surface to **4,000 feet** above the airport elevation.
- **Configuration:** Usually consists of two layers:
  - A core surface area with a 5-nautical-mile radius.
  - An upper shelf area with a 10-nautical-mile radius that extends from 1,200 feet to 4,000 feet above the airport elevation.
- **sUAS Requirement:** Prior authorization from ATC is required to operate within Class C airspace.

Class D Airspace

Class D airspace is established around airports that have an operational control tower but are not as busy as Class B or C airports.
- **Dimensions**: Generally extends from the surface to **2,500 feet** above the airport elevation.
- **Configuration:** Individually tailored, but often depicted as a single cylinder of airspace.
- **sUAS Requirement:** Prior authorization from ATC is required to operate within Class D airspace.

Class E Airspace

Class E is the "catch-all" category for controlled airspace that is not designated as Class A, B, C, or D. A significant portion of the airspace over the U.S. is Class E.

- **Authorization Requirement:** For sUAS operations, ATC authorization is **only required** for the Class E airspace that begins at the surface and is designated for an airport.
- Floors of Class E: Class E airspace can begin at various altitudes:
    - The surface (requires ATC authorization for sUAS).
    - 700 feet AGL.
    - 1,200 feet AGL (the most common floor).
    - 14,500 feet MSL in areas where it is not charted lower.
- **Ceiling:** Class E typically extends up to, but not including, 18,000 feet MSL.

Class G Airspace

Class G airspace is uncontrolled airspace. It is the portion of the airspace that has not been designated as Class A, B, C, D, or E.
- **Dimensions:** Extends from the surface up to the floor of the overlying controlled airspace (which is typically Class E at either 700 or 1,200 feet AGL).
- **ATC Control:** ATC has no authority or responsibility to control air traffic in Class G airspace.
- **sUAS Requirement:** No ATC authorization is required to operate an sUAS in Class G airspace.

Special Use Airspace (SUA)

Special Use Airspace is designated for activities that must be confined or where limitations are imposed on non-participating aircraft. It's important for remote pilots to identify and understand the rules for any SUA in their operating area.

> **Exam Tip**
> For the Part 107 exam, you must know the difference between Prohibited and Restricted areas and what is required to operate in them. For other types of SUA, you should be able to identify them and understand the nature of the activity within them.

Airspace Type	Chart ID	Purpose / Activity	sUAS Operating Rule
Prohibited	P-###	Security / National Welfare	Flight is **prohibited**.

REMOTE PILOT FAA PART 107 STUDY GUIDE

Restricted	R-###	Hazardous activities (e.g., artillery, gunnery)	Flight is restricted. **Permission from the using or controlling agency is required.**
Warning	W-###	Hazardous activity over water (>3 NM offshore)	No specific permission required, but flight is hazardous. Extreme caution is advised.
Military Operation Area (MOA)	Name (e.g., "Boardman MOA")	Military training activities (e.g., aerobatics, abrupt maneuvers)	No specific permission required, but flight is hazardous. Extreme caution is advised.
Alert	A-###	High volume of pilot training or unusual aerial activity	No specific permission required. All pilots are responsible for collision avoidance.
Controlled Firing Area (CFA)	Not Charted	Hazardous activities (e.g., ordnance disposal)	Activities are suspended when non-participating aircraft approach. No specific action required by the remote pilot.

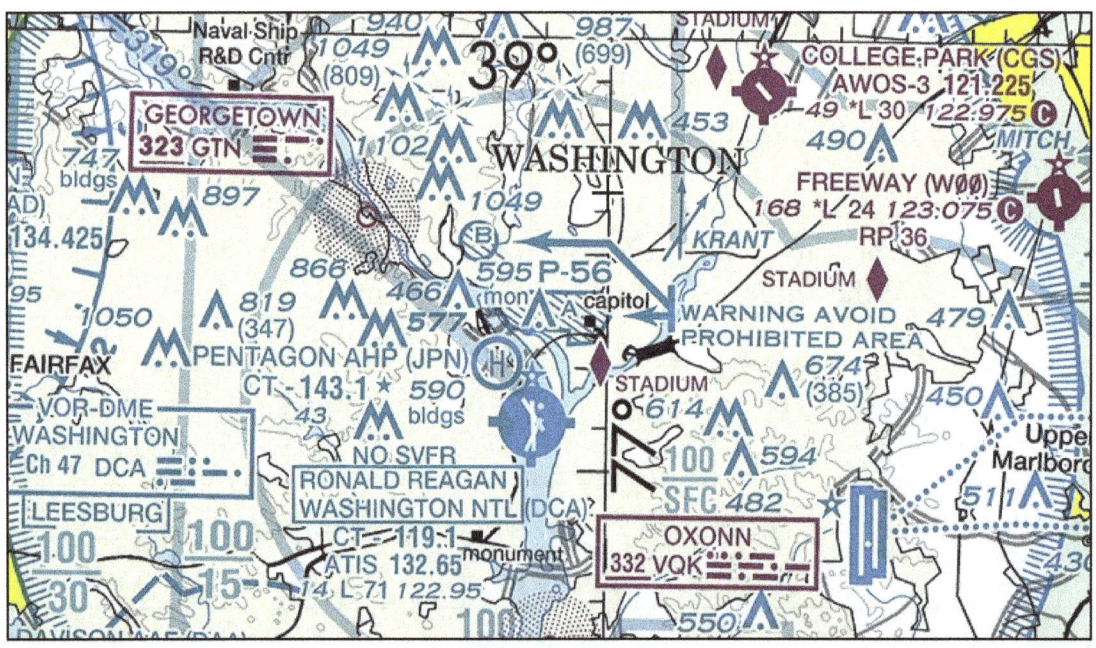

Figure 2-B. An example of a prohibited area, P-56 around Washington D.C.

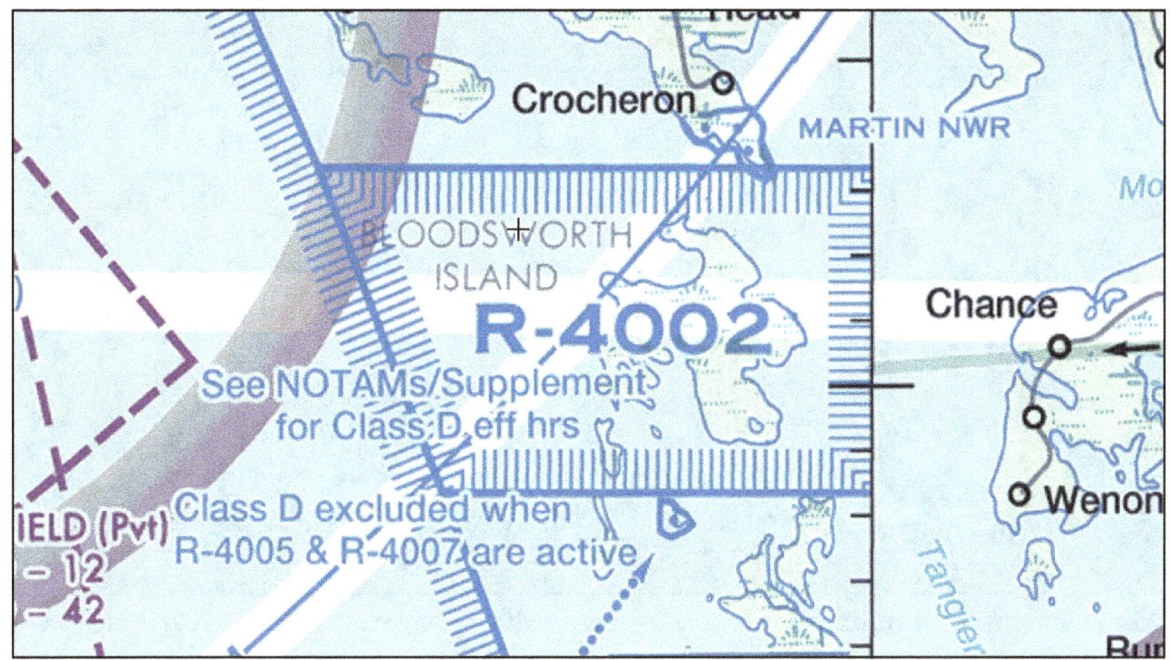

Figure 2-C. An example of a restricted area, R-4002 around Bloodsworth Island, Maryland.

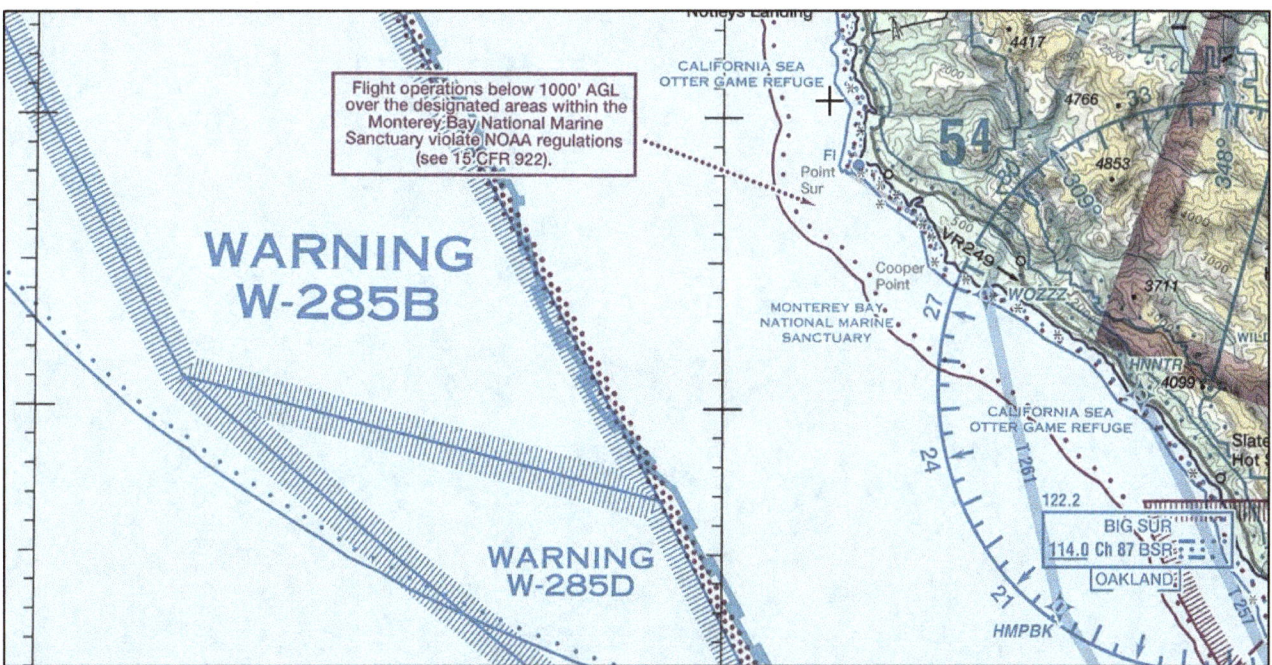

Figure 2-D. An example of a warning area, W-482B around San Francisco, California.

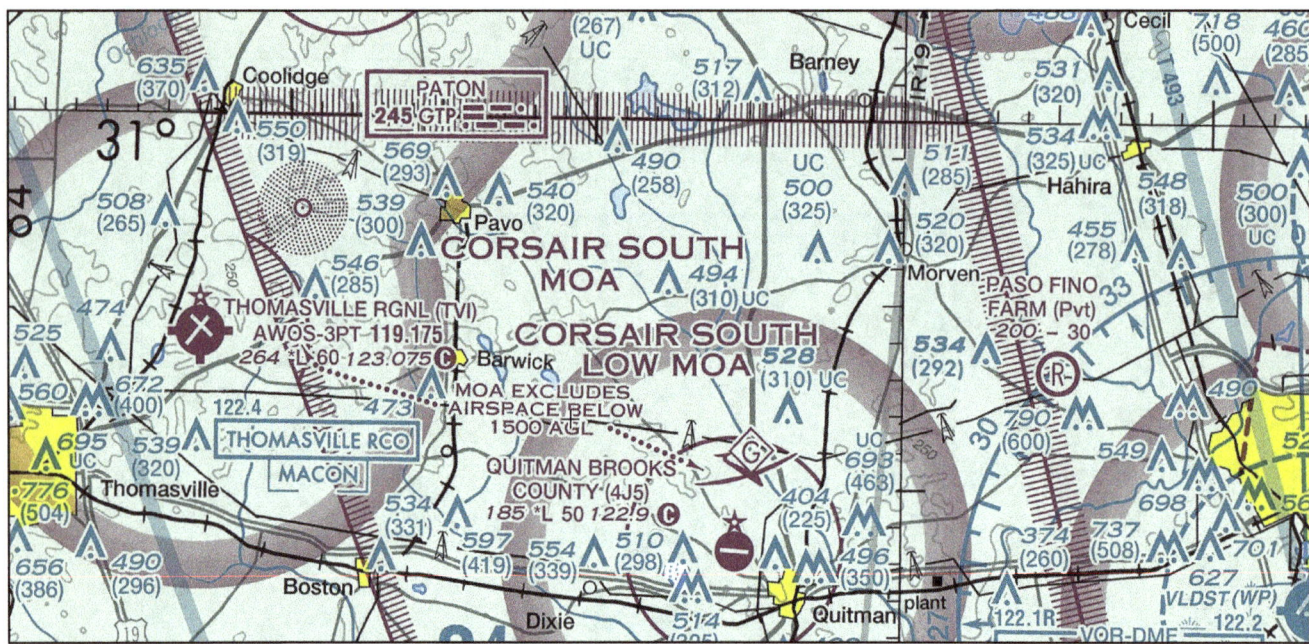

Figure 2-E. An example of military operations areas (MOA), Corsair South MOA and Corsair South Low MOA around Thomasville, Georgia.

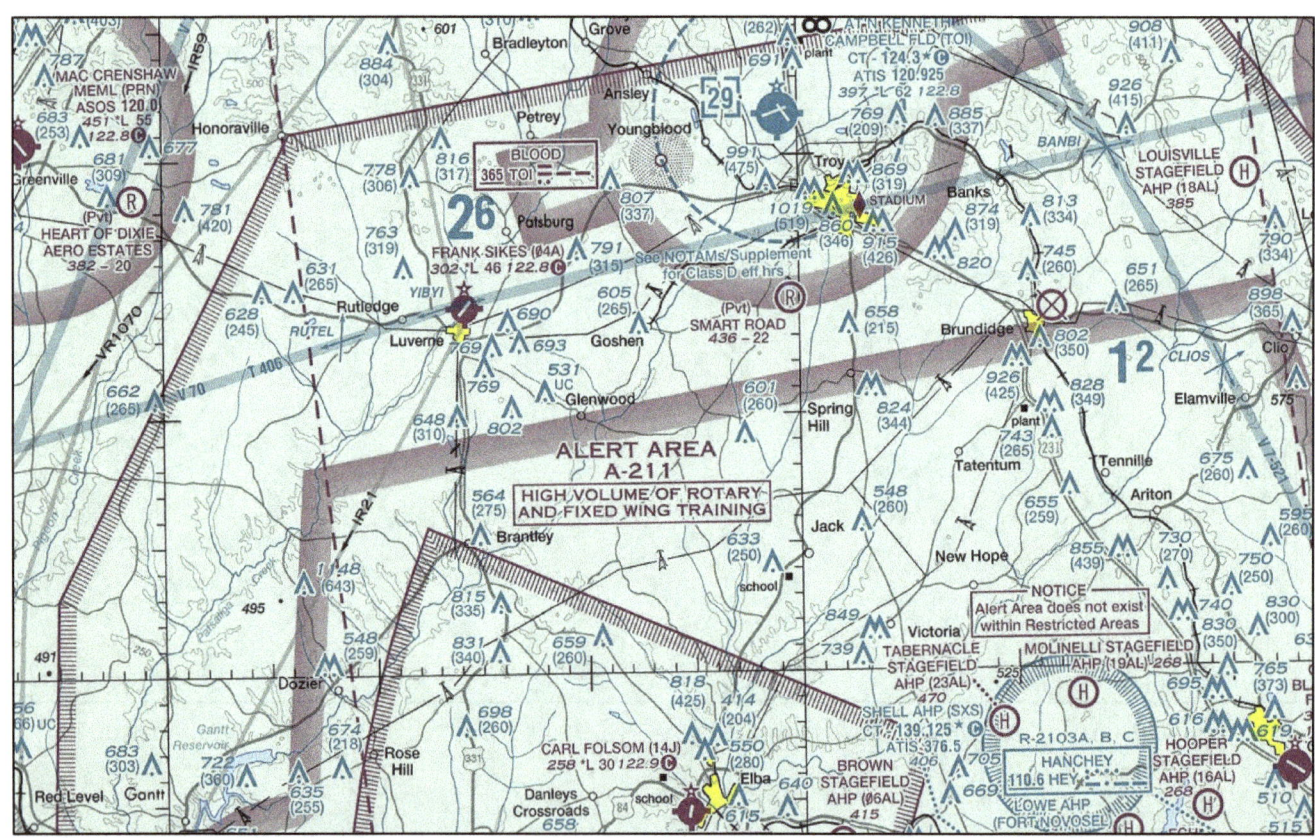

Figure 2-F. An example of an alert area, A-211 around a concentrated flight training area near Fort Rucker, Alabama.

Other Airspace Areas

Beyond the standard airspace classifications and Special Use Airspace, there are several other types of airspace areas and routes that remote pilots should be aware of.
- **Military Training Routes (MTRs):** Routes used by military aircraft for high-speed, low-altitude tactical training.
    - Identified as "IR" (IFR) or "VR" (VFR).
    - Routes with segments below 1,500 ft AGL use a four-digit number (e.g., VR1207).
    - Routes with segments above 1,500 ft AGL use a three-digit number (e.g., IR206).
    - Remote pilots should be extremely vigilant for fast-moving military traffic when operating near MTRs.
- **Temporary Flight Restrictions (TFRs):** Issued via NOTAM to temporarily restrict flight in certain areas for reasons like VIP movement, disaster relief, or major sporting events. It is the pilot's responsibility to check for TFRs before every flight.
- **National Security Areas (NSAs):** Established over locations requiring increased security (e.g., nuclear sites, government facilities). Pilots are requested to voluntarily avoid flying through NSAs. Flight may be temporarily prohibited by NOTAM.
- **Terminal Radar Service Areas (TRSAs):** Depicted with solid black lines on sectional charts. While primarily for manned aircraft, their presence indicates a higher volume of traffic around a terminal area.
- **Parachute Jump Operations:** Areas with frequent parachute jumping are depicted on sectional charts. Pilots should be alert for jump aircraft and parachutists.

Air Traffic Control (ATC) and the National Airspace System (NAS)

The primary purpose of the Air Traffic Control (ATC) system is to prevent collisions and to organize and expedite the flow of air traffic. While sUAS operators under Part 107 do not typically communicate directly with ATC via radio, they are still a part of the National Airspace System (NAS) and must comply with ATC instructions and authorizations.
- **Primary Function:** ATC's main goal is to ensure safe separation between aircraft operating within the system.
- **Authorizations:** For sUAS, the main interaction with ATC is through the process of obtaining authorization to operate in controlled airspace (Class B, C, D, and surface E) via systems like LAANC.
- **Emergency Authority:** ATC has the authority to issue instructions to any aircraft, including sUAS, to ensure safety. A remote pilot must comply with all ATC instructions.

Task A. Airspace Classification - Practice Questions

✓ The answer key is located at the end of this chapter on Page 73

1. What type of airspace is found around the nation's busiest airports, generally extending from the surface to 10,000 feet MSL?

    A. Class B.
    B. Class C.
    C. Class D.

2. Class C airspace typically consists of a core surface area and an upper shelf, and generally extends up to

    A. 10,000 feet MSL.
    B. 4,000 feet above the airport elevation.
    C. 2,500 feet above the airport elevation.

3. What are the typical dimensions of Class D airspace?

    A. Surface to 2,500 feet above the airport elevation.
    B. Surface to 4,000 feet above the airport elevation.
    C. Surface to 1,200 feet above the airport elevation.

4. Under which circumstance is a remote pilot required to obtain ATC authorization to operate in Class E airspace?

    A. When the Class E airspace begins at 700 feet AGL.
    B. When operating in any Class E airspace.
    C. When the Class E airspace is designated for an airport and begins at the surface.

5. A remote pilot is planning an operation in Class G airspace. Is ATC authorization required?

    A. Yes, authorization is always required.
    B. No, Class G is uncontrolled airspace and does not require ATC authorization.
    C. Only if the operation is within 5 miles of any airport.

6. A remote pilot is planning an operation that would enter a Restricted Area (R-4401). What

is required to conduct this flight?

   A. A waiver from the FAA.
   B. Prior authorization from Air Traffic Control.
   C. Permission from the using or controlling agency.

7. A remote pilot notices a thin gray line on their sectional chart labeled "VR1207." This indicates

   A. a published VFR route for transitioning through complex airspace.
   B. a Military Training Route where segments are below 1,500 feet AGL.
   C. a Victor airway used by IFR traffic.

8. What is the primary purpose of the Air Traffic Control (ATC) system?

   A. To prevent collisions and expedite the flow of traffic.
   B. To provide weather information to pilots.
   C. To manage airport ground operations.

TASK B. AIRSPACE OPERATIONAL REQUIREMENTS

Basic Weather Minimums

Under Part 107, the Remote PIC is responsible for ensuring that weather conditions are safe for flight. This includes adhering to specific, mandatory minimums for visibility and cloud clearance.

The standard weather minimums are:
- **Flight Visibility:** At least **3 statute miles**, as observed from the location of the control station.
- **Cloud Clearance:** The sUAS must remain at least:
    - **500 feet below** any clouds.
    - **2,000 feet horizontally** from any clouds.

The Remote PIC can use local aviation weather reports (like METARs) or other reliable means to determine these conditions before and during the flight. If the minimums cannot be met, the operation is not permitted.

ATC Authorizations and Operating Limitations

Operating an sUAS in the National Airspace System requires adherence to a standard set of operating limitations and, when necessary, obtaining authorization from Air Traffic Control (ATC).

Standard Operating Limitations (§107.51)
- **Maximum Groundspeed:** 100 mph (87 knots).
- **Maximum Altitude:** 400 feet AGL, unless operating within a 400-foot radius of a structure, in which case the sUAS may fly up to 400 feet above the structure's immediate uppermost limit.
- **Minimum Visibility:** 3 statute miles.
- **Cloud Clearance:** 500 feet below, 2,000 feet horizontally.

ATC Authorization (§107.41)
- **Requirement:** Prior authorization from ATC is required to operate in Class B, C, D, and the surface area of Class E airspace designated for an airport.
- **Basis for Approval:** The FAA approves or denies these requests based on factors like traffic density, controller workload, and the overall impact on the safety and efficiency of air traffic.

- **Method:** Authorization is typically obtained through the Low Altitude Authorization and Notification Capability (LAANC) system.

Operations Near Airports

Even when operating in uncontrolled airspace (Class G) where no ATC authorization is needed, remote pilots have a responsibility to be vigilant and courteous when flying near any airport, heliport, or seaplane base.

Under §107.43, no person may operate an sUAS in a manner that **interferes with operations and traffic patterns**.

> **Important Concept:** Interference vs. Collision
> "Interference" is a broader concept than just avoiding a collision. If the presence of an sUAS causes a manned aircraft pilot to alter their flight path, delay a takeoff or landing, or otherwise change their normal procedure, it is considered interference.

Best Practices for Operating Near Airports in Uncontrolled Airspace:
- Be aware of and avoid all traffic patterns and runway approach corridors.
- Yield the right-of-way to all manned aircraft, whether they are in the air or on the surface.
- Operate in such a way that manned aircraft pilots do not need to take any action to avoid a potential conflict.

Remaining Clear of Other Aircraft

The foundational safety principle for all pilots, including Remote Pilots in Command (Remote PICs), is to "see and avoid" other aircraft. Part 107 places the responsibility squarely on the remote pilot to yield the right of way to all other aircraft.

To satisfy this responsibility, the Remote PIC must:
- Know the location and flight path of their sUAS at all times.
- Be constantly aware of other aircraft, people, and property in the operating area.
- Maneuver the sUAS to avoid any potential collision.
- Take action early enough to ensure that pilots of manned aircraft do not need to take any evasive action.

Potential Flight Hazards

Operating an sUAS at low altitudes (below 500 feet AGL) exposes the aircraft to numerous ground-based hazards that may not be obvious or charted. Remote pilots must be extremely vigilant for these obstructions.

> **Exam Tip**
> Wires are a major hazard for low-altitude aviation. Remember that guy wires supporting towers can extend up to **1,500 feet horizontally** from the structure. The recommended safe distance is to avoid all skeletal structures by at least **2,000 feet horizontally**.

Common Low-Altitude Hazards:
- **Antenna Towers:** Tall, skeletal structures supported by nearly invisible guy wires.
- **Overhead Wires:** Power and utility lines that span rivers, canyons, and highways. They are often not marked or lighted if they are below 200 feet AGL.
- **Wind Turbines:** Large, tall structures that are often grouped in farms. While typically lit, not all turbines within a farm may have lights.
- **Meteorological (MET) Towers:** Thin, guyed towers erected for wind evaluation. They are often difficult to see and may not be marked.
- **Other Obstructions:** Temporary structures like construction cranes or new buildings may not yet be on aeronautical charts.

It is a critical part of preflight planning to check charts and NOTAMs for known obstructions and to maintain a sharp lookout for uncharted hazards during flight.

Common Aircraft Accident Causal Factors

The FAA has identified common factors that contribute to general aviation accidents. Many of these are directly applicable to sUAS operations and highlight the importance of pilot professionalism, planning, and alertness.

Top Causal Factors Relevant to sUAS Operations:
- Inadequate preflight preparation and/or planning.
- Failure to see and avoid objects or obstructions.
- Improper inflight decisions or planning.
- Misjudgment of distance and speed.
- Selection of unsuitable terrain (for takeoff, landing, or emergencies).

> **Important Concept:** Alertness
> Air collisions and accidents often happen in ideal weather conditions, possibly because clear visibility can encourage a false sense of security. Remote pilots must remain alert at all times, regardless of how good the weather is. If another aircraft appears too close, the safest action is to give way immediately rather than insisting on the right-of-way.

Avoiding Flight Beneath Unmanned Balloons

Unmanned free balloons pose a unique hazard to aircraft. Many have long suspension devices or trailing wire antennas that can extend far below the balloon itself. These subsystems are often invisible to a pilot until they are dangerously close.

- **Hazard:** The suspension lines and antennas below an unmanned balloon are difficult to see and can create a collision risk.
- **Safety Precaution:** Pilots should remain **well clear** of all unmanned free balloons and **avoid flying below them** at all times.
- **Reporting:** If you sight an unmanned free balloon, you are urged to report it to the nearest FAA facility to help ATC track its movement.

Emergency Airborne Inspection of Other Aircraft

While the AIM discusses procedures for manned aircraft assisting another aircraft in distress, this type of close-proximity flying is uniquely hazardous. It requires specialized training and a high degree of skill, especially when unplanned.

For sUAS operations under Part 107, there are no specific regulations addressing this scenario. However, given the inherent risks and the primary responsibility to yield the right of way to all manned aircraft, it is strongly recommended that Remote Pilots in Command **do not** attempt to conduct an in-flight inspection of a manned aircraft. Such an action could create a collision hazard and would likely be considered a careless or reckless operation.

Precipitation Static (P-Static)

Precipitation static, or P-static, is an electrical phenomenon that occurs when an aircraft in flight collides with uncharged particles like rain, snow, dust, or ash. This contact causes a buildup of a substantial negative electrical charge on the aircraft's skin.

If this charge cannot be safely dissipated, it can discharge from the aircraft's extremities (wingtips, antennas, propeller tips) in a phenomenon called "corona." This discharge creates radio frequency (RF) interference that can seriously degrade or cause the complete loss of communications and navigation equipment.

Symptoms of P-Static:
- Complete loss of VHF communications.
- Erroneous magnetic compass readings.
- High-pitched squeals or motor-boat sounds on audio.
- Erratic instrument readouts.
- "St. Elmo's Fire" (a visible plasma discharge) on the windshield or propellers.

While this is primarily a concern for manned aircraft with sensitive avionics, severe P-static could potentially interfere with an sUAS's control link or GPS reception.

Laser Operations

Lasers, even from miles away, can pose a serious threat to aviation safety by causing temporary vision impairment, distraction, or even permanent eye damage to pilots. The FAA prohibits the disruption of aviation activity by any person on the ground or in the air.
- **Hazard:** Unauthorized laser illumination of an aircraft can distract or blind the pilot.
- Pilot Action: Remote pilots should be aware of known laser activities (published in NOTAMs) and avoid them.
- **Reporting:** If an sUAS operation is illuminated by a laser, the event should be reported to the nearest ATC facility as soon as possible. Information to include would be the time, location, altitude, and color of the laser.

When a laser event is reported, ATC will broadcast a general caution warning to other aircraft in the area.

Avoiding Thermal Plumes

Exhaust plumes from power plants, factories, and other industrial facilities can create significant and often invisible hazards for low-flying aircraft.
- **Hazard:** These plumes consist of hot, unstable gases that can cause severe turbulence and vertical shear. Other risks include reduced visibility, engine contamination, and icing.
- **Extent:** The turbulent effects of a plume can extend more than **1,000 feet** above the top of the stack or cooling tower.
- **Risk Factors:** The hazard is most critical during low-altitude flight, especially in calm, cold air when the hot plume rises vertically with little dissipation.

Pilot Action: Remote pilots should be aware of the location of industrial facilities and avoid flying in the vicinity of their thermal plumes, particularly at low altitudes.

Flying in the Wire Environment

Wires are one of the most significant and difficult-to-see hazards for all low-altitude aviation, including sUAS operations.
- **Antenna Towers and Guy Wires:** Tall towers are often supported by guy wires that are nearly invisible. These wires can extend up to **1,500 feet horizontally** from the tower base. The recommended safety practice is to avoid all skeletal structures by at least **2,000 feet horizontally**.
- **Uncharted Obstructions:** Many towers and wires, particularly those below 200 feet AGL, are not required to be marked, lit, or depicted on aeronautical charts.
- **Constant Vigilance:** The remote pilot must remain extremely vigilant for wires at all times, as they can be present even in remote areas and may not appear on any preflight planning resources.

The NOTAM System

A **Notice to Air Missions (NOTAM)** is a time-critical alert containing essential information for flight operations. NOTAMs are issued for temporary situations or for information that is not yet published on aeronautical charts. It is a mandatory part of the Remote PIC's preflight action to obtain and review all relevant NOTAMs for their planned operational area.

Common Reasons for NOTAMs:
- Hazards such as airshows, parachute jumps, or rocket launches.
- Temporary Flight Restrictions (TFRs).
- Closed runways or taxiways.
- Inoperable navigation aids (e.g., VOR) or communication services (e.g., ATIS).
- Inoperable lights on tall obstructions.
- Military exercises resulting in airspace restrictions.

Types of NOTAMs
- **NOTAM (D):** These are the most common type of NOTAMs. They contain information about all public-use airports and navigational facilities. They are required to have a keyword at the beginning of the text, such as RWY (runway), OBST (obstruction), or AIRSPACE.

- **FDC NOTAMs:** Issued by the National Flight Data Center, these NOTAMs are regulatory in nature. They are used to issue amendments to charts, changes to procedures, and, most importantly, **Temporary Flight Restrictions (TFRs)**.

How to Obtain NOTAMs
Remote pilots can obtain NOTAMs from several sources, including:
- Calling a Flight Service Station (FSS).
- Using the FAA's PilotWeb online portal.
- Various third-party aviation websites and applications.

Interpreting NOTAMs
NOTAMs use a specific set of abbreviations and keywords to convey information concisely.

Keyword	Example	Meaning
RWY	RWY 3/21 CLSD	Runways 3 and 21 are closed.
TWY	TWY F LGTS OTS	Taxiway F lights are out of service.
OBST	OBST TOWER ... LGTS OTS	The lights on an obstruction (tower) are out of service.
COM	COM ATIS OTS	The Automatic Terminal Information Service is out of service.
AIRSPACE	AIRSPACE AIRSHOW ACFT AVOIDANCE ADZD WEF	Airspace restrictions are in effect for an airshow; avoidance is advised.

Equipment for Night Flight

Operating an sUAS outside of daylight hours requires the aircraft to be properly equipped and the pilot to be properly trained.

Key Definitions
- **Civil Twilight:** The 30-minute period immediately before sunrise and immediately after sunset.
- **Night:** The period between the end of evening civil twilight and the beginning of morning civil twilight.

Requirements for Twilight and Night Operations:
- **Pilot Training:** The Remote PIC must have completed an initial knowledge test or recurrent training that covers night operations topics, such as night physiology and visual illusions.
- **Aircraft Lighting:** The sUAS must be equipped with anti-collision lighting that is:
  - Visible for at least **3 statute miles**.
  - Has a flash rate sufficient to avoid a collision.

The Remote PIC is ultimately responsible for verifying the lights are operational and meet the visibility standard.

> **Important Concept:** Reducing Light Intensity
> The Remote PIC has the discretion to reduce the intensity of the anti-collision lights if they determine that the brightness is impairing their ability to maintain VLOS sight with the aircraft. However, the lights **may not be extinguished**.

Ground Structure Lighting

To ensure aviation safety, the FAA establishes standards for marking and lighting tall structures that could pose a hazard to aircraft.
- **When is Lighting Required?** Any structure that exceeds an overall height of **200 feet AGL** should generally be marked and/or lighted. The FAA may also recommend lighting for shorter structures if an aeronautical study determines they pose a particular hazard.
- **Guyed Structures:** Tall, skeletal towers are often supported by guy wires. These wires can extend a significant distance from the tower's base (e.g., up to 1,500-2,000 feet for a 2,000-foot tower). To avoid these nearly invisible wires, pilots should clear the tower by at least **2,000 feet horizontally**.
- **Standards:** The FAA recommends specific marking and lighting systems to provide an adequate level of safety. Commercial or decorative lighting should not be used as a substitute.

Unlit Ground Hazards

Remote pilots must be aware that many significant hazards to low-altitude flight are not marked or lighted. This is especially true for operations below 200 feet AGL.
- **The Hazard Zone:** At and below 200 feet AGL, there are numerous power lines, antenna towers, and other obstructions that are not required to be marked, lighted, or charted.

- **Common Unlit Hazards:**
  - **Overhead Wires:** Power and utility lines often do not meet the height standard (200 feet AGL) that requires them to be marked.
  - **Meteorological (MET) Towers:** These thin, temporary structures are often unlit and difficult to see.
  - **New Construction:** Temporary cranes or newly erected buildings may not yet be published on charts or in NOTAMs.

- **Pilot Responsibility:** Constant vigilance is the only defense against these hazards. The remote pilot must actively scan the operational area for uncharted and unlit obstructions.

Manned Aircraft Lighting

Manned aircraft are equipped with standard lighting to help other pilots see them at night and determine their direction of flight. This system will help a remote pilot's situational awareness.

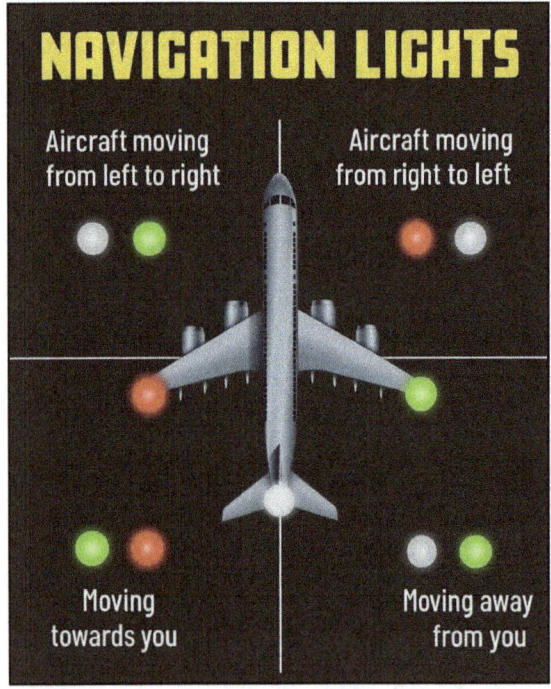

- **Position Lights:**
  - **Red Light:** On the left (port) wingtip.
  - **Green Light:** On the right (starboard) wingtip.
  - **White Light:** On the tail.
- **Anti-Collision Lights:** Flashing red or white lights, often on the top and bottom of the fuselage or on the tail.

Figure 2-I. Aircraft navigation lights diagram.

Interpreting Aircraft Direction:
You can determine an aircraft's general direction of movement by the combination of lights you see.

- **Red and Green light visible:** The aircraft is flying towards you.
- **Only White light visible:** The aircraft is flying away from you.
- **Green and White light visible:** The aircraft is moving from left to right across your field of view.
- **Red and White light visible:** The aircraft is moving from right to left across your field of view.

sUAS Lighting Requirements

The lighting requirements for sUAS are specific to operations conducted outside of daylight hours.

- **Daytime Operations:** Lighting is **not required** during the day. However, a remote pilot may choose to use lights to increase visibility.
- **Civil Twilight and Night Operations:** For any flight during civil twilight or at night, the sUAS must be equipped with anti-collision lighting that is visible for at least **3 statute miles**.
- **Remote PIC Responsibility:** Even if a manufacturer states the lights meet the standard, the Remote PIC is ultimately responsible for verifying before each flight that the lights are operational and meet the 3-statute-mile visibility requirement.
- **Dimming the Lights:** The Remote PIC may reduce the intensity of the anti-collision lights if they determine it is necessary for safety (e.g., to prevent the light from impairing their own night vision), but the lights **cannot be turned off**.

Task B. Airspace Operational Requirements - Practice Questions

✓ The answer key is located at the end of this chapter on Page 73

9. What is the minimum flight visibility required for sUAS operations?

   A. 1 statute mile.
   B. 3 statute miles.
   C. 5 statute miles.

10. Unless flown within a 400-foot radius of a structure, what is the maximum altitude a small unmanned aircraft may be operated?

    A. 400 feet AGL.
    B. 500 feet AGL.
    C. 1,200 feet AGL.

11. A remote pilot is operating in Class G airspace near a non-towered airport. A manned aircraft is on the downwind leg of the traffic pattern. What is the remote pilot's responsibility?

   A. The sUAS has the right-of-way because it is smaller.
   B. The remote pilot must ensure their sUAS does not interfere with the manned aircraft's operation.
   C. The remote pilot must announce their position on the CTAF.

12. The "see and avoid" concept requires that

   A. the remote pilot must take action to ensure other aircraft will not need to maneuver to avoid a collision.
   B. the remote pilot must be in radio communication with all aircraft in the vicinity.
   C. the sUAS must be equipped with an aircraft detection system.

13. Guy wires, which support structures like antenna towers, can extend horizontally for as much as

   A. 500 feet.
   B. 1,500 feet.
   C. 1 statute mile.

14. According to the AIM, one of the most frequent cause factors for general aviation accidents is

   A. failure to see and avoid objects or obstructions.
   B. improper operation of flight controls.
   C. using an unapproved model of aircraft.

15. What is the primary hazard associated with unmanned free balloons?

   A. They can release hazardous gases into the atmosphere.
   B. They can abruptly change direction and altitude.
   C. They often have invisible suspension devices or trailing antennas extending below them.

16. What is the recommended action for a Remote PIC if they are asked to perform an emergency airborne inspection of a manned aircraft?

A. Comply with the request, as assisting an aircraft in distress is a priority.
B. Decline the request, as close-proximity flight is hazardous and not addressed by Part 107.
C. Only perform the inspection if a Visual Observer is present.

17. Precipitation static is created when an aircraft in flight comes in contact with

A. other aircraft.
B. uncharged solid or liquid particles.
C. strong magnetic fields.

18. What is the primary hazard to pilots associated with laser illumination?

A. Electromagnetic interference with the control link.
B. Temporary vision impairment and distraction.
C. Overheating of the aircraft's camera sensor.

19. What is the primary hazard associated with flying an sUAS in the vicinity of a thermal plume from a power plant?

A. Radio frequency interference.
B. High winds and precipitation.
C. Significant air disturbances such as turbulence and vertical shear.

20. What is the recommended minimum horizontal distance a pilot should maintain from a tall, skeletal structure supported by guy wires?

A. 500 feet.
B. 1,500 feet.
C. 2,000 feet.

21. A remote pilot is checking preflight information and sees a NOTAM for their area that begins with "FDC." This type of NOTAM typically contains what kind of information?

A. Unverified aeronautical information.
B. Regulatory information, such as a Temporary Flight Restriction.
C. Changes to services, such as fuel availability.

22. To operate an sUAS at night, the aircraft must be equipped with anti-collision lighting that is visible for at least

A. 1 statute mile.
B. 3 statute miles.
C. 5 statute miles.

23. Generally, any structure that exceeds what height above ground level should be marked and/or lighted?

A. 100 feet AGL.
B. 200 feet AGL.
C. 400 feet AGL.

24. At and below what altitude are there numerous power lines, antenna towers, and other obstructions that are often not marked or lighted?

A. 200 feet AGL.
B. 400 feet AGL.
C. 500 feet AGL.

25. During a night operation, a remote pilot observes a manned aircraft with a red position light on the left and a green position light on the right. The aircraft is

A. flying towards the remote pilot.
B. flying away from the remote pilot.
C. crossing from right to left.

26. Is anti-collision lighting required for an sUAS operation conducted during the middle of the day?

A. No, lighting is not required for daytime operations.
B. Yes, all Part 107 operations require anti-collision lights.
C. Only if the flight is in controlled airspace.

ANSWER KEY FOR II. AIRSPACE CLASSIFICATION & OPERATING REQUIREMENTS

1. A. - Class B airspace surrounds the busiest airports and typically extends from the surface to 10,000 feet MSL.
2. B. - Class C airspace generally extends from the surface to 4,000 feet above the airport elevation.
3. A. - Class D airspace generally extends from the surface to 2,500 feet above the airport elevation.
4. C. - Authorization is only required for operations within the lateral boundaries of the surface area of Class E airspace designated for an airport.
5. B. - Class G is uncontrolled airspace, and ATC has no authority or responsibility to control traffic within it.
6. C. - No person may operate an sUAS in a restricted area without permission from the using or controlling agency.
7. B. - MTRs with no segment above 1,500 feet AGL are identified by four number characters.
8. A. - The primary purpose of the ATC system is to prevent a collision between aircraft operating in the system and to organize and expedite the flow of traffic.
9. B. - The minimum flight visibility, as observed from the location of the control station, must be no less than 3 statute miles.
10. A. - The altitude of the small unmanned aircraft cannot be higher than 400 feet above ground level, with a specific exception for structure inspections.
11. B. - A remote PIC is prohibited from operating an sUAS in a manner that interferes with operations and traffic patterns at any airport.
12. A. - A key part of the remote pilot's see-and-avoid responsibility is to ensure other aircraft do not need to maneuver to avoid the sUAS.
13. B. - Guy wires can extend about 1,500 feet horizontally from a structure, making them a significant hazard.
14. A. - Failure to see and avoid objects or obstructions is a leading cause of accidents and is a critical responsibility for remote pilots.
15. C. - The invisible subsystems extending below unmanned balloons create a potentially dangerous situation for other aircraft.
16. B. - Close-proximity, in-flight inspection of another aircraft is uniquely hazardous, and remote pilots should not attempt such a maneuver.

17. B. - P-static is caused by an aircraft coming in contact with uncharged particles such as rain, snow, fog, or dust.
18. B. - Illumination from laser operations can create temporary vision impairment miles from the actual location and can produce permanent eye damage.
19. C. - High temperature exhaust plumes can cause significant air disturbances such as turbulence and vertical shear.
20. C. - Because guy wires can extend up to 1,500 feet from a structure, it is recommended to avoid all skeletal structures horizontally by at least 2,000 feet.
21. B. - FDC NOTAMs are regulatory in nature and are used to issue information such as TFRs and changes to charts and procedures.
22. B. - For operations during civil twilight or at night, the small unmanned aircraft must have lighted anti-collision lighting visible for at least 3 statute miles.
23. B. - Any temporary or permanent structure that exceeds an overall height of 200 feet AGL should be marked and/or lighted.
24. A. - At and below 200 feet AGL, there are numerous obstructions that are not marked, lighted, or charted.
25. A. - Seeing both the red (left wing) and green (right wing) lights simultaneously means the aircraft is heading toward the observer.
26. A. - The regulations do not require small unmanned aircraft operating during the day to have illuminated anti-collision lighting.

III. WEATHER

TASK A. SOURCES OF WEATHER

Sources of Weather Information

A thorough preflight weather assessment is a critical responsibility for every Remote PIC. Aviation weather services are a combined effort of government agencies like the National Weather Service (NWS) and the Federal Aviation Administration (FAA), providing pilots with the data needed to make safe operational decisions.

Primary Weather Products
- **Surface Aviation Weather Observations (METARs):** This is a report of the current weather at a specific airport. It includes elements like wind, visibility, weather phenomena (rain, fog), sky condition (cloud cover), temperature, dew point, and altimeter setting. METARs provide a snapshot of conditions at a precise location.
- **Automated Weather Systems (AWOS/ASOS):** These automated systems are a primary source for generating METARs and provide continuous, up-to-date weather information from airports.

How to Obtain Weather Information
- **Flight Service Station (FSS):** The FSS is the primary source for preflight weather information and can be reached 24/7 by calling 1-800-WX BRIEF. Pilots can speak with a specialist to get a formal weather briefing tailored to their specific flight.
- **Internet Sources:** Numerous government and private websites provide access to METARs, forecasts, weather charts, and other aviation weather products.

Types of Weather Briefings
When contacting an FSS, a pilot should request one of three types of briefings depending on their needs.
  1. **Standard Briefing:** For initial flight planning, a pilot obtains a standard weather briefing. This provides a full picture of the situation, covering any adverse conditions, an overview of weather patterns, current conditions, and forecasts for the route and destination. It also includes information on winds aloft and any relevant NOTAMs. In situations where the weather is forecast to be unsafe, the briefer may state that "VFR

flight not recommended," though the pilot always makes the final go or no-go decision.
2. **Abbreviated Briefing:** If a flight is delayed after the initial briefing has been received, an abbreviated briefing can be used to get updated information. The pilot should tell the specialist the time of their previous briefing, which allows the briefer to provide only the new details that have changed since the original report.
3. **Outlook Briefing:** For trips planned much further ahead, such as six or more hours in the future, a pilot can request an outlook briefing. This provides forecast information based on large-scale weather trends to help with early planning. An outlook briefing should always be followed up with a standard briefing closer to the departure time to receive the most current details.

Aviation Routine Weather Reports (METAR)

A **METAR** is a report of the current surface weather conditions at an airport. It is presented in a standardized international format, allowing pilots worldwide to understand the information. METARs are typically issued hourly, but a special report, known as a **SPECI**, can be issued at any time if weather conditions are changing rapidly.

Understanding how to decode a METAR is a critical skill for any remote pilot. The report is presented in a specific, sequential order.

Decoding a METAR
Let's break down the following example:
METAR KGGG 161753Z AUTO 14021G26KT 3/4SM +TSRA BR BKN008 OVC012CB 18/17 A2970 RMK PRESFR

Component	Example	Meaning
Type of Report	METAR	Routine hourly report. (Could also be SPECI).
Station Identifier	KGGG	4-letter ICAO code. "K" indicates the contiguous U.S.
Date and Time	161753Z	The 16th day of the month at 1753 Coordinated Universal Time (UTC), also known as Zulu (Z) time.
Modifier	AUTO	The report was generated by an automated station. "COR" would mean a corrected report.

Wind	14021G26KT	Wind from **140** degrees (true north) at **21 knots**, with **gusts** to **26 knots**. VRB would mean variable direction.
Visibility	3/4SM	Prevailing visibility is **3/4 statute mile**.
Weather	+TSRA BR	**Heavy (+) Thunderstorm (TS)** with **Rain (RA)**. **Mist (BR)**. "-" means light, no sign means moderate.
Sky Condition	BKN008 OVC012CB	**Broken** clouds at **800 feet AGL**. **Overcast** at **1,200 feet AGL** with **Cumulonimbus (CB)** clouds.
Temperature/Dew Point	18/17	Temperature **18°C**, Dew Point **17°C**. "M" would indicate a minus (below zero) temperature.
Altimeter	A2970	Altimeter setting is **29.70 inches of mercury** ("Hg).
Remarks	RMK PRESFR	Remarks section. PRESFR means the pressure is falling rapidly.

> **Exam Tip**
> You must be able to decode METARs on the Part 107 exam. Pay special attention to wind (direction and speed), visibility, sky condition (cloud heights are in hundreds of feet AGL), and temperature/dew point. The closer the temperature and dew point are, the higher the relative humidity, and the more likely you are to see fog or low clouds.

Terminal Aerodrome Forecasts (TAF)

A **Terminal Aerodrome Forecast (TAF)** is a weather forecast for the area within a 5 statute mile radius of an airport. TAFs are typically issued for larger airports, are valid for a 24 or 30-hour period, and are updated four times a day (at 0000Z, 0600Z, 1200Z, and 1800Z). A TAF uses the same coding and abbreviations as a METAR.

Decoding a TAF
A TAF provides a forecast of expected wind, visibility, significant weather, and sky conditions. It also includes special groups to indicate significant changes.

TAF Group	Meaning
TAF or **TAF AMD**	Indicates a routine or **amended** forecast.
KPIR 111130Z	Station identifier (Pierre, SD), issued on the 11th day at 1130Z.
1112/1212	**Valid period:** From the 11th day at 1200Z until the 12th day at 1200Z.
15012KT P6SM BKN090	**Initial forecast:** Wind from 150° at 12 knots, visibility **greater than 6 statute miles**, broken clouds at 9,000 feet AGL.
TEMPO 1112/1114 5SM BR	**Temporary** conditions between 1200Z and 1400Z on the 11th: visibility 5 statute miles in mist.
FM1500 16015G25KT…	**From** 1500Z, a rapid and permanent change will occur: winds from 160° at 15 knots gusting to 25 knots…
PROB30 1200/1204…	**30% probability** between 0000Z and 0400Z on the 12th of thunderstorms and rain.

> **Exam Tip**
> Focus on understanding the valid time periods and the meaning of the change groups FM (From - a permanent change) and TEMPO (Temporary - fluctuations lasting less than an hour).

Weather Charts

Weather charts provide a graphical depiction of current and forecast weather over a large area, making them essential for seeing the "big picture" during preflight planning.

- **Surface Analysis Chart:** Issued every three hours, this chart shows the current surface weather. It depicts the positions of high and low-pressure systems, fronts, temperatures, dew points, and wind. Its key feature is the use of detailed station models, which allow a remote pilot to see the specific sky cover, pressure, temperature, dew point, wind, and present weather for various reporting points at a glance.
- **Weather Depiction Chart:** Also issued every three hours, this chart provides a graphical overview of flight conditions like VFR, MVFR, and IFR, which are derived

from METAR reports. IFR areas, where ceilings are below 1,000 feet or visibility is under 3 miles, are outlined with a solid line and shaded. MVFR areas, with ceilings from 1,000 to 3,000 feet or visibility between 3 to 5 miles, are outlined with a solid line but are not shaded, while VFR areas are not outlined at all.
- **Significant Weather Prognostic Charts ("Progs"):** These charts forecast significant weather hazards and are issued four times daily with 12-hour and 24-hour panels. For sUAS pilots, the low-level chart covering the surface to 24,000 feet is the most relevant. It helps a pilot anticipate hazards by showing forecast freezing levels, areas of turbulence, and regions of IFR and MVFR conditions along a planned route.

Automated Weather Observing Systems (ASOS/AWOS)

Automated weather stations are the backbone of the surface weather observation network in the United States. These systems provide continuous, real-time weather data from airports and other locations, forming the basis for METARs and other aviation weather reports.
- **Purpose:** To gather and disseminate current surface weather conditions automatically.
- **Types of Systems:**
    - **Automated Surface Observing System (ASOS):** Generally considered the primary, most sophisticated type of automated system, often used at major airports.
    - **Automated Weather Observing System (AWOS):** Comes in several levels (e.g., AWOS-1, AWOS-2, AWOS-3) with varying capabilities.
- **Data Provided:** These systems measure and report on key weather elements, including wind speed and direction, visibility, cloud height and coverage, temperature, dew point, altimeter setting, and precipitation.
- **Human Augmentation:** At some locations, a human weather observer may augment or back up the automated system, adding information that the sensors cannot detect (e.g., tornadoes, specific types of clouds).

For a remote pilot, the data from ASOS and AWOS stations are a primary source for determining the current, local weather conditions necessary for a safe and compliant preflight assessment.

Task A. Sources of Weather - Practice Questions

✓ The answer key is located at the end of this chapter on Page 90

1. A remote pilot is planning a flight for later in the afternoon and needs the most complete weather information for their planned route. Which type of weather briefing should be requested?

A. An abbreviated briefing.
B. An outlook briefing.
C. A standard briefing.

```
METAR KINK 121845Z 11012G18KT 15SM SKC 25/17 A3000

METAR KBOI 121854Z 13004KT 30SM SCT150 17/6 A3015

METAR KLAX 121852Z 25004KT 6SM BR SCT007 SCT250 16/15 A2991

SPECI KMDW 121856Z 32005KT 1 1/2SM RA OVC007 17/16 A2980 RMK RAB35

SPECI KJFK 121853Z 18004KT 1/2SM FG R04/2200 OVC005 20/18 A3006
```

Figure 3-A. Aviation Routine Weather Reports (METAR).

2. Refer to Figure 3-A above. What are the wind conditions at Wink, Texas (KINK)?

A. Calm.
B. 111° at 2 knots, gusts 18 knots.
C. 110° at 12 knots, gusts 18 knots.

```
TAF

KMEM 121720Z 1218/1324 20012KT 5SM HZ BKN030 PROB40 1220/1222 1SM TSRA OVC008CB
     FM122200 33015G20KT P6SM BKN015 OVC025 PROB40 1220/1222 3SM SHRA
     FM120200 35012KT OVC008 PROB40 1202/1205 2SM-RASN BECMG 1306/1308 02008KT BKN012
     BECMG 1310/1312 00000KT 3SM BR SKC TEMPO 1212/1214 1/2SM FG
     FM131600 VRB06KT P6SM SKC=

KOKC 051130Z 0512/0618 14008KT 5SM BR BKN030 TEMPO 0513/0516 1 1/2SM BR
     FM051600 18010KT P6SM SKC BECMG 0522/0524 20013G20KT 4SM SHRA OVC020
     PROB40 0600/0606 2SM TSRA OVC008CB BECMG 0606/0608 21015KT P6SM SCT040=
```

Figure 3-B. Terminal Aerodrome Forecasts (TAF).

3. Refer to Figure 3-B above. In the TAF for KOKC, the final forecast for the time period between 1600Z and 2200Z is for winds from

A. 180 degrees at 10 knots.
   B. 160 degrees at 10 knots.
   C. 180 degrees at 10 knots, with gusts to 20 knots.

4. A remote pilot is looking for a graphical representation of the current areas of IFR, MVFR, and VFR weather across the country. Which chart should be used?

   A. Weather Depiction Chart.
   B. Surface Analysis Chart.
   C. Significant Weather Prognostic Chart.

5. What is the primary role of automated weather systems like ASOS and AWOS?

   A. To provide long-range weather forecasts for flight planning.
   B. To gather and disseminate current surface weather observations.
   C. To track the movement of weather balloons.

TASK B. EFFECTS OF WEATHER ON PERFORMANCE

Weather Factors and Their Effects on Performance

The performance of an sUAS is directly and significantly affected by the characteristics of the atmosphere in which it operates. The most critical factor is air density, which is often expressed in aviation as density altitude.

Density Altitude
Density altitude is the vertical distance above sea level in a standard atmosphere at which a given air density is found. It's the altitude the aircraft "feels" like it is flying at.

> **Important Concept:** The Rule of Density Altitude
> - High Density Altitude = Thin air = Poor aircraft performance.
> - Low Density Altitude = Dense air = Good aircraft performance.

As air becomes less dense (higher density altitude), the performance of an sUAS is degraded in three key areas:
- **Power:** The engine or motors take in less air, reducing power output.
- **Thrust:** Propellers are less efficient in thin air and produce less thrust.
- **Lift:** The thin air exerts less force on the airfoils (wings and propellers), reducing lift.

Factor	Change That Increases Density Altitude (Worsens Performance)
Altitude	Higher elevation
Temperature	Higher temperature
Humidity	Higher humidity (moist air is less dense than dry air)
Pressure	Lower atmospheric pressure

Therefore, an sUAS will have the worst performance on a hot, humid day at a high-elevation airport. Conversely, it will perform best on a cold, dry day at a location at sea level.

Wind and Currents

The movement of air across the Earth's surface is a critical factor for all flight operations. This movement can be vertical (currents) or horizontal (wind), and it is primarily driven by differences in atmospheric pressure and temperature.

Wind Patterns
- **Pressure Systems:** Air flows from areas of high pressure to areas of low pressure. In the Northern Hemisphere, this flow is deflected by the Coriolis force, creating:
    - **High-Pressure Systems:** Clockwise (anticyclonic) circulation. Highs are typically associated with descending air and **good weather**.
    - **Low-Pressure Systems:** Counter-clockwise (cyclonic) circulation. Lows are typically associated with rising air, which leads to cloud formation and **bad weather**.

Convective Currents
Uneven heating of the Earth's surface creates localized vertical air movements called convective currents. These currents are a primary cause of low-level turbulence.
- **Causes:** Surfaces like pavement, sand, and barren land heat up quickly, creating rising columns of warm air (updrafts). Surfaces like water and vegetation heat up more slowly, resulting in cooler, descending air (downdrafts).
- **Effect on Flight:** When flying at low altitudes, an sUAS will experience turbulence when passing over these varied surfaces. Updrafts can cause the aircraft to "balloon" up, while downdrafts can cause it to sink unexpectedly.
- **Sea and Land Breezes:** This is a large-scale convective current that occurs in coastal areas.
- **Sea Breeze (Day):** Land heats faster than water. Warm air rises over the land and is replaced by cooler air flowing in from the sea, creating an **onshore** wind.
- **Land Breeze (Night):** Land cools faster than water. Warm air rises over the water and is replaced by cooler air flowing out from the land, creating an **offshore** wind.

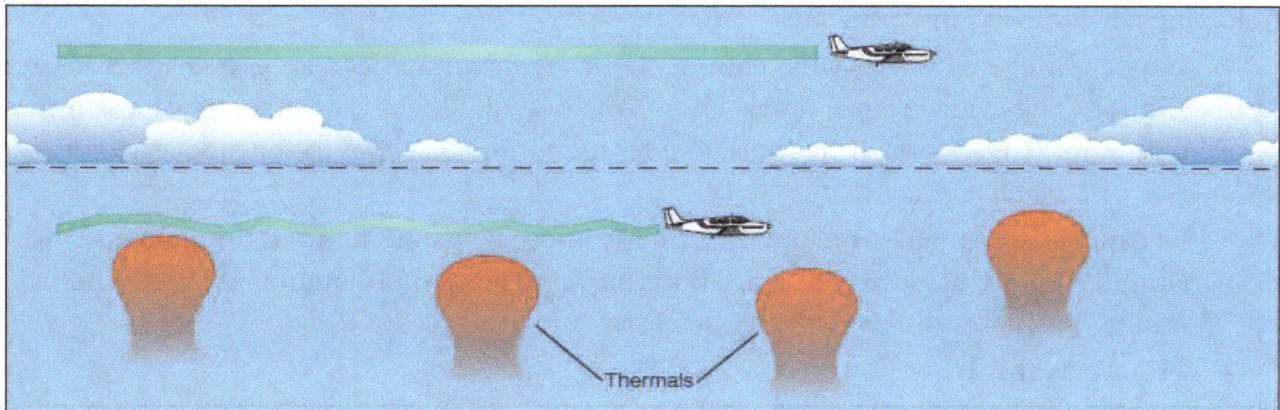

Figure 3-C. Convective turbulence avoidance.

Effects of Obstructions on Wind
Obstructions on the ground, both natural and man-made, disrupt the smooth flow of wind, creating mechanical turbulence.
- **Man-Made Obstructions:** Buildings, hangars, and other structures can cause severe turbulence, especially near airport runways. The intensity depends on the size of the building and the speed of the wind.
- **Mountainous Terrain:** Mountains have a large effect on wind flow.
- **Windward Side:** Air flowing up the windward side of a mountain generally creates updrafts.
- **Leeward Side:** Air flowing down the leeward (downwind) side of a mountain creates powerful, dangerous downdrafts and severe turbulence. **Pilots should be extremely cautious when operating on the leeward side of mountains**.

Atmospheric Stability, Pressure, and Temperature

The stability of the atmosphere is its tendency to resist or encourage vertical motion. This property is a primary driver of weather conditions.
- **Stable Air:** Resists vertical motion. If a parcel of air is forced to rise, it will be cooler (denser) than the surrounding air and will tend to sink back to its original level. Stable air is generally smooth and can lead to poor visibility as smoke, haze, and other pollutants are trapped near the surface. It is associated with **stratiform clouds** and steady precipitation.
- **Unstable Air:** Encourages vertical motion. If a parcel of air starts to rise, it will remain warmer (less dense) than the surrounding air and will continue to rise. This leads to turbulence, good surface visibility, and convective activity. It is associated with **cumuliform clouds**, showery precipitation, and thunderstorms.

To make informed operational decisions, remote pilots must have a firm grasp of the following key atmospheric principles.
- **Lapse Rate:** The rate at which atmospheric temperature decreases with an increase in altitude. The average lapse rate is about 2°C per 1,000 feet. The stability of an air mass is determined by comparing the actual temperature lapse rate to the adiabatic (cooling) rate of a rising parcel of air.
- **Temperature Inversion:** An atmospheric anomaly where temperature increases with altitude. An inversion acts as a lid, trapping weather and pollutants below it, often leading to poor visibility with fog, haze, or smoke.
- **Moisture and Dew Point:**

- o **Relative Humidity:** The amount of water vapor in the air compared to the maximum amount it could hold at that temperature.
- o **Dew Point:** The temperature to which air must be cooled to become 100% saturated.
- o **Temperature/Dew Point Spread:** When the temperature and dew point are close together, the air is nearly saturated, and visible moisture (fog, clouds, dew) is likely to form.
- **Frost:** Frost forms when moisture condenses on a surface whose temperature is below freezing. Frost on an sUAS disrupts the smooth flow of air, decreases lift, and increases drag. An sUAS must be completely free of frost before flight.

Air Masses and Fronts

An **air mass** is a large body of air that takes on the temperature and moisture characteristics of its source region. A front is the boundary line between two different air masses. The passage of a front always brings a change in weather.

Front Type	Description	Weather Characteristics
Cold Front	A cold, dense air mass advances and slides under a warmer air mass, lifting it rapidly.	Moves quickly (25-30 mph). Associated with a narrow band of weather. **Cumuliform clouds**, heavy rain showers, thunderstorms, and a sharp drop in temperature are common. Visibility is poor during passage but improves quickly behind the front.
Warm Front	A warm air mass advances and slides up and over a cooler air mass.	Moves slowly (10-25 mph). Associated with a wide area of weather. **Stratiform clouds** and drizzle are common, with poor visibility and fog. Embedded thunderstorms are possible in summer.
Stationary Front	Two air masses meet, but neither is strong enough to advance against the other.	The boundary remains in place for days. The weather is a mixture of conditions found in both warm and cold fronts.
Occluded Front	A fast-moving cold front overtakes a slower warm front.	Weather can often show characteristics of both a warm front and a cold front. It is often associated with widespread cloudiness and precipitation.

> **Important Concept:** Frontal Lifting
> The primary weather-producing mechanism of a front is the lifting of air. The type of weather depends on the stability of the air being lifted. If the lifted warm air is stable, you'll see stratiform clouds. If it's unstable, you'll see cumuliform clouds and thunderstorms. Cold fronts, with their steep leading edge, tend to cause more rapid and violent lifting, leading to more severe weather.

Thunderstorms

Thunderstorms are one of the most significant weather hazards to all aircraft, including sUAS. They produce a wide range of dangerous conditions, and remote pilots must understand their life cycle and associated risks. For a thunderstorm to form, three ingredients are required: sufficient water vapor, an unstable atmosphere, and an initial lifting action.

The Three Stages of a Thunderstorm
1. **Cumulus Stage:** Characterized by continuous **updrafts**. The lifting action begins, and a cumulus cloud grows vertically. There is no precipitation during this stage.
2. **Mature Stage:** This is the **most violent stage** of the thunderstorm's life. It begins when precipitation starts to fall from the cloud base, creating downdrafts. The storm now contains both strong updrafts and downdrafts, leading to extreme turbulence, heavy rain, lightning, and potential hail. The top of the cloud spreads out to form an anvil shape.
3. **Dissipating Stage:** Characterized primarily by **downdrafts**. The updrafts weaken and are replaced by downdrafts, causing the storm to weaken and "rain itself out."

> **Exam Tip**
> You must know the three stages of a thunderstorm and what defines them. Remember: Cumulus stage = updrafts only. Mature stage = updrafts and downdrafts (most dangerous). Dissipating stage = downdrafts only.

Thunderstorm Hazards
- **Turbulence:** The strong updrafts and downdrafts in the mature stage create violent turbulence that can cause a loss of control.
- **Tornadoes:** The most violent thunderstorms can produce tornadoes (if they touch land) or waterspouts (if they touch water). Any cloud connected to a severe thunderstorm carries a threat of violence.
- **Icing:** Strong updrafts carry water droplets high above the freezing level, creating supercooled water. This can lead to rapid and severe structural icing on an sUAS.

- **Hail:** Hailstones are formed when frozen water droplets are carried up and down within the storm, growing in size. Hail can be thrown for miles outside the main thunderstorm cloud, even in clear air, especially under the anvil. It can cause severe damage to an sUAS.
- **Lightning:** Every thunderstorm produces lightning, which can damage or destroy the electronic components of an sUAS.

Safety Rule: Never fly in, over, or under a thunderstorm. A good rule of thumb is to circumnavigate thunderstorms by at least **20 nautical miles**.

Fog

Fog is a cloud that is on or near the surface, and it poses a major hazard to sUAS operations by reducing visibility. Fog forms when the air is cooled to its dew point, causing water vapor to condense.

Type of Fog	Formation Process	Characteristics
Radiation Fog	The ground cools rapidly on clear, calm nights, cooling the air just above it to the dew point.	Forms in low-lying areas like valleys. Burns off as the sun rises and heats the ground.
Advection Fog	Warm, moist air moves over a cooler surface (like cool water or land).	Requires wind to form. Common in coastal areas. Can be persistent and deep.
Upslope Fog	Moist, stable air is forced up the side of a mountain or sloping terrain and is cooled to its dew point.	Requires wind. Can cover large areas and persist for a long time.
Steam Fog	Cold, dry air moves over warm water.	Evaporation from the water surface rises and immediately condenses, resembling smoke. Often associated with low-level turbulence and icing.

Ceiling and Visibility

- **Ceiling:** For aviation purposes, a ceiling is the height of the lowest layer of clouds reported as **broken** (BKN) or **overcast** (OVC). If the sky is obscured by fog or haze, the ceiling is the vertical visibility into the obscuration. Scattered (SCT) or few (FEW) clouds do not constitute a ceiling.
- **Visibility:** The greatest horizontal distance at which prominent objects can be seen with the naked eye.

For Part 107 operations, the minimum flight visibility is **3 statute miles**, and the sUAS must remain **500 feet below** any clouds. Therefore, a remote pilot must be able to determine both the reported visibility and the ceiling height to ensure a legal and safe flight.

Task B. Effects of Weather on Performance - Practice Questions

✓ The answer key is located at the end of this chapter on Page 90

6. What effect does high density altitude have on the efficiency of an sUAS propeller?

   A. Efficiency is increased.
   B. Efficiency is decreased.
   C. Efficiency is not affected by density altitude.

7. During the day, in a coastal area, what type of wind is most likely to be present?

   A. A land breeze, with wind flowing from the land to the sea.
   B. A sea breeze, with wind flowing from the sea to the land.
   C. A katabatic wind, with wind flowing downhill.

8. What are the characteristics of a stable air mass?

   A. Stratiform clouds, smooth air, and poor visibility.
   B. Cumuliform clouds, turbulence, and good visibility.
   C. Light winds, clear skies, and cold temperatures.

9. A remote pilot is expecting the passage of a cold front. What kind of weather conditions should they anticipate?

   A. A wide area of light drizzle and fog with stratiform clouds.
   B. A narrow band of towering cumulus clouds, heavy showers, and a sharp wind shift.

C. Several days of calm winds and clear skies.

10. Which stage of a thunderstorm is characterized by the presence of both updrafts and downdrafts and is considered the most violent?

   A. The mature stage.
   B. The cumulus stage.
   C. The dissipating stage.

11. A remote pilot is planning an early morning flight in a calm, low-lying valley on a clear night. What type of weather phenomenon should they be most concerned about?

   A. Advection fog.
   B. A thunderstorm.
   C. Radiation fog.

12. A METAR reports the sky condition as SCT025 BKN040 OVC080. What is the ceiling?

   A. 2,500 feet AGL.
   B. 4,000 feet AGL.
   C. 8,000 feet AGL.

ANSWER KEY FOR III. WEATHER

1. C. - A standard briefing provides the most complete information and a more complete weather picture and should be obtained prior to the departure of any flight.
2. C. - The METAR for KINK includes "11012G18KT," which decodes to 110° at 12 knots, gusts 18 knots.
3. A. - The forecast group "FM051600 18010KT" indicates that from 1600Z, the wind will be from 180 degrees at 10 knots.
4. A. - The Weather Depiction Chart is specifically designed to provide a graphic display of IFR, VFR, and marginal VFR (MVFR) weather.
5. B. - Automated weather sources, such as AWOS and ASOS, play a major role in the gathering of surface observations.
6. B. - In high density altitude (thinner air), a propeller is less efficient and produces less thrust.
7. B. - During the day, the land heats faster than the water, causing air to rise over the land and be replaced by cooler air from the sea, creating a sea breeze.
8. A. - Stable air resists vertical motion, leading to layered or stratiform clouds, smooth air, and the trapping of pollutants, which results in poor visibility.
9. B. - A cold front is characterized by a narrow band of weather, cumuliform clouds, showery precipitation, and a rapid change in wind and temperature.
10. A. - The mature stage is the most violent period, containing both strong updrafts and the downdrafts created by falling precipitation.
11. C. - Radiation fog typically forms in low-lying areas on clear, calm nights as the ground cools the air above it to the dew point.
12. B. - A ceiling is the lowest layer of clouds reported as broken or overcast; in this case, the broken layer is at 4,000 feet AGL.

IV. LOADING & PERFORMANCE

TASK A. LOADING AND PERFORMANCE

General Loading and Performance

Before every flight, the Remote PIC is responsible for verifying the sUAS is loaded correctly according to the manufacturer's weight and balance limitations. Operating an aircraft outside of these limits is unsafe and can lead to poor performance and loss of control.

Effects of Weight
Excessive weight degrades flight performance in almost every way. An overloaded sUAS will exhibit:
- Higher takeoff speed and a longer takeoff run.
- Reduced rate of climb.
- Lower maximum altitude.
- Shorter range and reduced cruising speed.
- Reduced maneuverability.
- A higher stalling speed.
- Longer landing distance.

The Remote PIC must always consider the impact of the aircraft's weight, especially when combined with performance-reducing conditions like high density altitude.

Effects of Balance (Center of Gravity - CG)
The **Center of Gravity (CG)** is the point where the entire weight of the aircraft is considered to be concentrated. Its location is critical for stability and control.
- **CG Location:** The CG is not a fixed point; it shifts as weight is added, removed, or moved. For an sUAS, this can happen when adding a payload or when a jettisonable load is dropped.
- **CG Limits:** The manufacturer establishes an allowable range for the CG. If the CG is outside these limits, the aircraft can become unstable and difficult or impossible to control.
- **PIC Responsibility:** The Remote PIC must determine the location of the CG before flight and understand how it might shift during the operation to ensure it remains within safe limits.

Load Factor

A **load factor** is the ratio of the total lift being produced by the aircraft to its actual weight. It is measured in Gs, where 1 G is the normal force of gravity. In straight-and-level, unaccelerated flight, the load factor is 1 G.

Any time an aircraft deviates from a straight flight path (e.g., in a turn, pull-up, or other maneuver), the load factor increases. This is important for two reasons:
- **Structural Stress:** High load factors impose stress on the aircraft's structure. It is possible for a pilot to impose a load that exceeds the structural limits of the aircraft, leading to failure.
- **Increased Stalling Speed:** An increased load factor increases the aircraft's stalling speed.

Load Factor in Turns
When an aircraft is in a level turn, it must produce lift equal to its weight plus the centrifugal force of the turn. This combined force is the load factor.
- As the **angle of bank increases**, the load factor increases exponentially.
- At a **60° bank angle**, the load factor is **2 Gs**. This means the aircraft's wings must produce lift equal to twice the aircraft's weight to maintain altitude.
- At a **70° bank angle**, the load factor is approximately **3 Gs**.

Load Factor and Stalling Speed
An aircraft stalls when its wing exceeds its **critical angle of attack (AOA)**, not because it is flying too slowly. However, stalling speed is directly related to load factor.
- **Stalling speed increases** in proportion to the square root of the load factor.
- An aircraft in a 60° bank (2 Gs) will stall at a speed approximately **40% higher** than its normal, straight-and-level stalling speed.
- This means an aircraft can be stalled at a very high airspeed if a high load factor is imposed, such as during a steep turn or an abrupt pull-up.

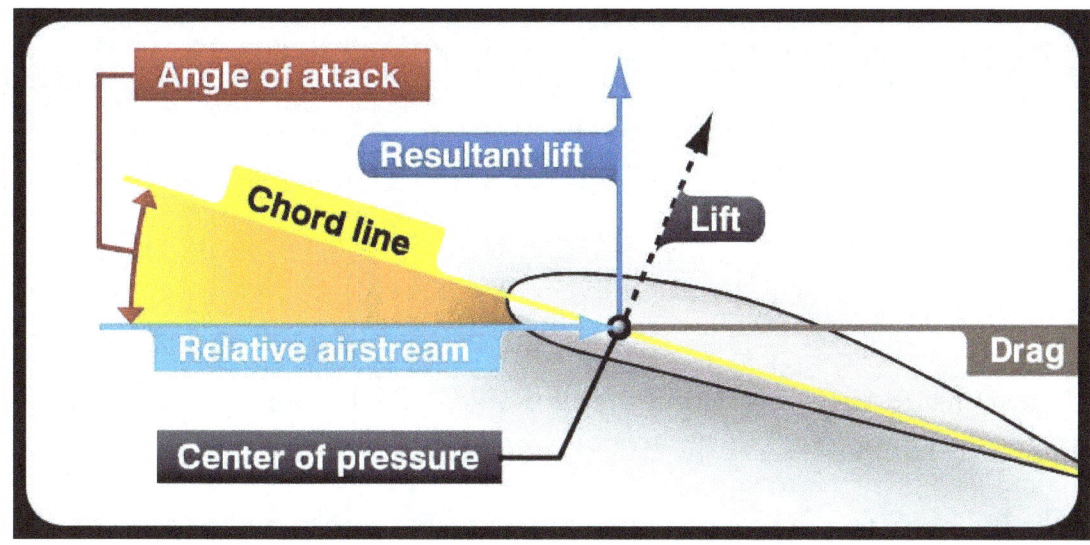

Figure 4-A. Diagram showing a normal angle of attack (AOA).

Balance, Stability, and Center of Gravity (CG)

Balance refers to the location of an aircraft's **Center of Gravity (CG)**, which is the single point at which the aircraft would balance if suspended. The proper location of the CG is critical for flight safety, stability, and control.

Longitudinal Balance (Forward and Aft CG)
The primary concern for a remote pilot is the fore-and-aft location of the CG. The manufacturer establishes a specific **CG range**, with a forward and an aft limit. Operating outside this range can have dangerous consequences.

Important Concept: CG and Stability

The location of the CG has a direct effect on the aircraft's longitudinal stability (its tendency to maintain a level pitch attitude).
- **Forward CG (Nose-Heavy):** Increases longitudinal stability. The aircraft will have a strong tendency to pitch down, requiring more back pressure on the controls to hold the nose up, especially during landing flare. This also results in a higher stalling speed.
- **Aft CG (Tail-Heavy):** Decreases longitudinal stability. The aircraft becomes less stable and may be difficult or impossible to recover from a stall. Control forces become very light, making it easy for the pilot to inadvertently overstress the aircraft.

CG Position	Stability	Control	Stall Recovery
Forward of Limit	Excessively stable	Difficult to raise the nose for takeoff/landing	Stall recovery is normal, but stalling speed is higher.
Aft of Limit	Unstable	Very light control forces (easy to overstress)	Stall recovery can become violent or impossible.

The Remote PIC must ensure the CG is within the allowable limits before flight and must consider how it might shift during flight (e.g., from dropping a payload).

Importance and Use of Performance Data

To ensure a safe flight, the Remote PIC must understand and use the performance data provided by the sUAS manufacturer. This information is essential for predicting how the aircraft will perform under various conditions.

Key Performance Considerations:
- **Weight and Balance (W&B):** The PIC must verify the aircraft is within its weight and CG limits before every flight.
- **Performance Data:** The manufacturer may provide data for takeoff, climb, range, endurance, and landing. This information allows the pilot to determine if a planned operation is feasible and safe.
- **Environmental Factors:** Performance data is critical for calculating the effects of non-standard conditions. For example, on a day with high density altitude (high elevation, hot temperature, high humidity), the manufacturer's performance charts might show that the maximum allowable takeoff weight must be reduced to ensure a safe climb.
- **Takeoff/Launch Area:** The PIC must also consider the launch environment, including the length and surface of the launch area, wind, and any obstacles.

If the manufacturer does not provide performance data, the pilot should seek out data from other users of the same model to use as a starting point for determining the aircraft's capabilities. Using this data is essential for safe and efficient operation.

Task A. Loading and Performance - Practice Questions

✓ The answer key is located at the end of this chapter on Page 96

1. What effect does an increase in aircraft weight have on takeoff performance?

   A. It results in a shorter takeoff run and a steeper angle of climb.
   B. It has no effect on takeoff performance.
   C. It results in a longer takeoff run and a reduced rate of climb.

2. When an sUAS is in a level, coordinated turn with a 60° bank angle, what is the load factor?

   A. 1G.
   B. 2Gs.
   C. 4Gs.

3. What is a characteristic of an sUAS that is loaded with its center of gravity aft of the allowable range?

   A. The sUAS will be unstable, and stall recovery may be difficult or impossible.
   B. The sUAS will be excessively stable.
   C. The sUAS will require excessive back pressure on the controls to take off.

4. Why is it critical for a remote pilot to use the manufacturer's performance data?

   A. To ensure the flight is as efficient as possible.
   B. To make practical use of the aircraft's capabilities and limitations for a safe operation.
   C. To verify the aircraft's registration is valid.

ANSWER KEY FOR IV. LOADING & PERFORMANCE

1. C. - Excessive weight reduces flight performance, leading to a longer takeoff run and a reduced rate and angle of climb.
2. B. - The load factor for any aircraft in a coordinated level turn at a 60° bank is 2 Gs.
3. A. - Loading in a tail-heavy condition has a serious effect upon longitudinal stability and reduces the capability to recover from stalls.
4. B. - The use of operational data in flying operations is essential for safe and efficient operation by allowing the pilot to understand the aircraft's capabilities and limitations.

V. OPERATIONS

TASK A. RADIO COMMUNICATIONS PROCEDURES

Airport Operations

Airports are categorized based on whether they have an operating Air Traffic Control (ATC) tower. This distinction determines the communication requirements and procedures for all aircraft operating in the vicinity, including sUAS.

- **Towered Airport:** An airport with an operating control tower. ATC is responsible for managing the flow of traffic. Manned aircraft are required to maintain two-way radio communication with the tower. For sUAS, operating in the controlled airspace of a towered airport (typically Class B, C, or D) requires **prior authorization from ATC**.
- **Nontowered Airport:** An airport without an operating control tower. Two-way radio communication is not required, but it is a standard and highly recommended practice for manned aircraft to self-announce their position and intentions on a designated **Common Traffic Advisory Frequency (CTAF)**.

Common Traffic Advisory Frequency (CTAF)

The Common Traffic Advisory Frequency (CTAF) is the designated radio frequency for pilots to communicate their positions and intentions when operating at a nontowered airport. Monitoring the CTAF is a critical tool for a remote pilot to build situational awareness of manned aircraft traffic in the area.

- **Purpose:** To allow pilots to coordinate with each other in the absence of a control tower.
- **Finding the Frequency:** The CTAF for an airport can be found on aeronautical charts (indicated by a "C" in a solid circle) and in the Chart Supplement.
- **Self-Announcing:** Manned aircraft pilots make self-announcement calls on the CTAF, typically starting from 10 miles out from the airport, during taxi, takeoff, and when flying in the traffic pattern.
- **Remote Pilot's Role:** While a remote pilot should not transmit on the CTAF (unless in an emergency), monitoring this frequency with a radio scanner or aviation radio provides invaluable, real-time information about the location and intentions of nearby manned aircraft.

UNICOM and ATIS

In addition to the CTAF, pilots use other frequencies to obtain important airport information.

Aeronautical Advisory Station (UNICOM)
- **What it is:** A non-government radio station that can provide airport advisory information at airports without a tower or FSS.
- **Services:** Upon request, a UNICOM operator can provide information on wind direction, the recommended runway, weather, and other airport conditions. At many airports, the UNICOM frequency also serves as the CTAF.

Automatic Terminal Information Service (ATIS)
- **What it is:** A continuous broadcast of recorded, non-control information in high-activity terminal areas (towered airports).
- **Purpose:** To reduce controller workload by automating the broadcast of routine information.
- **Content:** ATIS broadcasts include the airport name, a phonetic letter code (e.g., "Information Sierra"), time, and key weather information (wind, visibility, sky condition, temperature, dew point, altimeter setting). It also includes information on the active runways and instrument approaches.
- **How it's used:** Manned aircraft pilots listen to the ATIS before contacting the tower and inform the controller they have received the current information by stating the phonetic letter code (e.g., "with Information Sierra").

Aviation Communication: Call Signs, Phonetics, and Phraseology

While remote pilots are not expected to communicate on aviation frequencies except in an emergency, understanding the language of the sky is essential for interpreting the communications you will hear while monitoring the CTAF or other frequencies.

Aircraft Call Signs
- **Standard Format:** U.S. registered aircraft have an "N-number" (e.g., N123AB). In radio calls, this is often shortened.
- **General Aviation:** Typically use the aircraft manufacturer name followed by the last few numbers/letters of the registration (e.g., "Cessna Three-Alpha-Bravo").
- **Airliners:** Use the airline's name and flight number (e.g., "Southwest Seven-Eleven").

The Phonetic Alphabet

To avoid confusion between similar-sounding letters (like "B," "C," "D," "E"), aviation uses the ICAO phonetic alphabet. The registration N123AB would be spoken as "November-One-Two-Three-Alpha-Bravo."

Figure 5-A. Chart of the ICAO phonetic alphabet.

Standard Phraseology

Aviation communication uses standardized phraseology for clarity and brevity.

Category	Example	How It's Spoken
Altitudes (below 18,000 ft)	4,500 ft	"Four thousand five hundred"
Flight Levels (at/above 18,000 ft)	FL190	"Flight Level One Niner Zero"
Frequencies	122.1 MHz	"One two two point one"
Wind Direction	220°	"Wind two two zero"
Speeds	190 knots	"One niner zero knots"
Time	0920 UTC	"Zero niner two zero" (Zulu)

Task A. Radio Communications Procedures - Practice Questions

✓ The answer key is located at the end of this chapter on Page 134

1. At an airport with an operating control tower, who is responsible for providing the safe, orderly, and expeditious flow of air traffic?

    A. Air Traffic Control (ATC).
    B. The airport manager.
    C. The pilots of each aircraft.

2. What is the primary purpose of a Common Traffic Advisory Frequency (CTAF)?

    A. To receive weather updates from an automated system.
    B. To carry out airport advisory practices at an airport without an operating control tower.
    C. To communicate with Air Traffic Control for clearances.

3. What is a UNICOM station?

    A. A government-run Air Traffic Control facility.
    B. A non-government station that may provide airport advisory information.
    C. An automated system for broadcasting weather data.

4. The letter "N" in the phonetic alphabet is

    A. Nancy.
    B. November.
    C. Nine.

TASK B. AIRPORT OPERATIONS

Types of Airports

Airports are broadly categorized based on their operational control and accessibility.
- **Towered Airport:** An airport with an active Air Traffic Control (ATC) tower. ATC manages the flow of traffic, and manned aircraft are required to maintain two-way radio communication. sUAS operations in the associated controlled airspace (Class B, C, or D) require prior ATC authorization.
- **Nontowered Airport:** An airport without an operating control tower. Pilots are responsible for self-announcing their positions and intentions on a Common Traffic Advisory Frequency (CTAF).
- **Civil Airport:** Open to the general public.
- **Military/Federal Government Airport:** Operated by the military or other federal agencies.
- **Private Airport:** Restricted-use and not open to the general public.

Other specialized facilities include **heliports** (for helicopters) and **seaplane bases** (for aircraft operating on water).

Situational Awareness in the Airport Environment

For a remote pilot, maintaining situational awareness in the airport environment is paramount, even though they are not physically in a cockpit. This involves understanding and interpreting ATC communications and being vigilant against runway confusion.
- **Monitoring ATC:** Even if not required to communicate, monitoring the appropriate ATC or CTAF frequency with a radio scanner provides invaluable real-time information about the location, altitude, and intentions of manned aircraft.
- **Understanding Instructions:** The remote pilot should be familiar with standard aviation phraseology and procedures to understand the instructions being given to other aircraft. This helps build a mental picture of the traffic flow.
- **Runway Confusion:** This occurs when an aircraft mistakenly uses the wrong runway or a taxiway for takeoff or landing. It is a major hazard. Remote pilots operating near airports must be certain of the active runway's location and orientation to avoid interfering with traffic patterns.
- **Seeking Clarification:** Manned aircraft pilots are taught that if they are ever unsure of an ATC instruction, they should ask for clarification. Remote pilots should also prioritize safety by asking for clarification.

Runway Markings and Signage

Airports use a standardized system of markings and signs to provide guidance and instructions to pilots on the ground. Understanding these visual aids is essential for interpreting an airport diagram and maintaining situational awareness.

Signs

Airport signs are color-coded based on their purpose:

Sign Type	Description (Color)	Purpose
Mandatory Instruction	**Red** background, **White** text	Denotes an entrance to a runway or critical area. **MUST STOP** here until cleared by ATC or the area is clear.
Location	**Black** background, **Yellow** text	Identifies your current location (e.g., the taxiway or runway you are on).
Direction	**Yellow** background, **Black** text	Indicates the direction of intersecting taxiways.
Destination	**Yellow** background, **Black** text	Points toward a specific location, like a runway, terminal, or FBO.
Runway Distance Remaining	**Black** background, **White** number	Indicates the remaining runway length in thousands of feet.

Markings

- **Runway Designation:** Runways are numbered based on their magnetic heading, rounded to the nearest 10 degrees (e.g., Runway 36 is oriented approximately 360° magnetic). Parallel runways are designated with L (Left), C (Center), or R (Right).
- **Runway Holding Position Marking:** This is the most critical marking for a pilot on the ground. It consists of **four yellow lines (two solid, two dashed)** and indicates the boundary of the runway safety area.
    - When approaching the runway, the **solid lines are on your side**. You **must not cross** without clearance from ATC (at a towered airport) or until the runway is clear (at a nontowered airport).

o When exiting the runway, the **dashed lines are on your side**. You are clear of the runway once the entire aircraft has crossed both the solid and dashed lines.

Type of Sign	Action or Purpose	Type of Sign	Action or Purpose
4-22	**Taxiway/Runway Hold Position:** Hold short of runway on taxiway	(dashed/solid runway boundary)	**Runway Safety Area/Obstacle Free Zone Boundary:** Exit boundary of runway protected areas
26-8	**Runway/Runway Hold Position:** Hold short of intersecting runway	(ILS boundary marking)	**ILS Critical Area Boundary:** Exit boundary of ILS critical area
8-APCH	**Runway Approach Hold Position:** Hold short of aircraft on approach	J→	**Taxiway Direction:** Defines direction & designation of intersecting taxiway(s)
ILS	**ILS Critical Area Hold Position:** Hold short of ILS approach critical area	↙L	**Runway Exit:** Defines direction & designation of exit taxiway from runway
⊖	**No Entry:** Identifies paved areas where aircraft entry is prohibited	22↑	**Outbound Destination:** Defines directions to takeoff runways
B	**Taxiway Location:** Identifies taxiway on which aircraft is located	↖MIL	**Inbound Destination:** Defines directions for arriving aircraft
22	**Runway Location:** Identifies runway on which aircraft is located	(striped marker)	**Taxiway Ending Marker:** Indicates taxiway does not continue
4	**Runway Distance Remaining:** Provides remaining runway length in 1,000 feet increments	↙A G L→	**Direction Sign Array:** Identifies location in conjunction with multiple intersecting taxiways

Figure 5-B. Runway marking and sign chart.

Airport Traffic Patterns

To ensure the safe and orderly flow of traffic, aircraft operating at an airport follow a standard procedure known as the **traffic pattern**. This is a rectangular flight path around the airport, with each segment, or "leg," having a specific name. While a remote pilot will not be flying this pattern, understanding it is critical for anticipating the actions of manned aircraft.

The Five Legs of a Traffic Pattern
1. **Departure Leg:** The flight path straight out from the runway after takeoff.
2. **Crosswind Leg:** A flight path at a right angle to the departure end of the runway.
3. **Downwind Leg:** A flight path parallel to the runway but in the opposite direction of landing. This is where an aircraft is typically configured for landing.
4. **Base Leg:** A flight path at a right angle to the landing end of the runway, transitioning from the downwind leg.
5. **Final Approach:** The flight path in the direction of landing, aligned with the extended centerline of the runway.

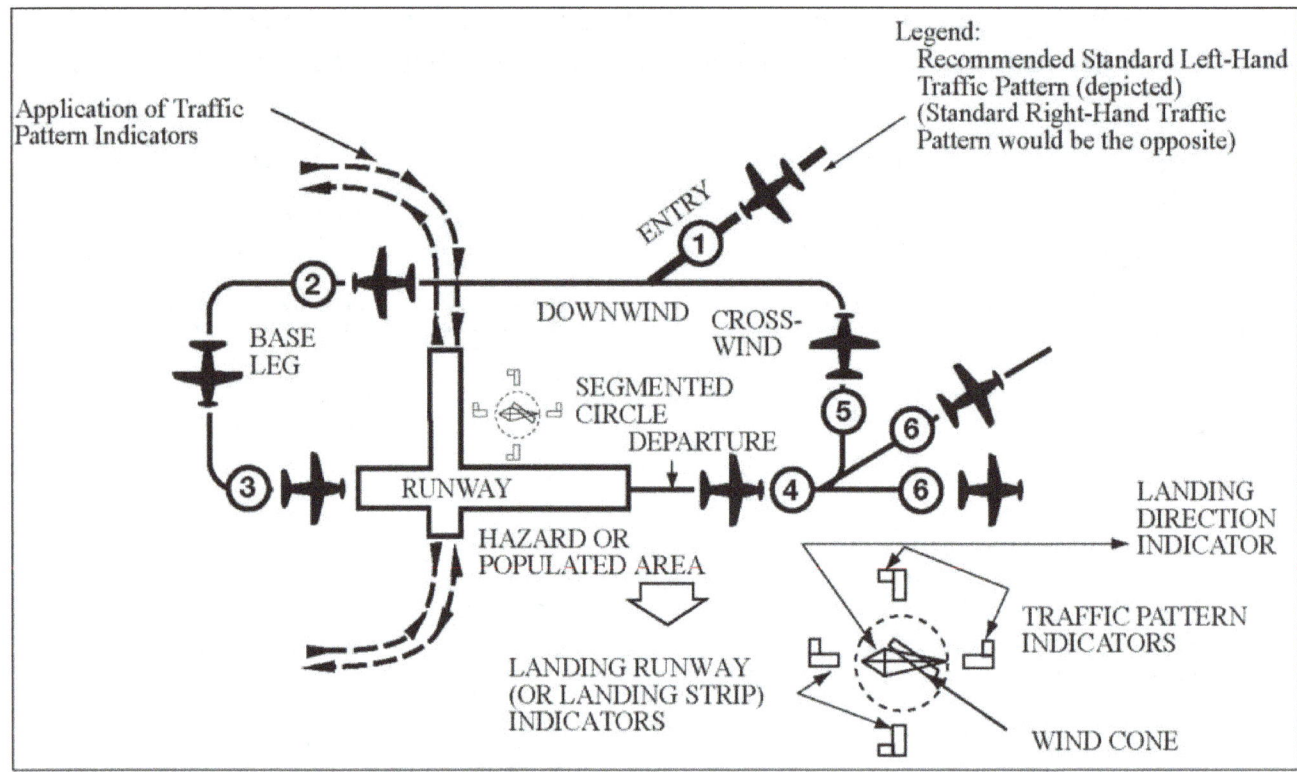

Figure 5-C. Traffic Pattern Operations – Single Runway

> **Important Concept: Standard Pattern Direction**
> Unless otherwise specified, all turns in a traffic pattern are made to the **left**. A "right traffic" pattern is non-standard and will be noted on aeronautical charts with "RP" and the runway number, or indicated by traffic pattern indicators on the ground at a non-towered airport.

Traffic Pattern Altitudes
- **Propeller-driven aircraft:** Typically fly the pattern at **1,000 feet AGL**.
- **Turbine-powered aircraft:** Typically fly at **1,500 feet AGL**.

Remote pilots must be aware of these altitudes and avoid interfering with aircraft flying the pattern.

Security Identification Display Areas (SIDA)

A Security Identification Display Area (SIDA) is a designated portion of an airport where security measures are in effect. Access to these areas, which often include ramps, aprons, and other operational zones, is strictly controlled. While Part 107 does not specifically regulate SIDA, a remote pilot whose operation requires them to be physically present within a SIDA must comply with all local airport security requirements, which may include obtaining a badge and undergoing a background check.

Sources for Airport Data

Before operating at or near any airport, a remote pilot must gather all available information about that location. This is a critical part of the preflight assessment.

The four primary sources for airport data are:
1. **Aeronautical Charts:** Provide a visual depiction of the airport, its runways, surrounding airspace, and key frequencies. The three main types are:
   - **Sectional Charts:** Most commonly used for VFR navigation (Scale 1:500,000).
   - **VFR Terminal Area Charts (TACs):** More detailed charts for navigating in or near busy Class B airspace (Scale 1:250,000).
   - **World Aeronautical Charts (WACs):** Less detailed charts for higher-speed aircraft (Scale 1:1,000,000).
2. **Chart Supplement U.S.:** Formerly known as the Airport/Facility Directory, this is the most comprehensive source of detailed information on public-use airports. It includes runway data, services available, operational hours, communication frequencies, and other critical notes.
3. **Notices to Air Missions (NOTAMs):** Provide time-critical information about temporary changes or hazards, such as runway closures or inoperative lights.
4. **Automatic Terminal Information Service (ATIS):** A continuous broadcast of current weather and airport information at towered airports.

Understanding Chart Symbols

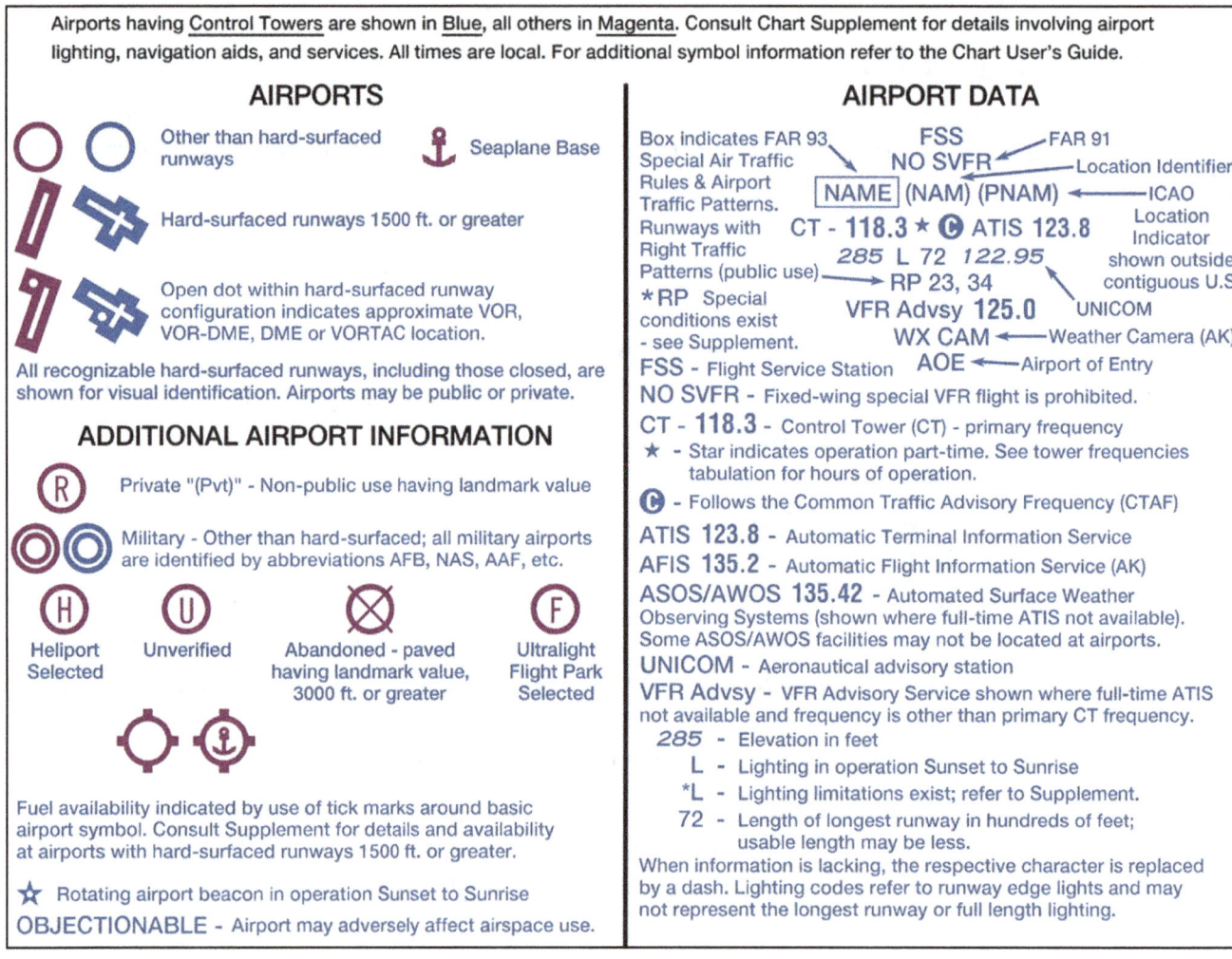

Figure 5-D. Legend of Sectional Chart for Airport Information

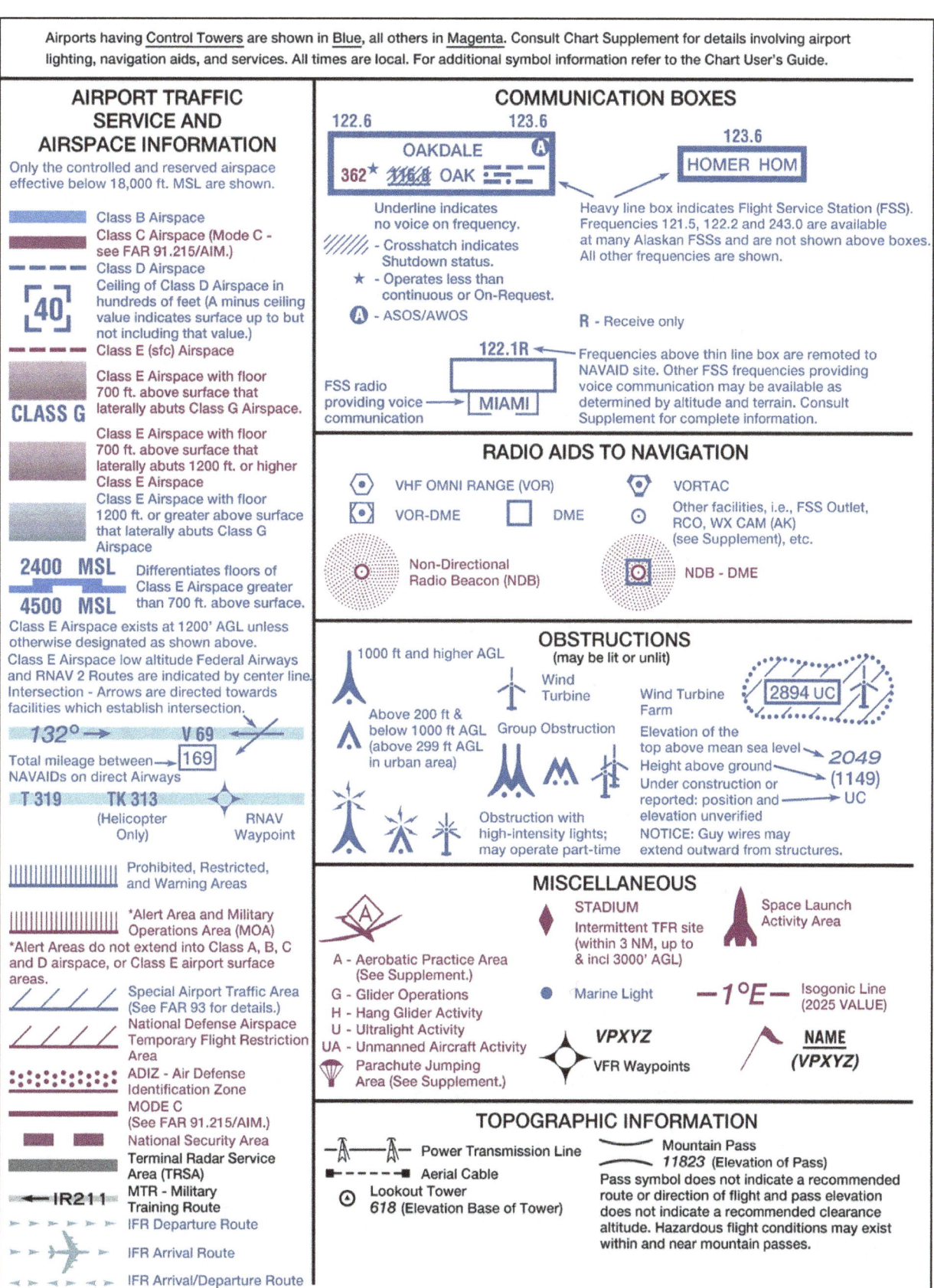

Figure 5-E. Legend of Sectional Chart for Airport Traffic

Wildlife Hazards

Strikes between aircraft and wildlife, particularly birds, pose a major and costly threat to aviation safety.
1. **Prevalence:** The vast majority of reported wildlife strikes involve birds. Waterfowl (ducks, geese), gulls, and raptors (hawks, vultures) cause the most damage.
2. **Pilot Responsibility:** Remote pilots should be vigilant for bird and other wildlife activity, especially during low-altitude operations. Bird activity is often greatest during the spring and fall migration seasons and can be concentrated near water sources.
3. **Reporting:** If an sUAS collides with wildlife, it is highly encouraged that the pilot report the strike to the FAA. This data helps the FAA track wildlife hazards and develop mitigation strategies.

Airport and Seaplane Base Lighting

Airport lighting is standardized to help pilots identify airports and navigate on the surface at night or in low visibility.
- **Airport Beacons:** Help pilots locate an airport at night. The color combination of the flashes indicates the type of airport:
    - **Civilian Land Airport:** Flashing **White** and **Green**.
    - **Water Airport:** Flashing **White** and **Yellow**.
    - **Heliport:** Flashing **White**, **Yellow**, and **Green**.
    - **Military Airport:** Two quick **White** flashes, then one **Green** flash.
- **Runway Lighting:**
    - **Runway Edge Lights:** White, except on instrument runways where the last 2,000 feet are amber.
    - **Runway End Lights:** Red lights marking the end of the runway.
- **Taxiway Lighting:**
    - **Taxiway Edge Lights:** Blue.
    - **Taxiway Centerline Lights:** Green.

Task B. Airport Operations - Practice Questions

✓ The answer key is located at the end of this chapter on Page 134

5. A remote pilot is planning to operate in the vicinity of an airport with an operating control tower. This type of airport is known as a

   A. nontowered airport.

B. private airport.
C. towered airport.

6. Why is it a good operating practice for a remote pilot to monitor the appropriate ATC or CTAF frequency when operating near an airport?

   A. To receive authorization for the flight.
   B. To improve situational awareness of manned aircraft operations.
   C. To provide traffic advisories to other pilots.

7. A sign with a red background and white characters indicates

   A. a mandatory instruction, such as an entrance to a runway.
   B. the current taxiway location.
   C. the direction to a specific destination.

8. A manned aircraft is flying parallel to the runway in the opposite direction of landing. Which leg of the traffic pattern is it on?

   A. Crosswind leg.
   B. Downwind leg.
   C. Upwind leg.

9. What is a Security Identification Display Area (SIDA)?

   A. A portion of an airport in which specific security measures are carried out.
   B. An area where aircraft are displayed for public viewing.
   C. The designated area for sUAS operations at an airport.

10. Which is the most comprehensive source of detailed information for a specific public-use airport?

    A. The Sectional Chart.
    B. The Chart Supplement U.S.
    C. The Aeronautical Information Manual (AIM).

11. Which group of birds is known to cause the most damage to civil aircraft in the United States?

    A. Waterfowl, gulls, and raptors.
    B. Pigeons and starlings.

C. Songbirds and sparrows.

12. A remote pilot observes an airport beacon that is flashing a white and green light. This indicates a

A. military airport.
B. heliport.
C. civilian land airport.

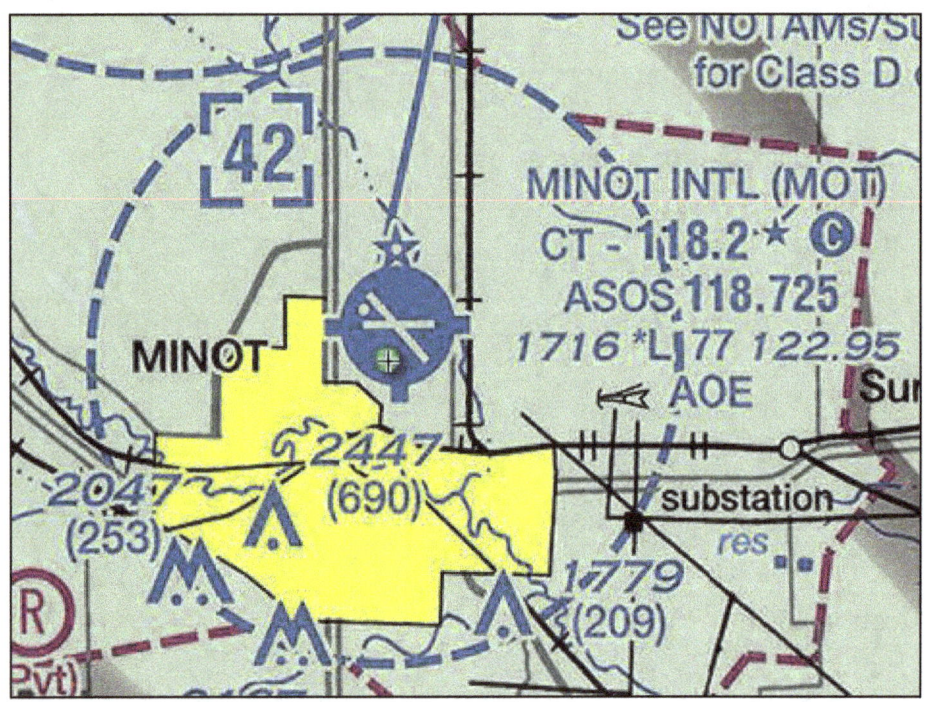

Figure 5-F. Sectional chart of Minot International Airport

13. Refer to Figure 5-F above. What is the ceiling of the Class D airspace surrounding Minot International Airport (MOT)?

A. 4,200 feet AGL.
B. 2,447 feet MSL.
C. 4,200 feet MSL.

TASK C. EMERGENCY PROCEDURES

Emergency Planning and Communication

While Part 107 does not mandate a specific emergency plan, a core responsibility of the Remote PIC is to be prepared for abnormal and emergency situations. This involves thorough preflight planning and a clear understanding of the sUAS's capabilities and limitations.

Key Elements of Emergency Preparedness:
- **Know Your Aircraft:** Be familiar with the manufacturer's stated limitations, including:
  - Operating temperature and weather limits (wind, rain).
  - Maximum altitude and range.
  - Battery endurance and power consumption.
  - Maximum weight.
- **Develop Procedures:** The PIC should have a plan for foreseeable abnormal and emergency situations, such as:
  - Loss of control link.
  - GPS signal loss.
  - Unexpected flight into bad weather.
  - Uncommanded flight maneuvers.
  - Loss of power or engine failure.
- **Crew Briefing:** Before the flight, the PIC must inform all crew members about emergency procedures, contingency plans, and their specific roles and responsibilities.

Characteristics and Hazards of Lithium Batteries

Most sUAS are powered by rechargeable lithium-polymer (LiPo) batteries. While they offer excellent performance, they also carry major risks if mishandled, damaged, or defective.

The Primary Hazard: Thermal Runaway
- **What it is:** A chain reaction where overheating in one battery cell generates enough heat to cause adjacent cells to overheat.
- **Causes:** Overcharging, physical damage (from a crash), short-circuiting, manufacturing defects, or exposure to extreme heat.
- **Result:** The battery can swell ("puff"), vent flammable electrolyte gas, ignite, and potentially explode. A LiPo fire can flare repeatedly as each cell ruptures.

Transportation and Handling:
- Lithium batteries are considered a Class 9 hazardous material, but most used in sUAS are excepted from the strictest shipping regulations.
- Always inspect batteries for damage before and after each flight. Look for swelling, punctures, or dented corners. **Never use or attempt to charge a damaged battery**.

Safe Charging, Usage, and Fire Risks of Lithium Batteries

Proper care and handling of LiPo batteries are essential for safety and for maximizing their lifespan.

Safe Charging
- **Never leave charging batteries unattended**. The risk of fire is greatest during the charging process.
- Charge at a safe rate, typically "**1C**" (1 times the battery's capacity). For a 1500mAh battery, a 1C charge rate is 1.5 amps.
- Use a charger specifically designed for LiPo batteries.
- Do not charge a battery that is damaged, puffy, or was involved in a crash.

Safe Usage and Storage
- **Storage Voltage:** For long-term storage (more than a day or two), LiPo batteries should be kept at a storage voltage (typically around 3.8 volts per cell), not fully charged or fully discharged. Leaving a battery fully charged for extended periods will degrade its performance and lifespan.
- **Temperature:** Heat is the enemy of LiPo batteries. Avoid leaving them in hot cars or in direct sunlight. Cold temperatures will temporarily reduce a battery's performance, leading to shorter flight times.
- **Lifespan:** LiPo batteries have a limited life, typically around 300 charge cycles. Signs that a battery should be retired include puffing, a major decrease in performance, or high internal resistance.

Loss of Aircraft Control Link and Fly-Aways

A "fly-away" occurs when the communication link between the control station and the sUAS is lost, and the aircraft does not behave as expected (e.g., it fails to return home or land). This can lead to a loss of the aircraft and create a major hazard.

While Part 107 does not have a specific reporting requirement for a simple fly-away, other regulations may apply depending on the outcome. Under **49 CFR 830.5**, the NTSB requires immediate notification for certain serious incidents.

NTSB notification is required for an sUAS operation if there is:
- **A flight control system malfunction or failure**. A complete loss of the control link is considered a flight control system malfunction under this rule and requires immediate NTSB notification.
- **Damage to property, other than the aircraft, estimated to exceed $25,000**. If a fly-away sUAS crashes and causes severe property damage, an NTSB report is required.

> **Exam Tip**
> Remember the distinction between FAA and NTSB reporting. The FAA requires a report within 10 days for accidents involving serious injury or property damage over $500. The NTSB requires immediate notification for the serious incidents listed in Part 830, which includes flight control failure and property damage over $25,000.

Loss of GPS Signal

Most sUAS rely heavily on the Global Positioning System (GPS) for stabilization, navigation, and automated functions like Return-to-Home (RTH). A loss of the GPS signal during flight can be a serious event if the pilot is not prepared.

Causes of GPS Signal Loss:
- **Interference:** Radio frequency (RF) interference from power lines, cell towers, or other wireless devices.
- **Obstructions:** Flying in "urban canyons" between tall buildings, in deep valleys, or under dense tree cover can block the sUAS's view of the satellites.
- **Space Weather:** Solar flares can disrupt GPS satellite signals.

Consequences and Recovery:
- **Loss of Position Hold:** The sUAS may drift with the wind, as it no longer knows its precise location.
- **Failure of Automated Modes:** Functions like RTH or waypoint navigation will not work.
- **Pilot Action:** If GPS is lost, the pilot must be prepared to immediately take manual control of the aircraft (often called "ATTI" or Attitude mode). The pilot must rely

solely on their own skill and VLOS to control the aircraft's position and bring it back safely.

Frequency Spectrums

The communication link between the control station and the sUAS operates on radio frequencies (RF). Understanding the basics of this spectrum is important for avoiding interference.

- **Common Frequencies:** Most consumer and professional sUAS operate in the unlicensed **2.4 GHz** and **5.8 GHz** frequency bands. These bands are also used by many other devices, such as Wi-Fi routers, which can be a source of interference.
- **Interference:** Operating in an area with many competing wireless signals (e.g., dense urban or office environments) can lead to a degraded or lost control link, potentially causing a fly-away.
- **Line of Sight (LOS):** The 2.4 GHz and 5.8 GHz bands are **line-of-sight**. Any physical obstruction (buildings, trees, hills) between the controller and the sUAS can block the signal and cause a loss of control. Maintaining VLOS, as required by Part 107, helps ensure a clear radio line of sight.
- **FCC Regulation:** The Federal Communications Commission (FCC) regulates the use of all frequency spectrums. While the 2.4 and 5.8 GHz bands are unlicensed for general use, other frequencies may require a specific license from the FCC.

Procedures for Operations Over People

Part 107 establishes four distinct categories for legally operating an sUAS over people. The Remote PIC is responsible for understanding these categories and ensuring the entire operation complies with the rules for the specific category being used.

Category	Key Requirement	Operations Over Open-Air Assemblies
Category 1	sUAS weighs **0.55 lbs or less** AND has no exposed rotating parts that could lacerate skin.	**Prohibited**, unless the operation complies with Remote ID rules.
Category 2	sUAS has an FAA-accepted DOC stating it will not cause injury greater than **11 ft-lbs** of kinetic energy upon impact.	**Prohibited**, unless the operation complies with Remote ID rules.

Category 3	sUAS has an FAA-accepted DOC stating it will not cause injury greater than **25 ft-lbs** of kinetic energy upon impact. **AND** operation is restricted.	**Strictly Prohibited.**
Category 4	sUAS has an **FAA-issued airworthiness certificate**.	**Prohibited**, unless the operation complies with Remote ID rules.

Category 3 Operational Restrictions
Category 3 is unique because of its strict operational limitations. To fly a Category 3 sUAS over people, one of the following conditions must be met:
- The operation is conducted over a **closed or restricted-access site**, and everyone within the site has been notified.
- **OR**, if not in a closed site, the sUAS **may not maintain sustained flight** over any non-participating person. This allows for brief transits but prohibits hovering over or repeatedly flying back and forth over people.

Procedures for Operations at Night

Operating an sUAS at night requires the Remote PIC to meet specific training requirements and for the aircraft to have special equipment. These procedures are designed to mitigate the risks associated with reduced visibility.

The two primary requirements for night operations are:
- **Pilot Training:** The Remote PIC must have completed an initial knowledge test or recurrent training after **April 6, 2021**. This updated curriculum includes topics on night operations, such as night physiology and visual illusions.
- **Aircraft Lighting:** The sUAS must be equipped with **anti-collision lighting** that is visible for at least **3 statute miles**.
  - The PIC is responsible for verifying the lights are operational and meet this standard before flight.
  - The PIC may **reduce the intensity** of the lights if they determine it is in the interest of safety (e.g., to avoid being blinded by the lights), but the lights **may not be extinguished**.

These same requirements also apply to operations during **civil twilight** (the 30-minute periods before sunrise and after sunset).

Task C. Emergency Procedures - Practice Questions

✓ The answer key is located at the end of this chapter on Page 134

14. As part of a thorough preflight, a remote pilot should have a plan for

   A. maximizing the aircraft's flight time.
   B. handling abnormal or emergency situations.
   C. posting flight videos to social media.

15. What is the primary hazard associated with lithium batteries?

   A. They can leak corrosive acid.
   B. They are susceptible to thermal runaway, which can lead to fire and explosion.
   C. They lose their charge very quickly in cold weather.

16. What is the safest recommended charge rate for a LiPo battery?

   A. 1C.
   B. 2C.
   C. The maximum rate the charger can provide.

17. A remote pilot experiences a complete loss of the control link, and the sUAS "flys away." It subsequently crashes into a building, causing an estimated $30,000 in damage. What action is required?

   A. The pilot must immediately notify the nearest NTSB office.
   B. The pilot must report the accident to the FAA within 10 days.
   C. Both an immediate NTSB notification and a 10-day FAA report are required.

18. Which of the following situations is most likely to cause a loss of GPS signal?

   A. Flying over a large, open field on a clear day.
   B. Flying between tall buildings in a dense urban area.
   C. Flying at a high altitude above 300 feet AGL.

19. What is a common cause of radio frequency interference for sUAS operations?

   A. Operating in an area with many Wi-Fi networks.
   B. Flying during a solar eclipse.

C. Flying in cold weather.

20. Which category of operations over people is strictly prohibited from being conducted over an open-air assembly under any circumstances?

   A. Category 1.
   B. Category 2.
   C. Category 3.

21. What are the two primary requirements for conducting an sUAS operation at night?

   A. The sUAS must weigh less than 4.4 pounds, and the pilot must use a Visual Observer.
   B. The pilot must have completed the required night training, and the sUAS must have anti-collision lights visible for 3 statute miles.
   C. The operation must be in Class G airspace, and the sUAS must be equipped with night-vision cameras.

TASK D. AERONAUTICAL DECISION-MAKING

Aeronautical Decision-Making (ADM)

Aeronautical Decision-Making (ADM) is a systematic mental process used by pilots to consistently determine the best course of action in response to a given set of circumstances. It is a structured approach to risk management and stress management.

Human factors are a leading cause of aviation accidents, with the vast majority occurring during the critical takeoff and landing phases of flight. Effective ADM is a pilot's primary tool for mitigating the risks associated with human error.

The Risk Management Process
Risk management is a continuous cycle that forms the core of ADM. It involves six steps:
1. **Identify Hazards:** Recognize any condition or event that could pose a threat.
2. **Assess Risks:** Determine the potential severity and probability of the identified hazards.
3. **Analyze Controls:** Consider what actions can be taken to mitigate the risks.
4. **Make Control Decisions:** Choose the best course of action.
5. **Use Controls:** Actively implement the chosen risk mitigation strategies.
6. **Monitor Results:** Continuously evaluate the effectiveness of the controls and adjust as needed.

Key Concept: Four Principles of Risk Management
1. Accept no unnecessary risk.
2. Make risk decisions at the appropriate level (the PIC is the final authority).
3. Accept risk when benefits outweigh the costs.
4. Integrate risk management into all phases of the operation.

Crew Resource Management (CRM)

Crew Resource Management (CRM) is the effective use of all available resources—human, hardware, and information—to ensure a safe and efficient flight operation. For a remote pilot, this means managing crew members (like a Visual Observer), using the sUAS's equipment and automation properly, and utilizing external information sources (like weather reports and ATC communications).
- **Team Environment:** CRM encourages open communication where all crew members are expected to contribute to situational awareness and safety.

- **Task Management:** The Remote PIC is responsible for delegating tasks appropriately to avoid work overload on any single crew member, including themselves. An overworked crew member is more likely to make a mistake.
- **Single-Pilot Resource Management (SRM):** For solo operations, the pilot must manage all resources on their own. This requires a high degree of discipline in planning, workload management, and using available information to maintain situational awareness.

The Remote PIC is the final authority and is directly responsible for the operation, but effective CRM/SRM is essential for making the best use of all available resources to support that authority.

Situational Awareness

Situational awareness is the accurate perception and understanding of all factors and conditions affecting the safety of the flight. It's not just knowing where you are, but understanding what is happening around you and what is likely to happen next.
- **Maintaining Awareness:** A pilot maintains situational awareness by monitoring all available information sources, such as radio communications, weather, aircraft status, and the surrounding environment.
- **Obstacles:** Fatigue, stress, and work overload are major obstacles to situational awareness. They can cause a pilot to fixate on one problem while ignoring other critical information.
- **Workload Management:** Effective workload management is key to maintaining situational awareness. This involves planning, prioritizing, and sequencing tasks to avoid becoming overloaded. A pilot who is "task saturated" is no longer aware of all inputs and is highly susceptible to making errors.

Hazardous Attitudes

A pilot's attitude has a direct impact on the quality of their decision-making. The FAA has identified five hazardous attitudes that can lead to poor judgment. Recognizing these attitudes in oneself and applying the correct antidote is a critical ADM skill.

Hazardous Attitude	The Thought	Antidote
Anti-authority	"Don't tell me what to do."	Follow the rules. They are usually right.

Impulsivity	"Do it quickly."	Not so fast. Think first.
Invulnerability	"It won't happen to me."	It could happen to me.
Macho	"I can do it." (Taking risks to impress others)	Taking chances is foolish.
Resignation	"What's the use?" (Feeling powerless)	I'm not helpless. I can make a difference.

Hazard Identification and Risk Assessment

A fundamental responsibility of the Remote PIC is to proactively identify hazards, assess the associated risks, and implement controls to mitigate those risks to an acceptable level. This is a continuous process that occurs before, during, and after every flight.

The Risk Assessment Process
The process is a logical, step-by-step method for managing risk:
1. **Hazard Identification:** Identify all potential hazards related to the operation. A hazard is any real or potential condition, event, or circumstance that could lead to an unplanned or undesired event. A helpful tool for this step is the **PAVE** checklist:
    - **Personal:** Use the **IMSAFE** checklist (Illness, Medication, Stress, Alcohol, Fatigue, Emotion) to assess your fitness for flight.
    - **Aircraft:** Is the sUAS, including all its components, in a condition for safe flight?
    - **enVironment:** Assess weather, terrain, obstacles, and airspace.
    - **External Pressures:** Are there pressures like deadlines or client demands that could negatively influence your decisions?
2. **Determine Severity and Likelihood:** For each identified hazard, assess two things:
    - **Severity:** How bad would the outcome be if the hazard occurred? (e.g., catastrophic, hazardous, minor).
    - **Likelihood:** How likely is it that the hazard will occur? (e.g., frequent, probable, remote).
3. **Develop Mitigations:** Create specific actions (controls) to reduce either the likelihood or the severity of the risk. For example, if the hazard is high winds, a mitigation could be to delay the flight until the winds subside.
4. **Verify Mitigations:** Ensure that the controls you've put in place do not create new, unforeseen hazards (this is known as **substitute risk**). The process is a continuous loop; after implementing mitigations, you re-evaluate the operation for any new hazards.

> **Important Concept:** Residual and Substitute Risk
> - **Residual Risk:** The amount of risk that remains *after* you have implemented your mitigation strategies. The goal is to reduce risk to an acceptable level, not necessarily to eliminate it entirely.
> - **Substitute Risk:** A new hazard that is created by the action you took to mitigate a different hazard. Always re-assess your plan after adding a mitigation.

This entire process should be constantly re-evaluated during the flight, with a thorough debriefing conducted post-flight to capture lessons learned.

Task D. Aeronautical Decision-Making - Practice Questions

✓ The answer key is located at the end of this chapter on Page 134

22. Aeronautical Decision-Making (ADM) is a

    A. checklist that must be completed before every flight.
    B. regulation that prohibits flying in hazardous weather.
    C. systematic approach to the mental process used by pilots to determine the best course of action.

23. Crew Resource Management (CRM) is the effective use of

    A. only the hardware and software of the sUAS.
    B. all available resources, including human, hardware, and information.
    C. only the personnel directly involved in the flight.

24. What is situational awareness?

    A. The ability to know the geographical location of the sUAS at all times.
    B. The accurate perception and understanding of all factors and conditions that affect safety.
    C. A pilot's knowledge of all Part 107 regulations.

25. A remote pilot decides to fly a mission despite being aware of weather that is forecast to be below legal minimums, thinking, "The forecast is probably wrong, and I'll be fine." This is an example of which hazardous attitude?

    A. Macho.

B. Impulsivity.
C. Invulnerability.

26. A remote pilot identifies high winds as a potential hazard for an upcoming flight. Deciding to wait until the wind speed decreases is an example of

A. hazard identification.
B. risk mitigation.
C. substitute risk.

TASK E. PHYSIOLOGY

Physiological Factors Affecting Safety

A remote pilot's physical condition is just as critical to flight safety as the mechanical condition of the sUAS. Factors like dehydration and heatstroke can severely impair judgment and performance.

Dehydration and Heatstroke
- **Dehydration:** A critical loss of water from the body. The first noticeable effect is **fatigue**, which impairs both physical and mental performance. Other symptoms include headache, cramps, sleepiness, and dizziness.
    - **Prevention:** Drink two to four quarts of water every 24 hours. Do not rely on the sensation of thirst, as it often arrives after dehydration has already begun. Limit diuretic drinks like coffee, tea, and alcohol.
- **Heatstroke:** A life-threatening condition where the body is unable to control its temperature. It can be caused by operating in hot conditions without proper hydration. The symptoms are similar to dehydration but can progress to complete collapse.
    - **Prevention:** Drink water at frequent intervals, even if you are not thirsty.

Drug and Alcohol Use

The FAA has strict, zero-tolerance rules regarding the use of drugs and alcohol by any crewmember, including the Remote PIC.

Alcohol
The regulations under **14 CFR §91.17** are clear and absolute:
- **"8 hours bottle to throttle":** You may not act as a crewmember within 8 hours after the consumption of any alcoholic beverage.
- **Blood Alcohol Concentration (BAC):** You may not act as a crewmember with a BAC of **0.04% or greater**.
- **"Under the influence":** You may not fly while under the influence of alcohol, regardless of the time passed or BAC level.
- **Hangovers:** A pilot is still considered to be under the influence while experiencing a hangover. Motor and mental responses are still impaired.
- **Altitude Effects:** Altitude multiplies the effects of alcohol. A single drink at altitude can have the same effect as two or three drinks at sea level.

Drugs (Prescription and Over-the-Counter)
- **The Rule (§91.17):** No person may act as a crewmember while using any drug that affects the person's faculties in any way contrary to safety.
- **Self-Assessment:** It is the pilot's responsibility to determine if a medication is safe for flight. The safest rule is not to fly while taking any medication unless it is approved by the FAA or an Aviation Medical Examiner (AME).
- **Over-the-Counter (OTC) Medications:** Many common OTC drugs, especially antihistamines (like Benadryl) and decongestants, can cause drowsiness and cognitive deficits, making them unsafe for flight.
- **Waiting Period:** For any new medication (OTC or prescribed), you should wait at least **five maximal dosing intervals** (e.g., if the dose is every 4-6 hours, wait at least 30 hours) to ensure you do not have any adverse side effects.

Hyperventilation

Hyperventilation is an excessive rate and depth of breathing that leads to an abnormal loss of carbon dioxide from the blood. It is often triggered by stress, anxiety, or fear.
- **Symptoms:** The symptoms of hyperventilation are very similar to those of **hypoxia** (oxygen deprivation) and include visual impairment, lightheadedness, dizziness, tingling sensations, and muscle spasms.
- **Cause:** A pilot encountering an unexpected or stressful situation may subconsciously increase their breathing rate.
- **Treatment:** The treatment is to restore the body's proper carbon dioxide level. This can be done by consciously slowing the breathing rate, breathing into a paper bag, or talking aloud. Recovery is usually rapid once the breathing rate returns to normal.

Because the symptoms are so similar to hypoxia, it is critical for a pilot to correctly diagnose the condition. If a pilot were experiencing these symptoms at high altitude in a manned aircraft, the first step would be to check their oxygen system before assuming hyperventilation.

Stress and Fatigue

Stress and fatigue are insidious physiological factors that can severely degrade a pilot's ability to make sound decisions and perform safely.

Stress
Stress is the body's response to a demand placed upon it.
- **Acute Stress:** A short-term, immediate "fight or flight" response to a perceived danger. A healthy person can normally cope with acute stress.
- **Chronic Stress:** Long-term, unrelenting stress from factors like financial worries or relationship problems. Chronic stress exceeds a person's ability to cope, causes performance to fall sharply, and can lead to emotional illness. A pilot experiencing chronic stress is not safe to fly.

Fatigue
Fatigue is a state of tiredness that can result from physical or mental exertion.
- **Acute Fatigue:** A normal, short-term tiredness from lack of sleep or strenuous effort. It is cured by adequate rest and sleep. A special type, **skill fatigue**, can disrupt the timing and smoothness of performing familiar tasks.
- **Chronic Fatigue:** Long-term, deep-seated tiredness that is not relieved by rest. It is often caused by continuous high-stress levels and requires medical treatment.

> **Exam Tip**
> Both chronic stress and chronic fatigue are medically disqualifying conditions. A pilot suffering from either condition should not fly and should seek medical attention. The **IMSAFE** checklist (Illness, Medication, Stress, Alcohol, Fatigue, Emotion) is a critical self-assessment tool to use before every flight.

Fitness for Flight and Factors Affecting Vision

A remote pilot's fitness for flight goes beyond just being free from illness; it includes ensuring their vision is not impaired by self-imposed stressors. This is especially critical for night operations.

Fitness for Flight
Under Part 107, no crewmember may participate in an sUAS operation if they know or have reason to know they have a physical or mental condition that would interfere with safety. This is a self-certification responsibility.
- **Prohibited Conditions:** Any condition that could render a crewmember incapable of performing their duties is disqualifying. Examples include:
  - Loss of dexterity needed to operate the controls.
  - Blurred vision.
  - Inability to maintain situational awareness due to illness or medication.
  - A debilitating condition like a severe migraine.

Factors Affecting Vision (Especially at Night)
- **Alcohol:** Impairs coordination and judgment, and degrades the eye's visual sensitivity.
- **Tobacco:** Smoking is the most significant self-imposed stressor for night vision. It introduces carbon monoxide into the bloodstream, which reduces the blood's oxygen-carrying capacity (a form of hypoxia). This can reduce a smoker's night vision by up to 20%.
- **Hypoglycemia:** Low blood sugar from missed meals can impair performance and shorten attention span.

Physiological Aspects of Night Operation

The human eye functions differently in low-light conditions. Understanding these differences is essential for safe night flying.

Rods and Cones
The retina contains two types of light-sensitive cells:
- **Cones:** Concentrated in the center of the retina (in an area called the fovea). They are responsible for color vision and sharp detail in bright light. They are not effective in dim light.
- **Rods:** Concentrated in the periphery of the retina. They are responsible for vision in low-light conditions and are very sensitive to movement, but they cannot discern color or sharp detail.

Night Vision Techniques
- **Dark Adaptation:** The process of the eyes adjusting to darkness. While cones adapt quickly, the rods can take approximately 30 minutes to fully adapt. A brief exposure to bright light can completely destroy this adaptation, requiring the process to start over.
- **Night Blind Spot:** Because there are very few rods in the center of the retina (the fovea), a blind spot exists in the center of your vision at night.
- **Off-Center Viewing:** To see an object at night, you must look **5° to 10° off-center** from the object. This technique focuses the image onto the peripheral part of the retina where the more light-sensitive rods are located.
- **Scanning:** At night, use a systematic scanning pattern, moving your eyes in short, regularly spaced movements at every **10-degree sector**. Do not fixate on any single point for more than a **2 to 3 seconds**.

Night Illusions

In the dark, with fewer visual cues, the brain can be tricked into perceiving things that are not real. A remote pilot must be aware of these common night illusions to avoid becoming disoriented.

Illusion	Cause	Prevention
Autokinesis	Staring at a single, stationary point of light against a dark background for several seconds.	The light will appear to move. Avoid fixating on one light; use a continuous visual scan.
False Horizon	Mistaking a sloped cloud formation, city lights, or stars for the actual horizon.	Use flight instruments for reference and be aware of the surrounding terrain and features.
Flicker Vertigo	A light flickering at a rate between 4 and 20 cycles per second (e.g., flying past a strobe light).	Can cause nausea and vertigo. Avoid looking at flickering lights; use proper scanning.
Reversible Perspective	At night, an aircraft may appear to be moving away when it is actually approaching.	Observe the aircraft's lights. If they are getting brighter, it is approaching.

Task E. Physiology - Practice Questions

✓ The answer key is located at the end of this chapter on Page 134

27. What is the first noticeable effect of dehydration?

   A. Fatigue.
   B. Dizziness.
   C. Headache.

28. A remote pilot had two beers at lunch and is scheduled for a flight 4 hours later. They feel fine, and their blood alcohol level is below 0.04%. Is this operation legal?

   A. No, a pilot must wait at least 8 hours after consuming any alcoholic beverage.
   B. Yes, because their blood alcohol level is below the legal limit.
   C. Yes, because only two beers were consumed.

29. A remote pilot has been working long hours and is feeling a deep sense of tiredness that is not relieved by a full night's sleep. They are likely suffering from

   A. acute fatigue.
   B. chronic fatigue.
   C. skill fatigue.

30. Which self-imposed stressor is known to have the most significant negative effect on night vision?

   A. Alcohol.
   B. Fatigue.
   C. Smoking.

31. To see an object clearly at night, a pilot must use off-center viewing by looking

   A. directly at the object.
   B. 5° to 10° off center of the object.
   C. through the top portion of their vision.

32. A remote pilot is conducting a night flight and stares at a single light on a distant tower for several seconds. The light appears to begin moving on its own. This illusion is called

   A. a false horizon.
   B. flicker vertigo.
   C. autokinesis.

TASK F. MAINTENANCE AND INSPECTION PROCEDURES

Basic Maintenance

sUAS maintenance includes all scheduled and unscheduled repairs, inspections, modifications, and software updates necessary to keep the aircraft in a condition for safe operation.

- **Manufacturer's Instructions:** Whenever possible, maintenance should be performed according to the manufacturer's instructions and recommended schedule.
- **Scheduled Maintenance:** The manufacturer may provide a schedule for periodic maintenance or replacement of components based on flight hours, cycles, or calendar time. If no schedule is provided, the operator should develop their own by tracking repairs and component time-in-service to establish a reliable maintenance protocol.
- **Unscheduled Maintenance:** This is maintenance required outside of the normal schedule, often discovered during a preflight inspection or after a mishap. Flight operations should not occur until any unscheduled maintenance issues are corrected.
- **Who Can Perform Maintenance:** The manufacturer may specify that certain tasks must be performed by them or an approved facility. However, for most tasks, the operator can perform the maintenance or use personnel with the appropriate expertise. If a component cannot be safely repaired, it should be replaced.

Preflight Inspection

Before every flight, the Remote PIC **must** conduct a preflight inspection to ensure the sUAS is in a condition for safe operation. This is a mandatory requirement under **§107.49**.

The inspection should be systematic and thorough, covering all components of the system. While the manufacturer's checklist is the primary guide, the FAA recommends that the PIC's inspection procedure includes, at a minimum, a check of the following:

- **Visual Condition:** General inspection for any visible damage.
- **Airframe and Control Surfaces:** Check for cracks, dents, and proper attachment of all parts.
- **Propulsion System:** Inspect propellers, rotors, and motors for any damage.
- **Power Supply:** Verify that the aircraft and control station batteries have adequate power for the planned flight.
- **Control Link:** Confirm a solid communication link is established between the control station and the aircraft.
- **GPS:** Verify the sUAS has acquired a signal from the minimum number of satellites specified by the manufacturer.

- **Payload:** Ensure any attached equipment, like a camera, is secure.
- **Registration Markings:** Check that they are displayed and legible.
- **Control Check:** After powering on, check for correct movement of control surfaces in response to controller inputs.
- **Low-Altitude Check:** Conduct a brief hover at a low altitude to check for any imbalances or irregular operation before proceeding with the mission.

Mitigating Mechanical Failures

A critical part of maintaining an sUAS is the ability to recognize the signs of an impending mechanical failure. The Remote PIC should be vigilant for these conditions during preflight and in-flight.

Condition	Potential Hazard	Recommended Action
Cracking or Delamination	Structural failure.	Inspect to determine the scope of damage and assess the need for repair.
Liquid/Fuel/Electrical Smell	Fire, loss of power.	Inspect to find the source. Do not fly until the issue is resolved.
Distorted/Bulging Battery	Abrupt power loss, fire, or explosion.	Do not use the battery. Inspect for damage and replace if necessary.
Diminishing Flight Time	Impending battery failure, abrupt power loss.	Inspect the battery's integrity; it may be at the end of its service life.
Delayed Control Inputs	Loss of control, fly-away.	Discontinue flight. Inspect and test the control link until reliable communication is established.
Loose/Missing Hardware	Structural failure, dropped object.	Secure or replace any loose or missing fasteners before flight.

Record Keeping

While not strictly mandated by Part 107 for all operations, keeping a logbook for the sUAS is a highly beneficial best practice.

Benefits of Record Keeping:
- **Establish a Maintenance Schedule:** By documenting repairs and time-in-service for components, an operator can develop a reliable scheduled maintenance program.
- **Track Service Life:** Helps in tracking the service life of critical components, such as batteries, motors, and propellers.
- **Identify Trends:** Methodical data collection can help identify systemic component failures before they lead to an accident.
- **Demonstrate Responsibility:** Provides a documented history of the aircraft's maintenance, reinforcing the owner/operator's commitment to safety.

Records should be kept for all components of the system, including the aircraft, control station, and any other support equipment.

Preflight Inspection for Night Operations

In addition to all the standard preflight inspection items, an operation that will take place during civil twilight or at night requires a specific check of the aircraft's lighting system.

The remote pilot must:
- Ensure the sUAS's **anti-collision light(s) are functioning properly** before the flight.
- Consider the **power consumption** of the lights. The PIC may need to reduce the planned flight duration to ensure there is enough battery power to keep the lights illuminated for the entire flight and still have enough power to land safely.

Manufacturer's Declaration of Compliance (DOC) for Category 2 and 3

For an sUAS to be eligible for Category 2 or 3 operations over people, the manufacturer or applicant must formally declare to the FAA that the aircraft meets the required safety standards. This is done via a **Declaration of Compliance (DOC)**.
- **Basis of the DOC:** The DOC is based on a **MOC**, which is the specific testing, analysis, or inspection method used to prove the aircraft meets the safety requirements.

- **MOC Acceptance:** An MOC must be accepted by the FAA before an applicant can use it to support a DOC.
- **Safety Requirements:** The MOC and DOC must address three key areas:
  1. The sUAS does not exceed the applicable **injury severity limit** (impact kinetic energy).
  2. The sUAS does not have any **exposed rotating parts** that could cause lacerations.
  3. The sUAS does not contain any **safety defects**.

Task F. Maintenance and Inspection Procedures - Practice Questions

✓ The answer key is located at the end of this chapter on Page 134

33. If a small UAS manufacturer does not provide a maintenance schedule, who is responsible for establishing one?

   A. The FAA.
   B. The Remote PIC for each flight.
   C. The sUAS operator.

34. According to Part 107, who is responsible for inspecting the sUAS to ensure it is in a condition for safe operation?

   A. The sUAS owner.
   B. The Remote PIC.
   C. The person who performed the last maintenance.

35. During a preflight inspection, a remote pilot notices that the casing of a LiPo battery is bulging. What is the correct course of action?

   A. Use the battery, but plan for a shorter flight time.
   B. Do not use the battery and assess the need for replacement.
   C. Charge the battery fully to see if the bulge goes down.

36. What is a primary benefit of keeping a maintenance logbook for an sUAS?

   A. It is required to be submitted to the FAA annually.
   B. It helps in establishing a reliable scheduled maintenance program.
   C. It increases the resale value of the sUAS.

37. What is a required preflight action for a remote pilot planning a night flight?

A. Ensure the anti-collision lights are functional.
   B. Notify the nearest airport of the operation.
   C. Calibrate the sUAS's camera for low-light conditions.

38. A Means of Compliance (MOC) is a method used to show that an sUAS

   A. meets the performance-based safety requirements for Category 2 or 3 operations.
   B. has been registered with the FAA.
   C. is compliant with the Remote ID rule.

ANSWER KEY FOR V. OPERATIONS

1. A. - ATC is responsible for providing the safe, orderly, and expeditious flow of air traffic at towered airports.
2. B. - A CTAF is a frequency designated for the purpose of carrying out airport advisory practices while operating to or from an airport without an operating control tower.
3. B. - UNICOM is a non-government air/ground radio communication station that may provide airport information at public use airports.
4. B. - The phonetic equivalent for the letter "N" is November.
5. C. - A towered airport is defined as an airport that has an operating control tower.
6. B. - Monitoring the correct frequency allows the remote pilot to build a mental picture of the air traffic in the vicinity, significantly enhancing safety.
7. A. - Mandatory instruction signs have a red background with a white inscription and denote an entrance to a runway, critical area, or prohibited area.
8. B. - The downwind leg is a flight path parallel to the landing runway in the opposite direction of landing.
9. A. - A SIDA is a portion of an airport in which security measures specified in federal regulations are carried out.
10. B. - The Chart Supplement U.S. provides the most comprehensive information on a given airport, including runway details, services, and operational notes.
11. A. - Waterfowl, gulls, and raptors are the bird species that cause the most damage to civil aircraft in the United States.
12. C. - Flashing white and green is the standard beacon combination for a civilian land airport.
13. C. - The number [42] inside the blue dashed box indicates that the ceiling of the Class D airspace extends up to, but does not include, 4,200 feet Mean Sea Level (MSL).
14. B. - A prudent remote pilot will have a plan to handle potential emergency or abnormal procedures.
15. B. - Overheating can cause thermal runaway, which can lead to the release of flammable electrolyte, ignition, and explosion.
16. A. - The safest way to charge a LiPo battery, and the one that puts the least amount of strain on it, is to charge at a rate of 1C.
17. C. - Because the property damage exceeded $25,000, immediate notification to the NTSB is required. An FAA report would also be required because the damage exceeded $500.
18. B. - Tall objects like buildings can block the drone's view of the sky and make it difficult

to receive a strong GPS signal.
19. A. - The 2.4 GHz and 5.8 GHz bands used by most sUAS are also used for computer wireless networks, and this interference can cause problems.
20. C. - Category 3 operations are not allowed over an open-air assembly of persons, and this prohibition is not subject to the Remote ID exception.
21. B. - Small UAS operations at night may occur only if the remote PIC has completed the appropriate training and the sUAS is equipped with the required anti-collision lighting.
22. C. - ADM is a systematic approach to the mental process used by pilots to consistently determine the best course of action in response to a given set of circumstances.
23. B. - CRM is a component of ADM in which the pilot makes effective use of all available resources: human resources, hardware, and information.
24. B. - Situational awareness is the accurate perception and understanding of all the factors and conditions within the five fundamental risk elements that affect safety.
25. C. - The belief that "accidents happen to others, but never to me" is the hazardous attitude of invulnerability.
26. B. - Developing controls to reduce the risk identified is the mitigation step of the risk assessment process.
27. A. - The first noticeable effect of dehydration is fatigue, which in turn makes top physical and mental performance difficult, if not impossible.
28. A. - The regulations require a minimum of 8 hours to pass between drinking alcohol and piloting an aircraft.
29. B. - Chronic fatigue extends over a long period, is not relieved by adequate rest, and usually has psychological roots or an underlying disease.
30. C. - Of all the self-imposed stressors, cigarette smoking most decreases visual sensitivity at night, potentially causing a 20% loss in night vision capability.
31. B. - To see an object clearly at night, the pilot must expose the rods to the image, which is done by looking 5° to 10° off center.
32. C. - Autokinesis is caused by staring at a single point of light against a dark background for more than a few seconds.
33. C. - If the manufacturer does not provide scheduled maintenance instructions, the operator should establish a scheduled maintenance protocol.
34. B. - The remote PIC must inspect the small UAS to ensure that it is in a condition for safe operation prior to each flight.
35. B. - A distorted battery casing may indicate impending failure, such as an abrupt power loss or explosion, and it should not be used.

36. B. - By documenting repairs and time-in-service, an operator can establish a reliable maintenance schedule for the sUAS and its components.
37. A. - The remote pilot must ensure the small unmanned aircraft anti-collision light(s) function(s) properly prior to any flight that will occur at night.
38. A. - An MOC is a method to show that a small unmanned aircraft meets the safety requirements for operations over people, such as not exceeding the injury severity limit.

PRACTICE TESTS

Now it's time to put your knowledge into practice. The following **3 practice exams** are designed to give you a realistic preview of the official FAA knowledge test. To get the most benefit from them, your goal should be to simulate the actual testing environment as closely as possible. This approach does more than just test your knowledge; it helps you build the mental stamina and confidence needed for test day. Each exam mirrors the structure of the real thing, consisting of **60 multiple-choice questions** drawn from the core subject areas.

To begin, find a **two-hour window** of completely uninterrupted time. The official test has a two-hour limit, so training yourself to focus for this duration is a critical part of your preparation. Settle in at a quiet desk or table, and clear it of any materials that aren't permitted during the actual exam. Put away books, notes, and all personal electronic devices, leaving only your approved testing aids like a plotter or a basic calculator.

As you work through the questions, use the provided answer sheet to record your selections. This gets you accustomed to tracking your answers separately from the questions themselves. After you have completed all 60 questions, use the answer key to grade your performance. Remember, the benchmark for passing the official exam is a score of **70%**, which translates to **answering a minimum of 42 questions correctly**.

Finally, view your results as a powerful study tool. Scoring the test is just the first step; the real learning comes from carefully analyzing your mistakes. Pay close attention to the questions you answered incorrectly and look for patterns. Are you consistently struggling with a specific topic, such as weather or regulations? Use this valuable feedback to target your weaker areas and focus your final review where it will have the greatest impact.

PRACTICE TEST 1: ANSWER SHEET

1. Ⓐ Ⓑ Ⓒ
2. Ⓐ Ⓑ Ⓒ
3. Ⓐ Ⓑ Ⓒ
4. Ⓐ Ⓑ Ⓒ
5. Ⓐ Ⓑ Ⓒ
6. Ⓐ Ⓑ Ⓒ
7. Ⓐ Ⓑ Ⓒ
8. Ⓐ Ⓑ Ⓒ
9. Ⓐ Ⓑ Ⓒ
10. Ⓐ Ⓑ Ⓒ
11. Ⓐ Ⓑ Ⓒ
12. Ⓐ Ⓑ Ⓒ
13. Ⓐ Ⓑ Ⓒ
14. Ⓐ Ⓑ Ⓒ
15. Ⓐ Ⓑ Ⓒ
16. Ⓐ Ⓑ Ⓒ
17. Ⓐ Ⓑ Ⓒ
18. Ⓐ Ⓑ Ⓒ
19. Ⓐ Ⓑ Ⓒ
20. Ⓐ Ⓑ Ⓒ
21. Ⓐ Ⓑ Ⓒ
22. Ⓐ Ⓑ Ⓒ
23. Ⓐ Ⓑ Ⓒ
24. Ⓐ Ⓑ Ⓒ
25. Ⓐ Ⓑ Ⓒ
26. Ⓐ Ⓑ Ⓒ
27. Ⓐ Ⓑ Ⓒ
28. Ⓐ Ⓑ Ⓒ
29. Ⓐ Ⓑ Ⓒ
30. Ⓐ Ⓑ Ⓒ
31. Ⓐ Ⓑ Ⓒ
32. Ⓐ Ⓑ Ⓒ
33. Ⓐ Ⓑ Ⓒ
34. Ⓐ Ⓑ Ⓒ
35. Ⓐ Ⓑ Ⓒ
36. Ⓐ Ⓑ Ⓒ
37. Ⓐ Ⓑ Ⓒ
38. Ⓐ Ⓑ Ⓒ
39. Ⓐ Ⓑ Ⓒ
40. Ⓐ Ⓑ Ⓒ
41. Ⓐ Ⓑ Ⓒ
42. Ⓐ Ⓑ Ⓒ
43. Ⓐ Ⓑ Ⓒ
44. Ⓐ Ⓑ Ⓒ
45. Ⓐ Ⓑ Ⓒ
46. Ⓐ Ⓑ Ⓒ
47. Ⓐ Ⓑ Ⓒ
48. Ⓐ Ⓑ Ⓒ
49. Ⓐ Ⓑ Ⓒ
50. Ⓐ Ⓑ Ⓒ
51. Ⓐ Ⓑ Ⓒ
52. Ⓐ Ⓑ Ⓒ
53. Ⓐ Ⓑ Ⓒ
54. Ⓐ Ⓑ Ⓒ
55. Ⓐ Ⓑ Ⓒ
56. Ⓐ Ⓑ Ⓒ
57. Ⓐ Ⓑ Ⓒ
58. Ⓐ Ⓑ Ⓒ
59. Ⓐ Ⓑ Ⓒ
60. Ⓐ Ⓑ Ⓒ

PRACTICE TEST 1: QUESTIONS

1. According to 14 CFR Part 107, what is the definition of a "small unmanned aircraft"?

    A. An unmanned aircraft weighing 55 pounds or more.
    B. An unmanned aircraft weighing less than 55 pounds on takeoff, including everything that is on board or attached to the aircraft.
    C. Any aircraft that can be flown without a human pilot on board, regardless of weight.

2. Prior to every flight, the Remote PIC must assess the operating environment. This assessment must include which of the following?

    A. Local weather conditions, airspace, and any flight restrictions.
    B. The price of fuel and the client's budget.
    C. The availability of Wi-Fi for software updates.

3. When operating a small unmanned aircraft in Class G airspace, what is required?

    A. Authorization from Air Traffic Control (ATC).
    B. A transponder with altitude-reporting capability.
    C. No authorization from ATC is required.

4. What is the minimum flight visibility required for sUAS operations, as observed from the control station?

    A. 1 statute mile.
    B. 3 statute miles.
    C. 5 statute miles.

5. An FAA accident report is required if an incident results in damage to property, other than the sUAS itself, with a cost greater than

    A. $250 to repair or replace the property, whichever is lower.
    B. $500 to repair or replace the property, whichever is lower.
    C. $1,000 to repair or replace the property, whichever is higher.

6. To operate an sUAS in Class D airspace, the remote pilot must first obtain

    A. authorization from Air Traffic Control (ATC).
    B. permission from the airport manager.

C. a certificate of waiver from the FAA.

Figure 1-20.

7. Refer to Figure 1-20 above. You are planning an sUAS operation within Alert Area A-381. What frequency should be used to monitor the high volume of helicopter and seaplane traffic?

   A. 122.9 MHz.
   B. 119.5 MHz.
   C. 123.025 MHz.

8. Refer to Figure 1-20 above. What is the length of the longest runway at Winnie Stowell (T90) airport?

A. 3,600 feet.
   B. 2,400 feet.
   C. 3,000 feet.

9. Under what condition is it permissible to operate an sUAS from a moving land vehicle?

   A. When operating over a congested, urban area.
   B. When transporting another person's property for compensation.
   C. When operating over a sparsely populated area.

10. What are the minimum cloud clearance requirements for sUAS operations?

    A. 500 feet above and 2,000 feet horizontally from clouds.
    B. 1,000 feet below and 1,000 feet horizontally from clouds.
    C. 500 feet below and 2,000 feet horizontally from clouds.

11. How does an aft (rearward) Center of Gravity (CG) affect the stability of an unmanned aircraft?

    A. It increases longitudinal stability, making the aircraft more stable.
    B. It has no effect on stability but increases maneuverability.
    C. It decreases longitudinal stability, making the aircraft less stable and potentially difficult to control.

12. Refusal to submit to an alcohol test when requested by a law enforcement officer is grounds for

    A. a mandatory 30-day waiting period before re-application.
    B. a written warning for the first offense.
    C. suspension or revocation of the Remote Pilot Certificate.

13. If a Visual Observer is used during an sUAS operation, what must the Remote PIC ensure?

    A. The VO holds a valid Remote Pilot Certificate.
    B. The VO and the Remote PIC maintain effective communication with each other at all times.
    C. The VO is positioned at least 50 feet away from the Remote PIC.

14. To operate an sUAS within a Restricted Area, the remote pilot must have permission from

A. the nearest Air Traffic Control facility.
B. the controlling agency of the Restricted Area.
C. the local airport authority.

15. Which weather phenomenon is typically associated with an unstable air mass?

    A. Smooth air and steady precipitation.
    B. Stratiform clouds and poor visibility.
    C. Turbulence and showery precipitation.

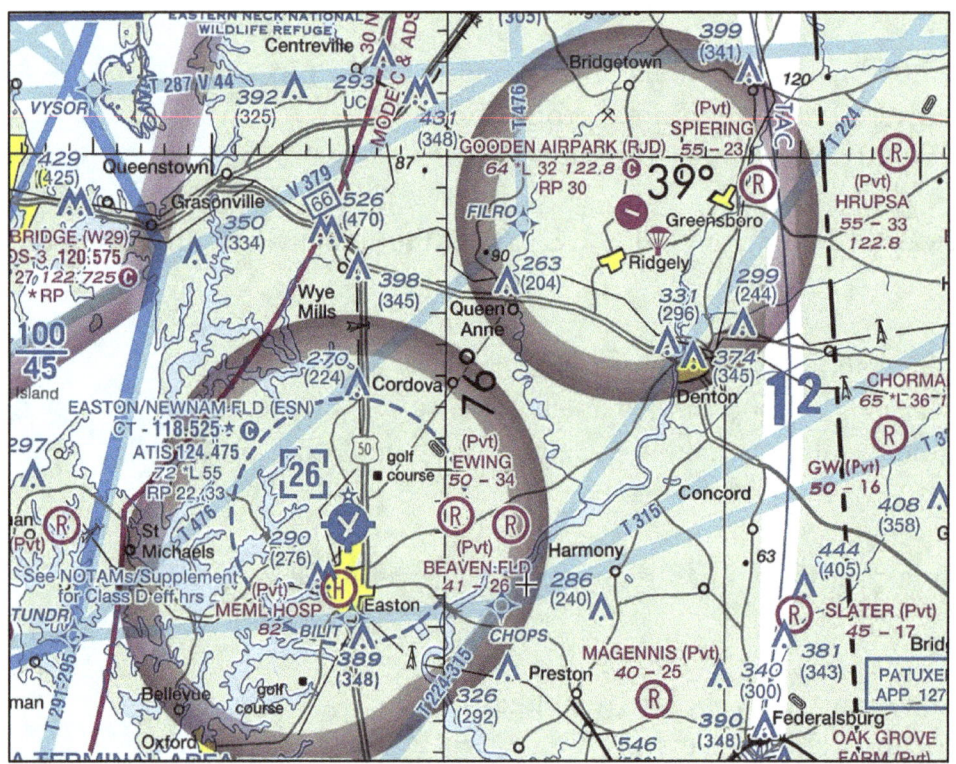

Figure 1-21.

16. Refer to Figure 1-21 above. What is the ATIS frequency for Easton/Newnam Field (ESN)?

    A. 124.475 MHz.
    B. 118.525 MHz.
    C. 122.725 MHz.

17. Refer to Figure 1-21 above. The airspace directly overlying Easton/Newnam Field (ESN) is of what classification from the surface up to 2,600 feet MSL?

A. Class E.
B. Class D.
C. Class G.

18. Unless otherwise authorized, what is the maximum groundspeed for a small unmanned aircraft?

    A. 87 knots (100 mph).
    B. 100 knots (115 mph).
    C. 55 knots (63 mph).

19. To maintain currency as a Remote PIC, you must complete recurrent aeronautical knowledge training within the previous

    A. 12 calendar months.
    B. 24 calendar months.
    C. 36 calendar months.

20. To operate an sUAS during civil twilight, the aircraft must be equipped with

    A. a flashing red beacon visible for 1 statute mile.
    B. anti-collision lighting visible for at least 3 statute miles.
    C. two-way radio communication equipment.

21. What is a primary purpose of a Temporary Flight Restriction (TFR)?

    A. To provide a safe environment for the operation of disaster relief aircraft.
    B. To establish permanent routes for commercial air traffic.
    C. To designate areas for sUAS training exercises only.

22. What is the primary cause of all changes in the Earth's weather?

    A. The movement of air masses.
    B. Variations in solar energy received by the Earth's surface.
    C. The rotation of the Earth on its axis.

23. A remote pilot is operating in the vicinity of a non-towered airport. To ensure situational awareness, the pilot should monitor the airport's Common Traffic Advisory Frequency (CTAF). What is the primary purpose of the CTAF?

    A. To receive instructions from a remote air traffic controller.

B. For pilots of manned aircraft to self-announce their position and intentions.
C. To obtain automated weather broadcasts only.

24. When must a current remote pilot certificate be in the pilot's personal possession or readily accessible at the control station?

    A. Only when flying for commercial purposes.
    B. Only when a Visual Observer is also present.
    C. Anytime the person is acting as the Remote PIC.

25. What is a "load factor" in relation to an aircraft?

    A. The total weight of the payload the aircraft is carrying.
    B. The ratio of the total lift being produced by the aircraft to its total weight.
    C. The maximum amount of time an aircraft can remain airborne.

26. A person without a Part 107 certificate may operate an sUAS for a commercial operation under what specific condition?

    A. If they are directly supervised by a Remote PIC who can immediately take direct control.
    B. As long as the operation is conducted in Class G airspace.
    C. Provided the sUAS weighs less than 0.55 pounds.

27. What type of weather briefing should be requested when the proposed departure time is 6 or more hours away?

    A. A Standard Briefing.
    B. An Abbreviated Briefing.
    C. An Outlook Briefing.

28. What is a characteristic of stable air?

    A. Stratiform clouds and poor surface visibility.
    B. Good surface visibility.
    C. Cumuliform clouds.

29. What is the maximum altitude a remote pilot can fly an sUAS above a 1,200-foot tall television tower?

    A. 400 feet AGL.

B. 1,600 feet AGL.
C. 1,200 feet AGL.

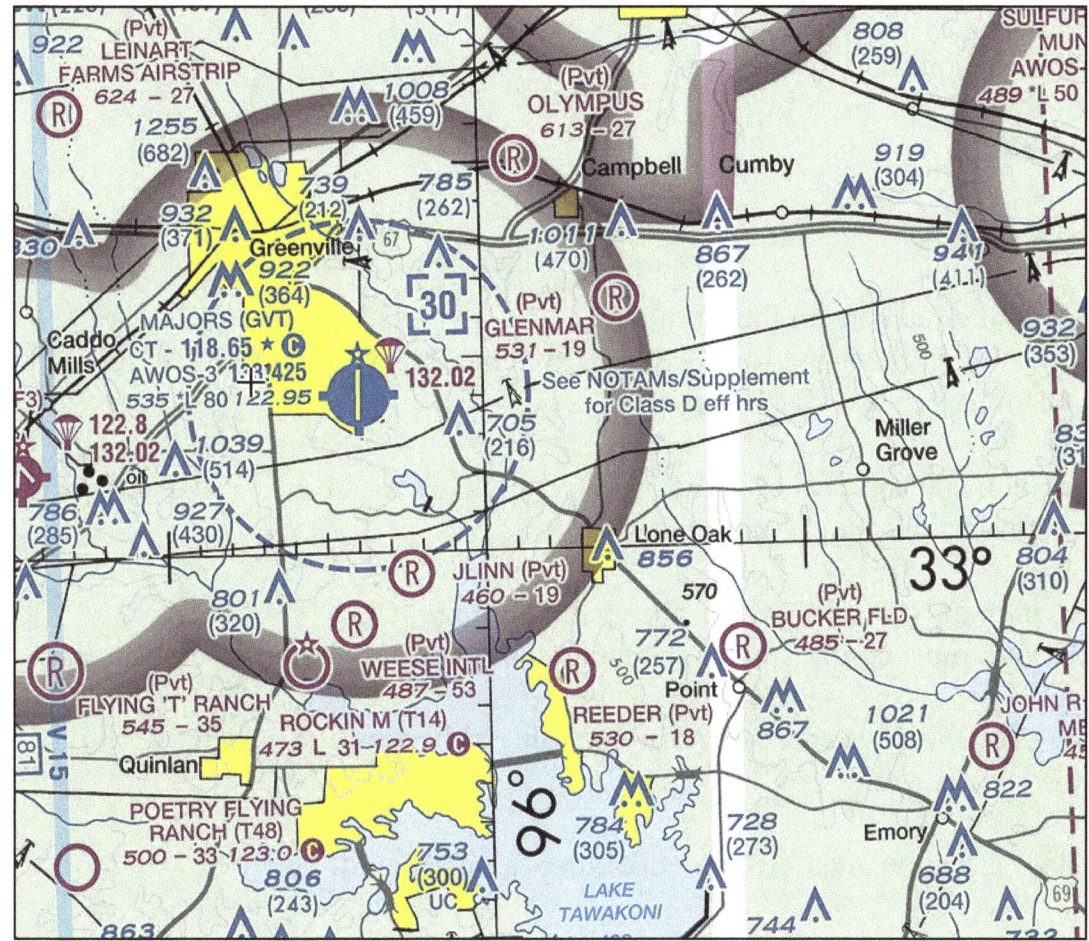

Figure 1-22.

30. Refer to Figure 1-22 above. What are the approximate coordinates of Majors Airport (GVT)?

A. 33°05'N, 96°05'W.
B. 33°30'N, 96°30'W.
C. 32°55'N, 95°55'W.

31. Refer to Figure 1-22 above. What are the approximate coordinates of the town of Emory?

A. 32°53'N, 95°46'W.
B. 33°05'N, 96°05'W.
C. 32°58'N, 95°45'W.

REMOTE PILOT FAA PART 107 STUDY GUIDE | 145

32. The responsibility for preventing a hazardous situation from developing during an sUAS flight rests with

   A. all crewmembers equally.
   B. the owner of the sUAS.
   C. the Remote PIC.

33. What is "density altitude"?

   A. The altitude read directly from the altimeter.
   B. The pressure altitude corrected for nonstandard temperature.
   C. The height of the aircraft above the ground.

34. An sUAS operation is planned near a Military Operations Area (MOA). What is the remote pilot's responsibility concerning the MOA?

   A. The remote pilot must obtain a waiver to operate in the MOA.
   B. The remote pilot must contact the controlling agency for permission to fly near the MOA.
   C. The remote pilot should exercise extreme caution and be aware that military flight activities may be present.

35. What is the likely effect on an sUAS if it encounters a microburst?

   A. A powerful downdraft and significant wind shear, posing a severe hazard to the aircraft.
   B. A strong updraft followed by a period of calm air.
   C. A gradual increase in airspeed followed by a gentle downdraft.

36. When a control tower located at an airport in Class D airspace ceases operation for the night, what happens to the airspace classification?

   A. The airspace reverts to Class E or a combination of Class E and G.
   B. The airspace designation is suspended until the tower reopens.
   C. The airspace remains Class D.

37. A remote pilot is hired to inspect a cell tower. The client provides a company-owned sUAS and states that it is ready for flight. What is the remote pilot's responsibility?

   A. To trust the client's assessment and proceed with the flight immediately.

B. To perform a preflight inspection of the sUAS to ensure it is in a condition for safe operation.
C. To ask the client for the maintenance logs before flying.

38. What is the definition of "night" for the purposes of Part 107 operations?

    A. The time between one hour after sunset and one hour before sunrise.
    B. The time between official sunset and official sunrise.
    C. The time between the end of evening civil twilight and the beginning of morning civil twilight.

39. Which of these is a potential consequence of operating an sUAS with an overloaded payload?

    A. Increased maneuverability.
    B. Shorter takeoff run and improved climb rate.
    C. Reduced endurance and higher stalling speed.

40. A remote pilot is planning a flight in an area where a Notice to Air Missions (NOTAM) has been issued for a temporary flight restriction. The remote pilot must

    A. comply with the provisions of the NOTAM.
    B. contact the nearest FSS for verbal permission to fly.
    C. operate at an altitude below 200 feet AGL to avoid the restriction.

41. During a flight, the remote pilot experiences a "flyaway," where the sUAS does not respond to control inputs. What is a critical part of the emergency response?

    A. Immediately turn off the control station to reset the connection.
    B. Attempt to regain control by flying another sUAS nearby to observe it.
    C. Notify any available crewmembers and ATC, if applicable, of the situation.

42. Crew Resource Management (CRM) is the effective use of all available resources to ensure a safe outcome. For a remote pilot, these resources include

    A. human resources, hardware, and information.
    B. only the hardware and software of the sUAS.
    C. the Remote PIC's judgment exclusively.

43. What are the typical vertical limits of Class C airspace?

A. Surface to 2,500 feet AGL.
B. Surface to 4,000 feet AGL.
C. 1,200 feet AGL to 10,000 feet MSL.

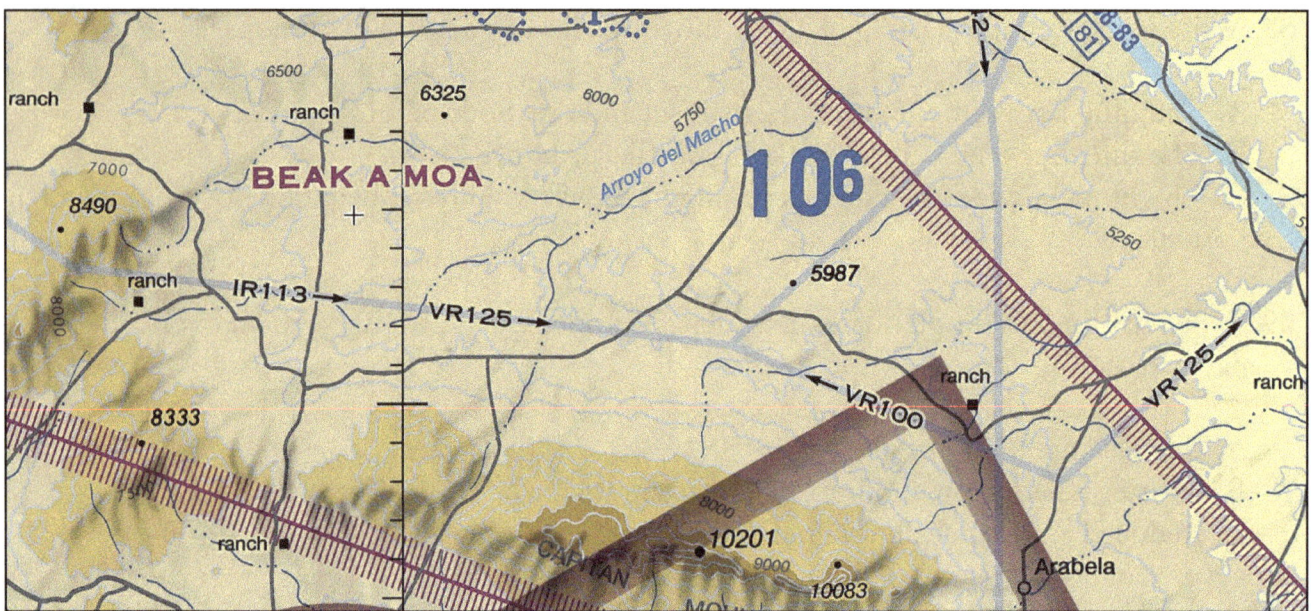

Figure 1-23.

44. Refer to Figure 1-23 above. You are planning an sUAS operation near the military training routes labeled VR125 and IR113. What is a key characteristic of these routes?

   A. They are used for military training, with at least one segment of each route operating above 1,500 feet AGL.
   B. They are used exclusively for military training conducted below 1,500 feet AGL.
   C. They are reserved for high-altitude, supersonic military operations only.

45. Refer to Figure 1-23 above. The chart depicts both IR and VR military training routes. What is the fundamental difference between an IR route (like IR113) and a VR route (like VR125)?

   A. IR routes are exclusively for high-altitude operations, while VR routes are for low-altitude operations.
   B. IR routes are flown under Instrument Flight Rules (IFR), while VR routes are flown under Visual Flight Rules (VFR).
   C. IR routes are flown from East to West, while VR routes are flown from West to East.

46. A remote pilot on a hot, humid day begins to experience a headache, fatigue, and dizziness. These are symptoms of what physiological condition?

A. Hyperventilation.
B. Hypoxia.
C. Dehydration.

47. Which type of fog is dependent on the presence of wind for its formation and continued existence?

A. Radiation fog.
B. Advection fog.
C. Steam fog.

48. What is a potential consequence of making a fraudulent or intentionally false entry in any record or report required by Part 107?

A. A mandatory fine of $500.
B. A requirement to retake the initial aeronautical knowledge test.
C. Suspension or revocation of the Remote Pilot Certificate.

49. During a preflight inspection, you notice that the casing of a lithium battery is slightly swollen or "puffed." What is the correct course of action?

A. Use the battery, but for a shorter flight time.
B. Do not use the battery and dispose of it according to manufacturer or safety guidelines.
C. Charge the battery fully to see if the swelling reduces.

50. What is the first step in the Aeronautical Decision-Making (ADM) and risk management process?

A. Assessing the level of risk.
B. Implementing risk controls.
C. Identifying hazards.

51. Which of the following is a recommended technique for maintaining situational awareness during an sUAS operation?

A. Focusing exclusively on the video feed from the aircraft's camera.
B. Monitoring radio communications and frequently scanning the airspace and operating environment.
C. Relying solely on the Visual Observer to identify all potential hazards.

52. What three conditions are necessary for the formation of a thunderstorm?

   A. High pressure, a stable temperature lapse rate, and fog.
   B. Sufficient moisture, an unstable lapse rate, and a lifting action.
   C. Low humidity, a temperature inversion, and calm winds.

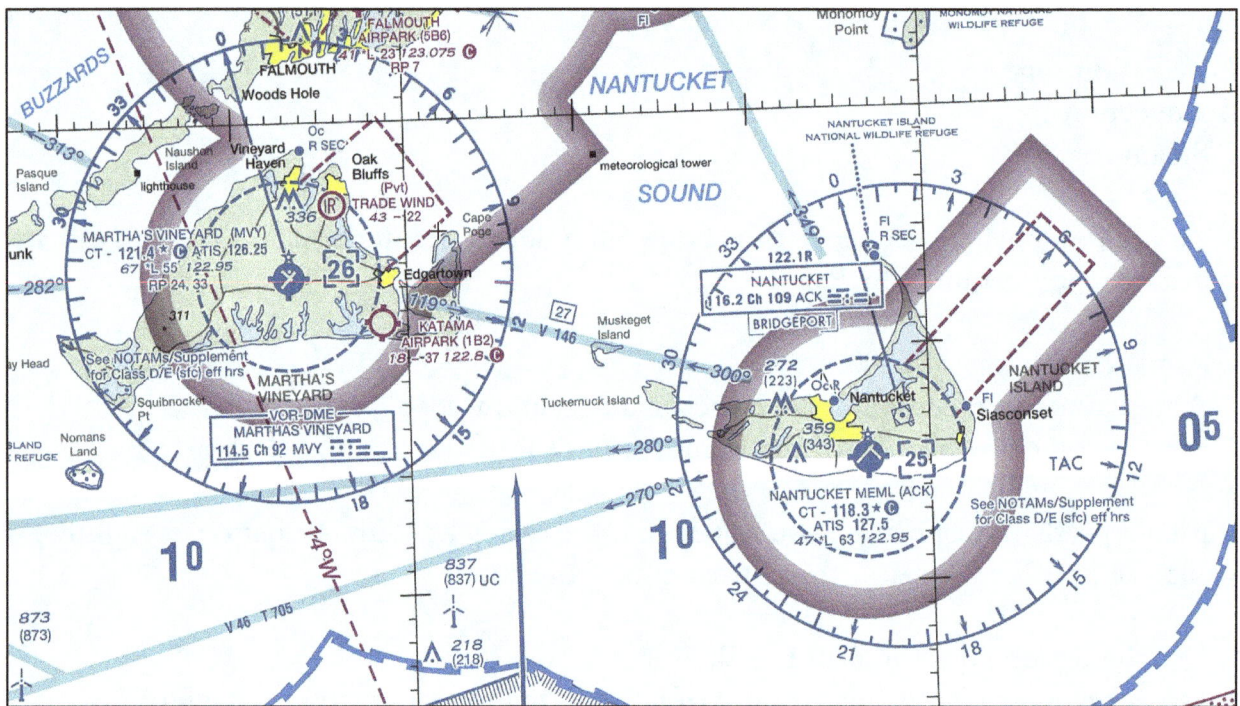

Figure 1-24.

53. Refer to Figure 1-24 above. The airspace directly overlying Nantucket Memorial (ACK) airport is designated as Class D. What is the ceiling of this airspace?

   A. 2,600 feet AGL.
   B. 2,500 feet MSL.
   C. 2,500 feet AGL.

54. Refer to Figure 1-24 above. You are planning to operate an sUAS over the town of Edgartown, just east of the Martha's Vineyard (MVY) Class D airspace. What is the floor of the controlled airspace in this location?

   A. The surface.
   B. 1,200 feet AGL.
   C. 700 feet AGL.

150 | REMOTE PILOT FAA PART 107 STUDY GUIDE

55. When an aircraft is in a coordinated, level turn at a 60-degree bank, the load factor is

   A. 1.5 Gs.
   B. 2.0 Gs.
   C. 4.0 Gs.

56. How is Class E airspace that begins at the surface depicted on a sectional chart?

   A. A dashed magenta line.
   B. A dashed blue line.
   C. A solid magenta line.

57. Which hazardous attitude is characterized by the thought, "Rules do not apply in this situation"?

   A. Invulnerability.
   B. Resignation.
   C. Anti-authority.

58. A remote pilot is planning to inspect a wind turbine that is 350 feet tall. The operation will remain within a 400-foot radius of the turbine. What is the highest altitude the sUAS is permitted to fly?

   A. 400 feet AGL.
   B. 750 feet AGL.
   C. 400 feet above the turbine's nacelle.

59. An abnormal increase in the volume of air breathed in and out, often caused by a stressful situation, can lead to a condition known as

   A. hyperventilation.
   B. dehydration.
   C. hypoxia.

60. If a remote pilot loses the command and control link with the sUAS, what is the expected behavior of the aircraft?

   A. It will follow a pre-set lost link procedure, such as returning to home, landing, or hovering.
   B. It will continue on its last commanded heading and altitude indefinitely.
   C. It will immediately shut down and fall to the ground.

PRACTICE TEST 1: ANSWER KEY

1. B. - Part 107 defines a small unmanned aircraft (sUAS) as an unmanned aircraft weighing less than 55 pounds, which includes the aircraft, payload, and any other attached equipment at the time of takeoff.
2. A. - According to 14 CFR §107.49, the Remote PIC must assess the operating environment, which includes checking local weather, airspace classifications, flight restrictions, and the location of persons and property on the surface.
3. C. - Class G is uncontrolled airspace, and operations under Part 107 do not require ATC authorization to fly in this class of airspace.
4. B. - 14 CFR §107.51 specifies that the minimum flight visibility must be no less than 3 statute miles from the location of the control station.
5. B. - 14 CFR §107.9 requires a report to the FAA within 10 days for any accident that causes damage to any property, other than the sUAS, if the cost to repair or replace it is more than $500.
6. A. - 14 CFR §107.41 prohibits sUAS operations in Class B, C, or D airspace without prior authorization from Air Traffic Control.
7. C. - The information box for Alert Area A-381, located in the lower portion of the chart, specifies to contact (CTC) 123.025 MHz due to the high volume of traffic.
8. A. - The airport data for Winnie Stowell (T90) reads "24 *L 36 122.9 C". The number "36" after the runway lighting symbol (*L) indicates the length of the longest runway in hundreds of feet, which is 3,600 feet.
9. C. - Part 107 permits operation from a moving land or water-borne vehicle, provided the operation is conducted over a sparsely populated area and is not transporting property for compensation or hire.
10. C. - 14 CFR §107.51 requires that the small unmanned aircraft must be kept at least 500 feet below the clouds and 2,000 feet horizontally from them.
11. C. - An aft CG reduces the aircraft's longitudinal stability. This can make it difficult to recover from stalls and may lead to control difficulties, as the aircraft becomes tail-heavy.
12. C. - According to 14 CFR §107.59, refusing to submit to an alcohol test is grounds for the denial of an application for a remote pilot certificate or the suspension or revocation of an existing certificate.
13. B. - When a VO is used, the crew must maintain effective communication at all times to ensure the VO can relay hazards to the Remote PIC in a timely manner.
14. B. - Operations in a Restricted Area are not permitted unless the remote pilot has

obtained permission from the using or controlling agency, as they are responsible for the activities within that airspace.

15. C. - Unstable air is characterized by vertical air movement, which leads to turbulence, the formation of cumuliform clouds, and showery precipitation.

16. A. - The airport data block for Easton/Newnam Field (ESN) shows "ATIS 124.475," which is the frequency for the Automated Terminal Information Service.

17. B. - The dashed blue circle surrounding the airport indicates the presence of Class D airspace. The number [26] inside the blue brackets indicates the ceiling of this Class D airspace is 2,600 feet MSL.

18. A. - 14 CFR §107.51 limits the groundspeed of a small unmanned aircraft to no more than 87 knots, which is equivalent to 100 miles per hour.

19. B. - A Remote PIC must pass a recurrent knowledge test or complete online training within 24 calendar months to continue exercising the privileges of their certificate.

20. B. - For operations during periods of civil twilight or at night, the sUAS must have lighted anti-collision lighting that is visible for at least 3 statute miles.

21. A. - TFRs are issued to protect persons and property in the air or on the surface from a hazard, such as providing a safe environment for disaster relief operations, or to provide security for major events.

22. B. - Nearly all weather is a result of heat exchange. Uneven heating of the Earth's surface by the sun is the driving force behind atmospheric circulation, which in turn creates weather phenomena.

23. B. - The CTAF is a designated frequency for pilots to communicate their positions and intentions to other aircraft in the vicinity of a non-towered airport, enhancing safety through shared situational awareness.

24. C. - 14 CFR §107.7 requires the Remote PIC to have their remote pilot certificate in their physical possession and readily accessible whenever exercising the privileges of that certificate.

25. B. - Load factor is the force applied to an aircraft's structure, measured in Gs (gravity). It represents the ratio of the lift being generated to the aircraft's weight and increases during maneuvers like turns or pull-ups.

26. A. - A non-certificated person may operate the flight controls of an sUAS under Part 107, provided they are under the direct supervision of a Remote PIC and the Remote PIC has the ability to immediately take direct control of the aircraft.

27. C. - An Outlook Briefing is intended for planning purposes when a flight is proposed for 6 or more hours in the future. It provides initial forecast information that can help in making

a go/no-go decision.

28. A. - Stable air resists vertical movement, which tends to trap smoke, dust, and other pollutants, leading to poor visibility. This stability also favors the development of widespread, layered clouds (stratiform).

29. B. - Part 107 allows an sUAS to be flown up to 400 feet above the uppermost limit of a structure, provided it remains within a 400-foot radius of that structure. Therefore, 1,200 feet + 400 feet = 1,600 feet AGL.

30. A. - Majors (GVT) airport is located slightly north of the 33°N latitude line and west of the 96°W longitude line. Following the tick marks, its position is approximately 33°05'N, 96°05'W.

31. A. - The town of Emory is located just south of the 33°N latitude line and just east of the 96°W longitude line. By interpolating between the marked lines of latitude and longitude, its position is found to be approximately 32°53'N, 95°46'W.

32. C. - The Remote PIC is directly responsible for, and is the final authority as to, the operation of the sUAS. This includes identifying and mitigating risks before and during the flight.

33. B. - Density altitude is a measure of air density. It is calculated by starting with pressure altitude and then correcting for temperature deviations from the standard atmosphere.

34. C. - While entry into an active MOA is not prohibited for VFR traffic (including sUAS), it is critical for pilots to be vigilant. MOAs are used for military training, which can include high-speed, acrobatic maneuvers.

35. A. - A microburst is a small-scale, intense downdraft that, upon reaching the surface, spreads outward in all directions. This creates severe wind shear and is extremely dangerous to all aircraft, especially at low altitudes.

36. A. - When a control tower at a Class D airport closes, the airspace designation changes. It typically becomes a Class E surface area, or reverts to Class G up to a specific altitude with Class E above it.

37. B. - The Remote PIC is required by regulation to conduct a preflight check of the sUAS before each flight to verify it is safe to operate, regardless of who owns the aircraft or who performed the last maintenance.

38. C. - For Part 107, night is specifically defined as the period from the end of evening civil twilight to the beginning of morning civil twilight, as published in the Air Almanac.

39. C. - Exceeding the aircraft's weight limits adversely affects performance in almost every way. It requires more power to fly, thus reducing endurance, and it increases the speed at which the wings will stall.

40. A. - NOTAMs, including those for TFRs, are regulatory in nature. A remote pilot must comply with all restrictions and procedures outlined in the NOTAM unless they have a specific waiver or authorization.

41. C. - In a flyaway situation, communication is key. The Remote PIC should immediately notify crewmembers and, if operating under an ATC authorization, inform ATC so they can warn other aircraft of the potential hazard.

42. A. - CRM is a comprehensive approach that involves using all available resources, which includes other crewmembers (human), the aircraft and control station (hardware), and data such as weather reports, charts, and manuals (information).

43. B. - Class C airspace is generally configured from the surface to 4,000 feet above the airport elevation (AGL), with an outer shelf that typically starts at 1,200 feet AGL.

44. A. - Military Training Routes (MTRs) with three-digit identifiers (e.g., 125, 113) have at least one segment that operates above 1,500 feet AGL. MTRs with four-digit identifiers operate entirely at or below 1,500 feet AGL.

45. B. - The letters in a Military Training Route designation indicate the flight rules under which the route is operated. "IR" stands for Instrument Route, and "VR" stands for Visual Route.

46. C. - Headache, fatigue, cramps, and dizziness are common symptoms of dehydration. Flying in hot and humid conditions increases the body's rate of water loss, making it crucial for pilots to stay hydrated.

47. B. - Advection fog forms when moist air moves over a colder surface, and wind is required to transport the air mass. Radiation fog, by contrast, forms on calm, clear nights.

48. C. - 14 CFR §107.5 states that falsifying records is a basis for the suspension or revocation of any certificate or waiver, denial of an application, or a civil penalty.

49. B. - A swollen or damaged lithium battery indicates a potential internal failure. It should not be used, charged, or stored, and must be disposed of properly.

50. C. - The risk management process begins with identifying potential hazards in all areas of the operation (e.g., pilot, aircraft, environment). Only after hazards are identified can they be assessed and mitigated.

51. B. - Situational awareness is the accurate perception of all factors affecting the flight. This requires the Remote PIC to integrate information from multiple sources, including monitoring the aircraft, the environment, and communications.

52. B. - For a thunderstorm to develop, there must be a source of moisture, an unstable atmosphere (where temperature decreases rapidly with altitude), and a mechanism to lift the air, such as a front or surface heating.

53. B. - The dashed blue circle around Nantucket Memorial (ACK) indicates Class D airspace. The number [25] within the blue brackets signifies that the ceiling of this Class D airspace extends up to, but does not include, 2,500 feet MSL.

54. C. - Edgartown is located within the faded magenta ring (vignette) but outside the dashed blue Class D circle. This vignette indicates that the floor of the Class E controlled airspace begins at 700 feet AGL.

55. B. - In a 60-degree level bank, the lift required to maintain altitude is twice the aircraft's weight, resulting in a load factor of 2.0 Gs. This significantly increases the stalling speed.

56. A. - A dashed magenta line on a sectional chart indicates that Class E airspace begins at the surface. This is typically found around airports that do not have an operating control tower but do have a weather observer and an instrument approach procedure.

57. C. - The anti-authority attitude is found in people who do not like being told what to do and may disregard rules they feel are unnecessary. The antidote is to remember that rules are usually in place for a reason.

58. B. - The rule allows flight up to 400 feet above the structure's uppermost limit. Therefore, the maximum altitude is the height of the turbine (350 feet) plus 400 feet, which equals 750 feet AGL.

59. A. - Hyperventilation is an excessive rate and depth of breathing that leads to an abnormal loss of carbon dioxide from the blood. It can be triggered by stress and cause symptoms like dizziness and tingling sensations.

60. A. - Modern sUAS are programmed with lost link procedures to ensure predictable behavior if the control link is lost. These procedures are designed to mitigate risk by having the aircraft execute a safe, pre-determined action.

PRACTICE TEST 2: ANSWER SHEET

1. Ⓐ Ⓑ Ⓒ   16. Ⓐ Ⓑ Ⓒ   31. Ⓐ Ⓑ Ⓒ   46. Ⓐ Ⓑ Ⓒ

2. Ⓐ Ⓑ Ⓒ   17. Ⓐ Ⓑ Ⓒ   32. Ⓐ Ⓑ Ⓒ   47. Ⓐ Ⓑ Ⓒ

3. Ⓐ Ⓑ Ⓒ   18. Ⓐ Ⓑ Ⓒ   33. Ⓐ Ⓑ Ⓒ   48. Ⓐ Ⓑ Ⓒ

4. Ⓐ Ⓑ Ⓒ   19. Ⓐ Ⓑ Ⓒ   34. Ⓐ Ⓑ Ⓒ   49. Ⓐ Ⓑ Ⓒ

5. Ⓐ Ⓑ Ⓒ   20. Ⓐ Ⓑ Ⓒ   35. Ⓐ Ⓑ Ⓒ   50. Ⓐ Ⓑ Ⓒ

6. Ⓐ Ⓑ Ⓒ   21. Ⓐ Ⓑ Ⓒ   36. Ⓐ Ⓑ Ⓒ   51. Ⓐ Ⓑ Ⓒ

7. Ⓐ Ⓑ Ⓒ   22. Ⓐ Ⓑ Ⓒ   37. Ⓐ Ⓑ Ⓒ   52. Ⓐ Ⓑ Ⓒ

8. Ⓐ Ⓑ Ⓒ   23. Ⓐ Ⓑ Ⓒ   38. Ⓐ Ⓑ Ⓒ   53. Ⓐ Ⓑ Ⓒ

9. Ⓐ Ⓑ Ⓒ   24. Ⓐ Ⓑ Ⓒ   39. Ⓐ Ⓑ Ⓒ   54. Ⓐ Ⓑ Ⓒ

10. Ⓐ Ⓑ Ⓒ   25. Ⓐ Ⓑ Ⓒ   40. Ⓐ Ⓑ Ⓒ   55. Ⓐ Ⓑ Ⓒ

11. Ⓐ Ⓑ Ⓒ   26. Ⓐ Ⓑ Ⓒ   41. Ⓐ Ⓑ Ⓒ   56. Ⓐ Ⓑ Ⓒ

12. Ⓐ Ⓑ Ⓒ   27. Ⓐ Ⓑ Ⓒ   42. Ⓐ Ⓑ Ⓒ   57. Ⓐ Ⓑ Ⓒ

13. Ⓐ Ⓑ Ⓒ   28. Ⓐ Ⓑ Ⓒ   43. Ⓐ Ⓑ Ⓒ   58. Ⓐ Ⓑ Ⓒ

14. Ⓐ Ⓑ Ⓒ   29. Ⓐ Ⓑ Ⓒ   44. Ⓐ Ⓑ Ⓒ   59. Ⓐ Ⓑ Ⓒ

15. Ⓐ Ⓑ Ⓒ   30. Ⓐ Ⓑ Ⓒ   45. Ⓐ Ⓑ Ⓒ   60. Ⓐ Ⓑ Ⓒ

PRACTICE TEST 2: QUESTIONS

1. Which of the following is the correct definition of a "control station" according to 14 CFR Part 107?

   A. An interface used by the remote pilot to control the flight path of the small unmanned aircraft.
   B. The physical location where the Remote PIC is standing during the flight.
   C. Any FAA-approved structure used for housing and launching a small unmanned aircraft.

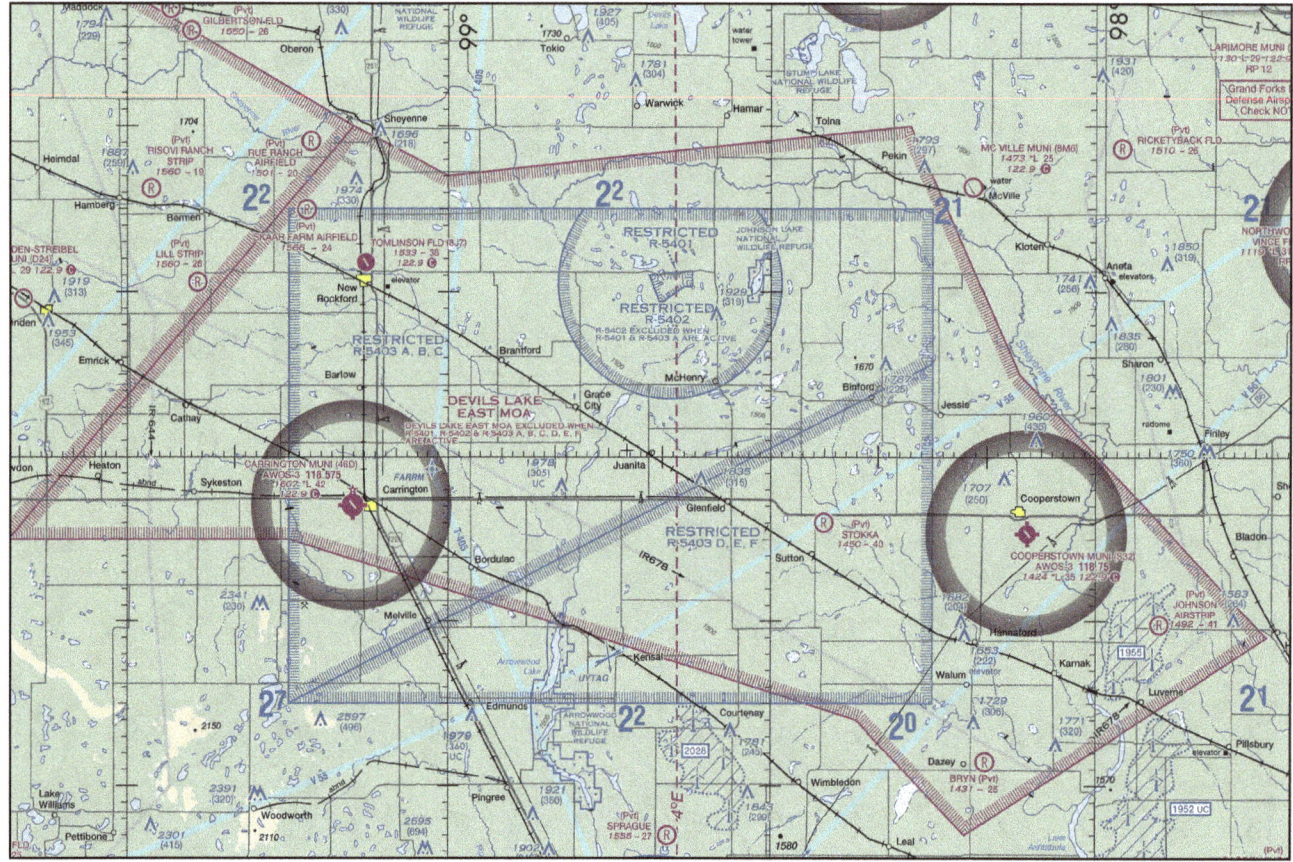

Figure 2-20.

2. Refer to Figure 2-20 above. A note for the DEVILS LAKE EAST MOA states that it is excluded when several restricted areas are active. What does this imply for a remote pilot?

   A. The MOA and the restricted areas are never active at the same time.
   B. The MOA is only active when the restricted areas are inactive.
   C. Pilots must get permission for both the MOA and the restricted areas to fly there.

158 | REMOTE PILOT FAA PART 107 STUDY GUIDE

3. Refer to Figure 2-20 above. What is the classification of the airspace from the surface up to 699 feet AGL over Carrington Muni (46D)?

   A. Class G.
   B. Class E.
   C. Class D.

4. A remote pilot is preparing for a flight and notices that the forecast includes high winds. What is the pilot's responsibility regarding this information?

   A. Proceed with the flight as planned, as sUAS are not significantly affected by wind.
   B. Assess the operating environment and determine if the flight can be conducted safely within the sUAS's operating limits.
   C. Obtain a waiver from the FAA to fly in high wind conditions.

5. What is the general dimension of the airspace designated as Class D around an airport?

   A. Surface to 10,000 feet MSL with a 10-nautical-mile radius.
   B. Surface to 4,000 feet AGL with a 5-nautical-mile radius.
   C. Surface to 2,500 feet AGL with a radius tailored to the instrument procedures at that airport, typically around 4 nautical miles.

6. Which combination of conditions will result in the highest density altitude?

   A. High temperature, high humidity, and low-pressure setting.
   B. Low temperature, low humidity, and high-pressure setting.
   C. High temperature, low humidity, and high-pressure setting.

7. What is a potential consequence of operating an sUAS that is loaded in a manner that puts its center of gravity (CG) forward of the forward limit?

   A. The aircraft will be less stable and may be difficult to recover from a stall.
   B. The aircraft will be overly stable, potentially making it difficult to raise the nose for landing.
   C. The aircraft will have a shorter endurance but increased maneuverability.

8. Within how many calendar days must an sUAS accident be reported to the FAA?

   A. 30 days.
   B. 10 days.
   C. 24 hours.

9. The "see and avoid" concept requires that the Remote PIC must

   A. yield right-of-way to all other aircraft.
   B. only be aware of other sUAS operations.
   C. fly at a predetermined altitude to avoid all traffic.

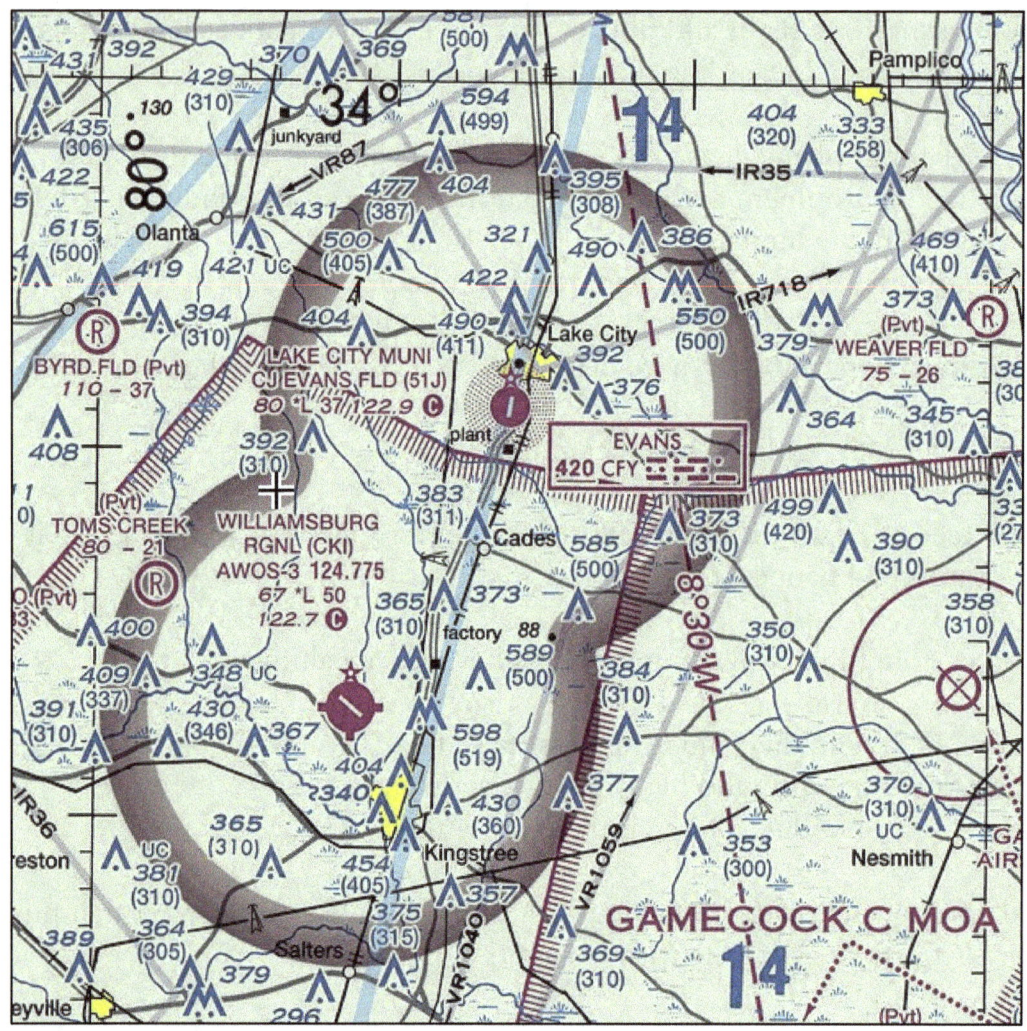

Figure 2-21.

10. Refer to Figure 2-21 above. What are the approximate geographic coordinates of Williamsburg RGNL (CKI) airport?

   A. 33°30'N, 79°30'W.
   B. 33°43'N, 79°51'W.
   C. 34°05'N, 80°05'W.

11. Refer to Figure 2-21 above. You are planning an operation that will enter the GAMECOCK C MOA. What does this airspace designation mean?

    A. All flight is prohibited without prior authorization.
    B. It is an Alert Area with a high volume of student pilot training.
    C. It is a Military Operations Area where pilots should exercise extreme caution.

12. What is the primary purpose of a Military Operations Area (MOA)?

    A. To prohibit all civilian air traffic for national security.
    B. To separate certain military training activities from IFR traffic.
    C. To provide a designated area for sUAS testing and development.

13. During a night operation, the Remote PIC notices that the anti-collision lights are making it difficult to see the sUAS's attitude and position. What action is the pilot permitted to take?

    A. Reduce the intensity of the anti-collision lights if it is in the interest of safety.
    B. Turn off the anti-collision lights for the remainder of the flight.
    C. Land the aircraft immediately, as this indicates a system malfunction.

14. While reviewing a METAR, a remote pilot sees the code "SCT030." What does this indicate?

    A. A scattered cloud layer with its base at 300 feet AGL.
    B. A scattered cloud layer with its base at 3,000 feet AGL.
    C. A solid overcast ceiling at 3,000 feet MSL.

15. An increase in the load factor on an sUAS will cause

    A. the aircraft to stall at a higher speed.
    B. the aircraft to stall at a lower speed.
    C. no change in the stalling speed.

16. What is the floor of Class G airspace?

    A. The surface.
    B. 700 feet AGL.
    C. 1,200 feet AGL.

17. What is a primary characteristic of an unstable air mass?

A. Smooth air.
B. Widespread stratiform clouds.
C. Good surface visibility outside of precipitation.

18. If a Remote PIC deviates from a Part 107 rule to respond to an in-flight emergency, what must they do after the incident?

    A. Immediately land and cease all flight operations for 24 hours.
    B. Submit a detailed report to the NTSB within 48 hours.
    C. Send a written report to the FAA upon request.

19. An sUAS must be registered with the FAA if its takeoff weight is

    A. 0.55 pounds or more.
    B. more than 0.55 pounds.
    C. 1 pound or more.

20. A stall occurs when the wing exceeds its critical

    A. airspeed.
    B. load factor.
    C. angle of attack.

21. What is the most effective way for a remote pilot to scan for traffic?

    A. Staring at a single point in the sky where traffic is expected.
    B. A series of short, regularly spaced eye movements to search different 10-degree sectors of the sky.
    C. Continuously and rapidly scanning the sky from horizon to horizon.

22. A remote pilot is asked to inspect a 500-foot radio tower. The client wants the sUAS to circle the very top of the tower. What is the maximum altitude the remote pilot can operate the sUAS to conduct this inspection?

    A. 500 feet AGL.
    B. 400 feet AGL.
    C. 900 feet AGL.

23. A remote pilot is operating on a clear day. Suddenly, the sUAS experiences a total loss of the GPS signal. What is the most appropriate initial response?

A. Continue operating the sUAS normally, but be prepared to take manual control.
B. Immediately activate the "Return to Home" function.
C. Declare an in-flight emergency to the nearest ATC facility.

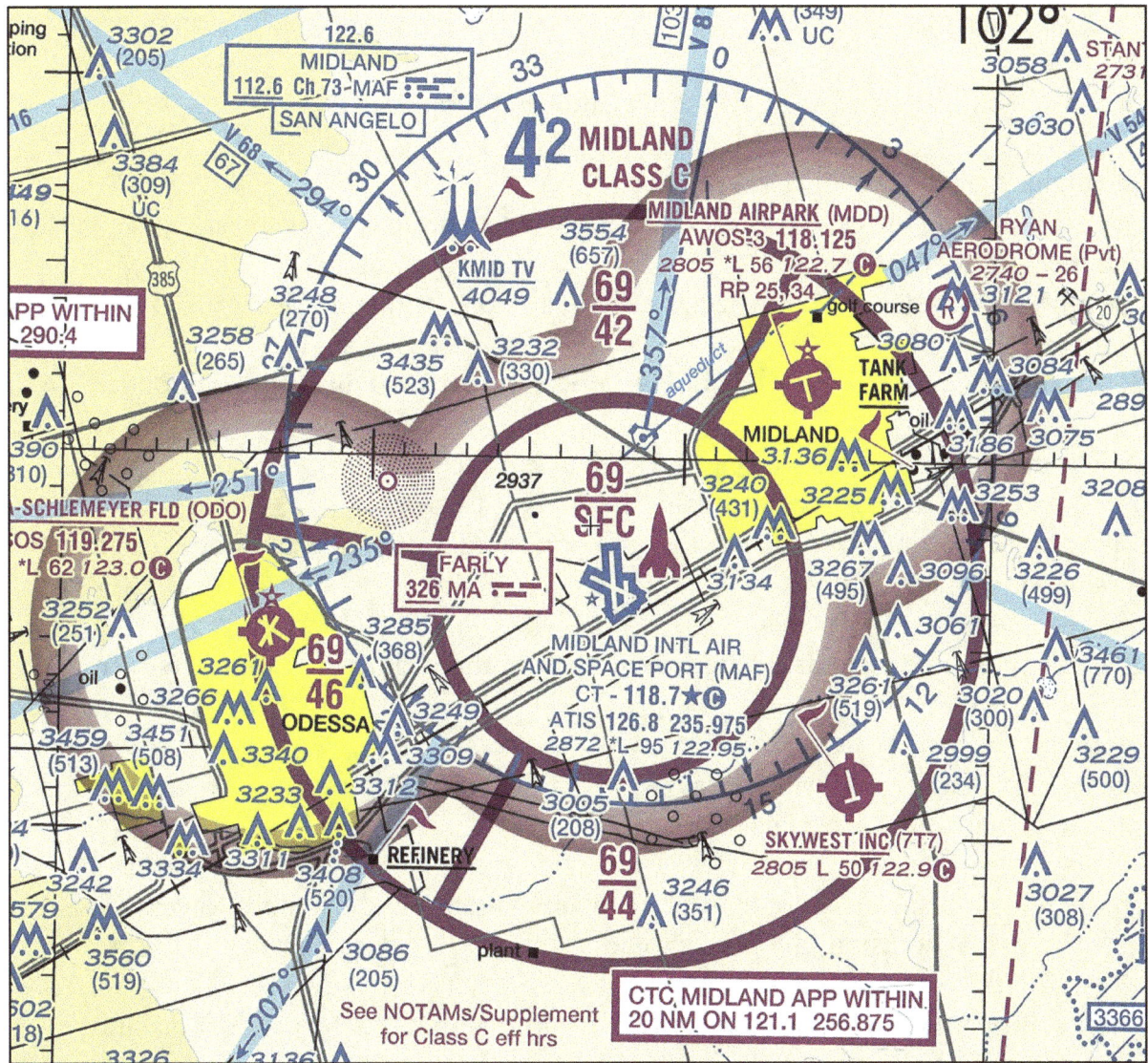

Figure 2-22.

24. Refer to Figure 2-22 above. What is the Common Traffic Advisory Frequency (CTAF) for Midland Intl Air and Space Port (MAF)?

A. 118.7 MHz.
B. 126.8 MHz.
C. 122.95 MHz.

25. Refer to Figure 2-22 above. What is the length of the longest runway at Midland Intl Air and Space Port (MAF)?

   A. 9,500 feet.
   B. 5,000 feet.
   C. 2,872 feet.

26. What is a "ceiling" defined as in aviation weather reports?

   A. The highest altitude of any cloud layer.
   B. The height of the lowest layer of clouds reported as broken or overcast, or the vertical visibility into an obscuration.
   C. The altitude at which visibility becomes less than 3 statute miles.

27. Under what condition may an object be dropped from a small unmanned aircraft?

   A. Only if the object is soft and weighs less than 8 ounces.
   B. If prior authorization is received from the FAA for every drop.
   C. If precautions are taken to ensure that the object will not create an undue hazard to persons or property.

28. What is the primary danger associated with flying in the vicinity of a thunderstorm?

   A. Radio interference.
   B. Extreme turbulence and wind shear.
   C. Reduced engine performance.

29. A remote pilot is planning an operation in an area with several tall, unlit towers. To mitigate the risk of collision, the pilot should

   A. fly only during the brightest part of the day and maintain a safe standoff distance.
   B. request a NOTAM to be issued for the flight.
   C. rely on the sUAS's GPS map to avoid the obstacles.

30. Which type of special use airspace is flight through completely forbidden for all aircraft?

   A. Prohibited Area.
   B. Restricted Area.
   C. Warning Area.

31. To satisfy the requirement for maintaining VLOS, the remote pilot must be able to see the sUAS with

   A. vision unaided by any device other than corrective lenses.
   B. the use of binoculars or a first-person view (FPV) camera.
   C. the assistance of a remote camera operator.

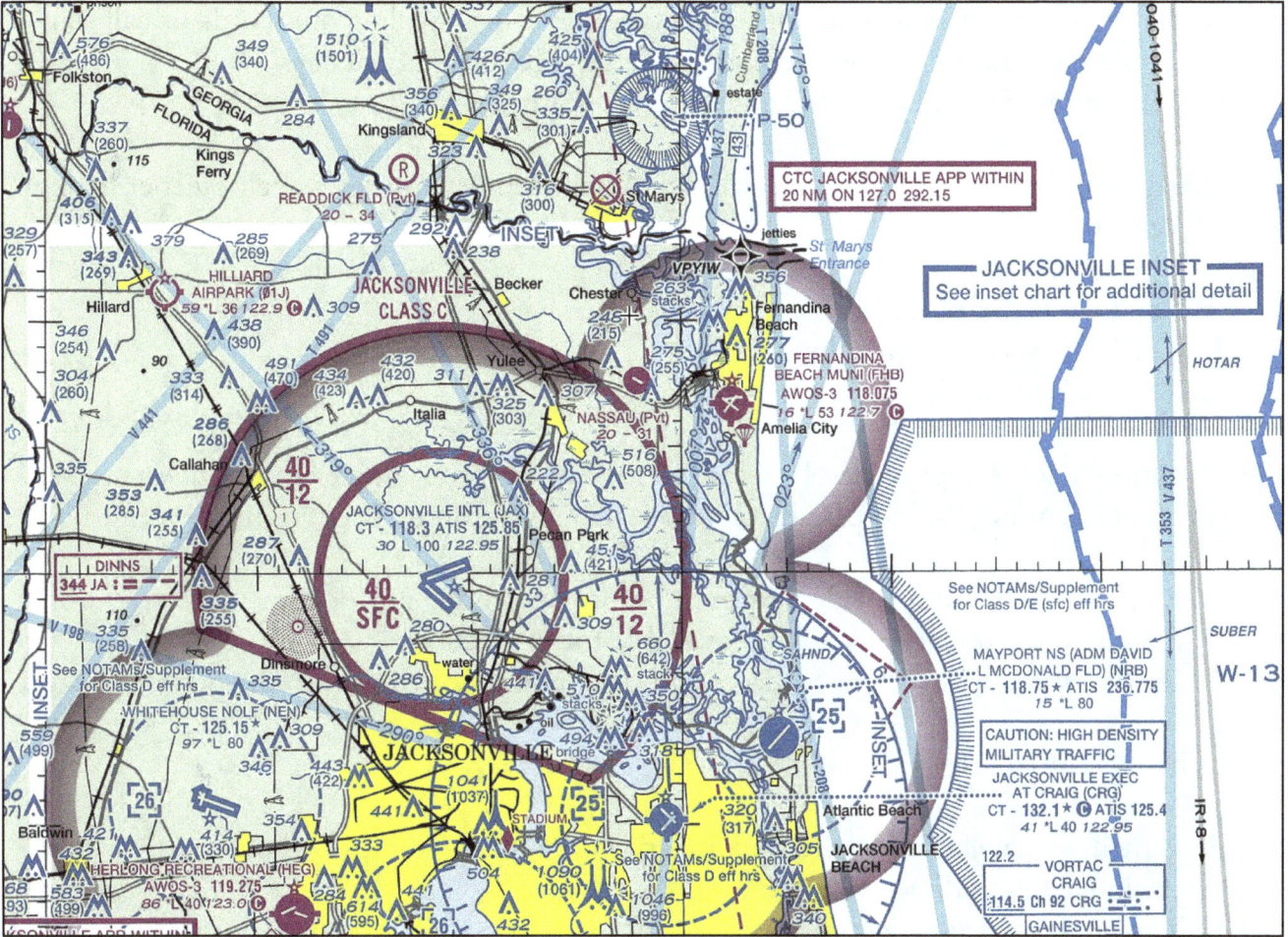

Figure 2-23.

32. Refer to Figure 2-23 above. What type of special use airspace is the area designated as P-50, located northeast of Kingsland?

   A. Restricted Area.
   B. Prohibited Area.
   C. Military Operations Area.

33. Refer to Figure 2-23 above. What are the floor and ceiling of the outer shelf of the Jacksonville Class C airspace?

A. The floor is 1,200 feet MSL, and the ceiling is 4,000 feet MSL.
   B. The floor is the surface, and the ceiling is 4,000 feet MSL.
   C. The floor is 1,200 feet AGL, and the ceiling is 4,000 feet AGL.

34. What is the purpose of the phonetic alphabet in aviation communication?

   A. To ensure clarity and avoid misunderstandings when spelling out words or call signs.
   B. To shorten transmissions and increase radio frequency efficiency.
   C. To communicate in a coded language for security purposes.

35. What happens to the load factor on an sUAS as it enters a progressively steeper bank in a level turn?

   A. The load factor decreases.
   B. The load factor remains the same.
   C. The load factor increases.

36. A remote pilot is approached by a federal law enforcement officer who requests to see the pilot's remote pilot certificate and the sUAS registration. The remote pilot must

   A. Request the officer provide a warrant before presenting any documents.
   B. State that the documents are not available for inspection.
   C. Present the remote pilot certificate and registration documents for inspection.

37. What is "autokinesis"?

   A. A night visual illusion where a stationary light appears to move when stared at for a prolonged period.
   B. The tendency for an aircraft to automatically return to a level flight attitude.
   C. A flight maneuver involving a rapid change in direction and altitude.

38. What is the primary difference between a "standard" and an "abbreviated" weather briefing from a Flight Service Station?

   A. A standard briefing is for VFR flights, while an abbreviated briefing is for IFR flights.
   B. An abbreviated briefing is used to update a previous standard briefing or to inquire about a specific piece of information.
   C. A standard briefing is a condensed version of an abbreviated briefing.

39. A small unmanned aircraft may not be operated over any human beings unless

A. The human beings are provided with hard hats.
B. The operation is conducted during daylight hours only.
C. The person is directly participating in the operation or is located under a covered structure.

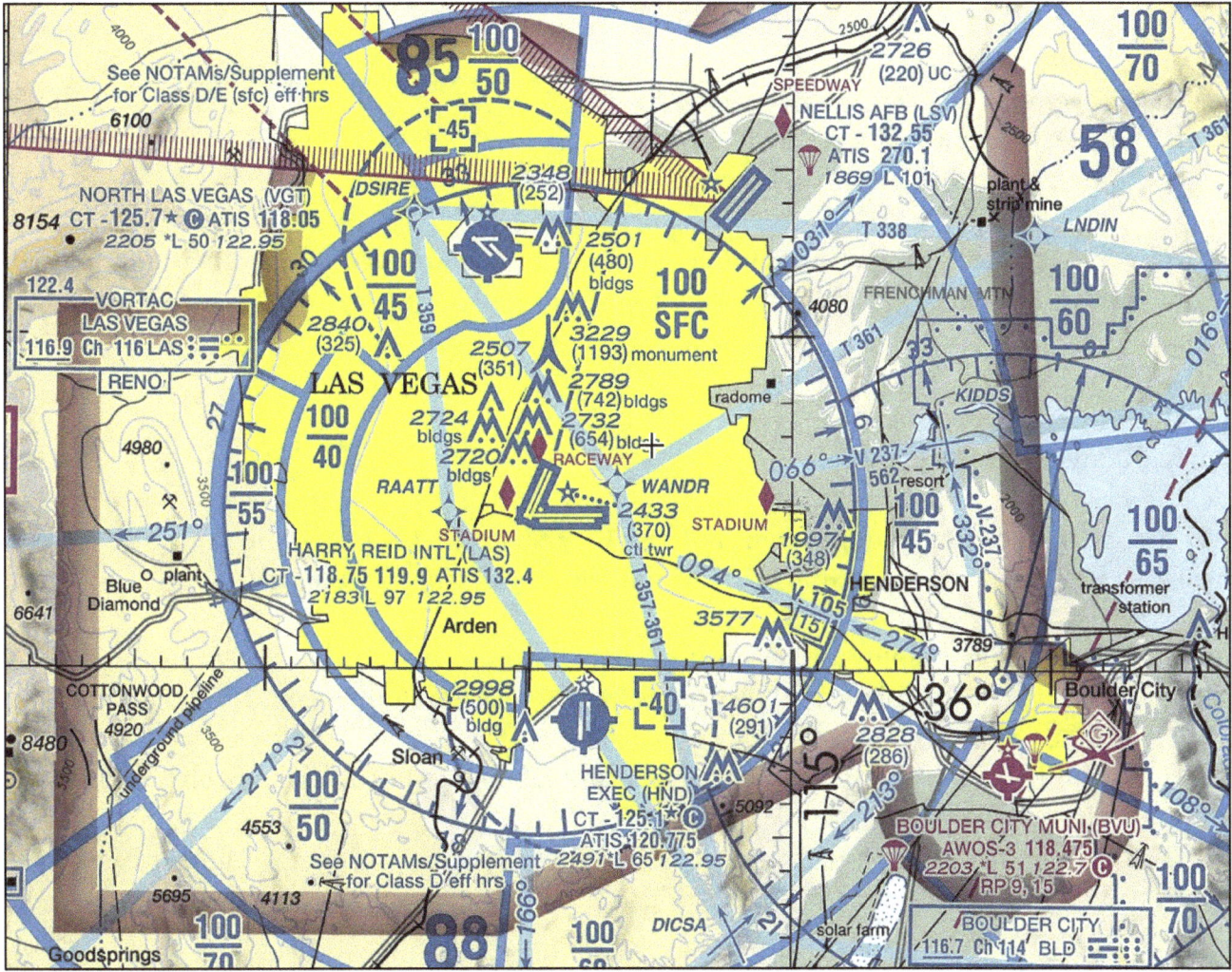

Figure 2-24.

40. Refer to Figure 2-24 above. What is the frequency for the Las Vegas VORTAC?

   A. 118.75 MHz.
   B. 116.9 MHz.
   C. 132.4 MHz.

41. Refer to Figure 2-24 above. What is the ATIS frequency for Henderson Exec (HND) airport?

A. 120.775 MHz.
B. 125.1 MHz.
C. 122.95 MHz.

42. What is the correct radio call sign for a civil aircraft with the registration number N123AB?

    A. "November One Two Three Alpha Bravo."
    B. "Niner One Two Three Adam Boy."
    C. "November One Twenty-Three AB."

43. Which of the following is an example of a performance-reducing factor that is amplified by excess weight?

    A. Lower stalling speed.
    B. Shorter takeoff run.
    C. Reduced rate of climb.

44. A remote pilot is planning a flight in Class G airspace that is below the floor of overlying Class E airspace. What are the visibility and cloud clearance requirements?

    A. 1 statute mile visibility and clear of clouds.
    B. 3 statute miles visibility, 500 feet below, 1,000 feet horizontal, and 2,000 feet above clouds.
    C. 3 statute miles visibility, 500 feet below, and 2,000 feet horizontally from clouds.

45. The PAVE checklist is a tool used in Aeronautical Decision-Making (ADM) to assess risk. What do the letters in PAVE stand for?

    A. **P**ilot, **A**ircraft, **V**isibility, **E**nvironment.
    B. **P**ilot, **A**ircraft, en**V**ironment, **E**xternal pressures.
    C. **P**rocedures, **A**ircraft, **V**isibility, **E**mergency.

46. During which stage of a thunderstorm are there both strong updrafts and downdrafts, resulting in the most severe hazards?

    A. The cumulus stage.
    B. The mature stage.
    C. The dissipating stage.

47. What is the effect of a heavier payload on an sUAS's endurance and maneuverability?

    A. Endurance is increased, and maneuverability is increased.
    B. Endurance is decreased, and maneuverability is reduced.
    C. Endurance is increased, but maneuverability is reduced.

48. A remote pilot plans to fly in an Alert Area. What is the pilot's responsibility?

    A. Obtain permission from the controlling agency before entering.
    B. Remain clear of the Alert Area at all times.
    C. Be aware that the area may contain a high volume of pilot training or unusual aerial activity and be equally responsible for collision avoidance.

49. A crewmember begins to experience the symptoms of hyperventilation. What is the recommended course of action?

    A. Have the person breathe rapidly into a paper bag.
    B. Administer a small amount of supplemental oxygen.
    C. Have the person consciously control their breathing rate to be slower and shallower.

50. While reviewing a Terminal Aerodrome Forecast (TAF), you see the code "WS020/31045KT". What does this mean?

    A. Wind shear is forecasted at 2,000 feet AGL, with the wind at that altitude from 310 degrees at 45 knots.
    B. The wind will be from 020 degrees at 31 knots, gusting to 45 knots.
    C. Weather services are forecasting wind speeds of 20 to 31 knots.

51. What does a mandatory instruction sign at an airport look like?

    A. Yellow background with black characters.
    B. Black background with yellow characters.
    C. Red background with white characters.

52. A remote pilot wants to conduct an operation that is not allowed under the standard rules of Part 107, such as flying beyond VLOS. The pilot must request a

    A. Temporary Flight Restriction (TFR).
    B. Certificate of Waiver (CoW).
    C. Special Flight Permit.

53. What is the recommended practice when flying near a NSA?

   A. Pilots are requested to voluntarily avoid flying through the depicted NSA.
   B. Pilots must obtain ATC clearance before entering an NSA.
   C. sUAS operations are prohibited within 5 nautical miles of any NSA.

54. While flying at night, a remote pilot notices that the lights of a distant town on a dark, featureless terrain appear to be stars in the sky. This can lead to which illusion?

   A. Autokinesis.
   B. False horizon.
   C. Flicker vertigo.

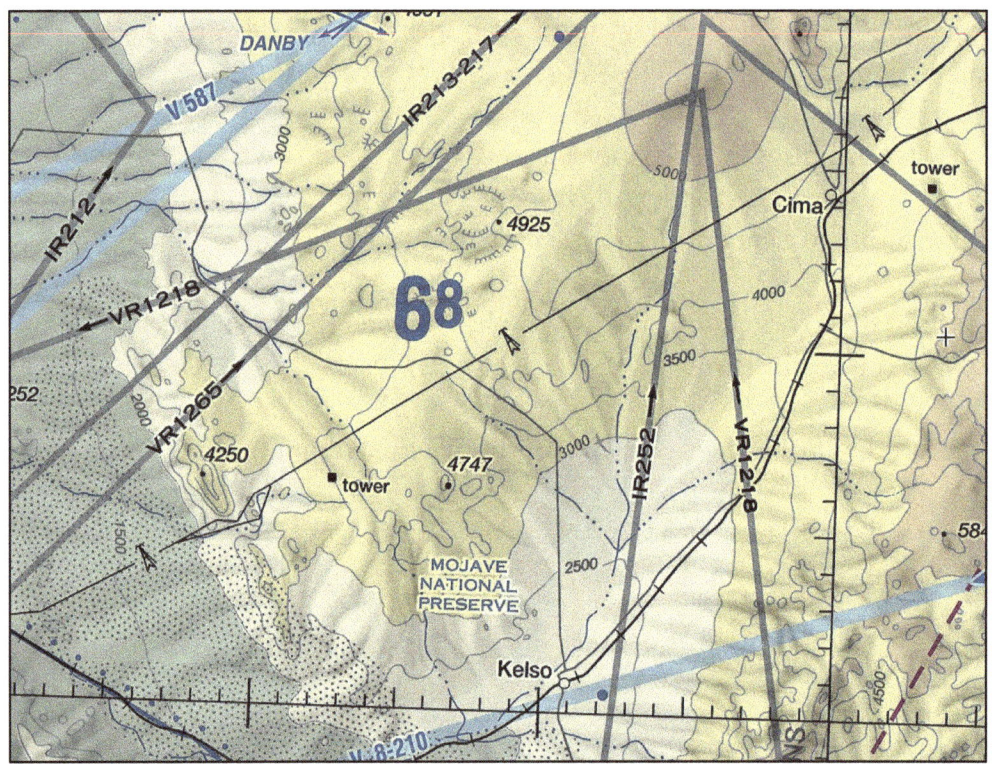

Figure 2-25.

55. Refer to Figure 2-25 above. You are planning an sUAS operation in the vicinity of the military training routes VR1218 and VR1265. What is the defining operational altitude characteristic of these routes?

   A. They are used for high-altitude training, exclusively above 10,000 feet MSL.
   B. They are flown entirely at or below 1,500 feet AGL.
   C. They have segments that operate both above and below 1,500 feet AGL.

56. Refer to Figure 2-25 above. What is the significance of the large blue number 68 in the center of the chart?

   A. It is the minimum safe altitude for the area, 6,800 feet AGL.
   B. It is the floor of the overlying controlled airspace, 6,800 feet MSL.
   C. It is the Maximum Elevation Figure, indicating the highest feature in that quadrant is 6,800 feet MSL.

57. If an unmanned aircraft is subjected to a load factor of 3 Gs, its stalling speed will be

   A. the same as in straight-and-level flight.
   B. approximately 1.73 times its normal stalling speed.
   C. 3 times its normal stalling speed.

58. A remote pilot is hired to film a local marathon. The FAA has issued a TFR over the entire race route. To operate the sUAS in the TFR, the pilot must

   A. fly below 100 feet AGL to stay clear of manned aircraft.
   B. have a Certificate of Waiver or Authorization that specifically permits flight in that TFR.
   C. be in constant communication with the race director.

59. The IMSAFE checklist is a self-assessment tool to determine fitness for flight. What does the "F" stand for?

   A. Fitness.
   B. Food.
   C. Fatigue.

60. What weather phenomenon is characterized by a shallow layer of smooth, stable air where the temperature increases with altitude?

   A. A cold front.
   B. A temperature inversion.
   C. A microburst.

PRACTICE TEST 2: ANSWER KEY

1. A. - A control station is defined as the interface, such as a remote control transmitter, used by the remote pilot or person manipulating the controls to control the flight path of the sUAS.
2. B. - The note explicitly states the MOA is excluded (inactive) when the listed restricted areas are active. This means a pilot must check the status of the restricted areas to determine if the MOA itself is active.
3. A. - The faded magenta circle around Carrington Muni (46D) indicates that Class E airspace begins at 700 feet AGL. Therefore, the airspace from the surface up to 699 feet AGL is Class G.
4. B. - Part of the preflight assessment required by 14 CFR §107.49 includes evaluating local weather conditions to ensure the sUAS can be operated safely and within its performance limitations.
5. C. - Class D airspace is generally a cylinder from the surface up to 2,500 feet above the airport elevation. Its lateral dimensions are individually tailored, but a 4 NM radius is typical.
6. A. - High density altitude (thin air) is caused by high temperatures, high humidity (moist air is less dense than dry air), and low atmospheric pressure. These conditions significantly decrease aircraft performance.
7. B. - A forward CG increases longitudinal stability, which can make the aircraft "nose-heavy." This may require excessive back pressure on the controls to maintain altitude and make it difficult to flare for landing.
8. B. - According to 14 CFR §107.9, a report must be made within 10 calendar days of any operation that results in at least serious injury to any person or property damage exceeding $500.
9. A. - The "see and avoid" responsibility requires the Remote PIC to remain clear of and yield the right-of-way to all other aircraft, including airborne vehicles, to prevent a collision hazard.
10. B. - Williamsburg RGNL (CKI) airport is located north of the 33°30'N latitude line and east of the 80°00'W longitude line. By interpolating between the marked lines, its position is approximately 33°43'N, 79°51'W.
11. C. - The magenta comb-like lines delineate a Military Operations Area (MOA). While sUAS flight is not prohibited, these areas are used for military training activities, and pilots must be vigilant and exercise extreme caution.
12. B. - MOAs are established to contain certain non-hazardous military training activities.

VFR traffic, including sUAS, may enter an active MOA but should exercise extreme caution.

13. A. - 14 CFR §107.29 allows the Remote PIC to reduce the intensity of the anti-collision lighting if they determine that, because of operating conditions, it would be in the interest of safety to do so. The lights may not be extinguished.

14. B. - In a METAR, "SCT" means scattered clouds (3/8 to 4/8 of the sky covered). The number "030" indicates the height of the cloud base in hundreds of feet above ground level (AGL), so 30 x 100 = 3,000 feet AGL.

15. A. - An increased load factor, such as in a steep turn, requires the wings to produce more lift to maintain altitude. This increased demand on the wings means the critical angle of attack will be reached at a higher airspeed, thus increasing the stall speed.

16. A. - Class G is uncontrolled airspace that extends from the surface up to the floor of the overlying controlled airspace (typically Class E at 700 or 1,200 feet AGL, or in some remote areas, 14,500 feet MSL).

17. C. - Unstable air is characterized by vertical movement, which tends to lift pollutants and moisture upwards. This vertical mixing generally results in good surface visibility between any showers that may form.

18. C. - After deviating from a rule during an emergency, the Remote PIC is only required to submit a written report explaining the deviation if requested to do so by the FAA.

19. B. - Part 48 requires registration for all small unmanned aircraft weighing more than 0.55 pounds (250 grams) and less than 55 pounds. An aircraft weighing exactly 0.55 pounds does not require registration.

20. C. - A stall is an aerodynamic condition that occurs when the smooth airflow over the wing is disrupted by exceeding the critical angle of attack, resulting in a loss of lift. It can happen at any airspeed.

21. B. - The most effective scanning method involves a series of short, systematic eye movements that bring successive areas of the sky into the central visual field. This technique helps to detect potential traffic without the eyes becoming fixated.

22. C. - 14 CFR §107.51 allows a remote pilot to operate an sUAS higher than 400 feet AGL if it is flown within a 400-foot radius of a structure and does not fly more than 400 feet above the structure's immediate uppermost limit. Therefore, 500 feet (tower height) + 400 feet = 900 feet AGL.

23. A. - A loss of GPS signal does not necessarily constitute an emergency or a lost link situation. The pilot should be prepared to operate the aircraft in a mode that does not rely on GPS (e.g., ATTI or manual mode) and maintain VLOS to control the aircraft safely.

24. A. - In the airport data block for MAF, the frequency 118.7 is followed by a "C" in a

solid circle, which designates it as the Common Traffic Advisory Frequency for that airport.

25. A. - The airport data for MAF includes "*L 95". The number "95" indicates the length of the longest runway in hundreds of feet, which is 9,500 feet.

26. B. - A ceiling is a measurement of the height of the base of the lowest cloud layer that covers more than half the sky (broken or overcast). It is a critical piece of information for determining flight conditions.

27. C. - 14 CFR §107.23 prohibits dropping any object from an sUAS in a manner that creates an undue hazard. The remote pilot is responsible for ensuring the safety of the operation.

28. B. - Thunderstorms contain powerful updrafts and downdrafts, which create severe turbulence and dangerous wind shear. These conditions can easily exceed an sUAS's performance capabilities and cause a loss of control.

29. A. - Hazard mitigation is a key component of the Remote PIC's responsibilities. For unlit obstacles, the best mitigation is to ensure maximum visibility by flying during the day and maintaining a safe distance from all known towers.

30. A. - Prohibited Areas are established for national security reasons (e.g., over the White House). Flight of aircraft within a Prohibited Area is not permitted under any circumstances.

31. A. - 14 CFR §107.31 requires that the Remote PIC, person manipulating the controls, or the visual observer must be able to see the unmanned aircraft with their own eyes, aided only by glasses or contact lenses if needed.

32. B. - The area is enclosed by blue comb-like lines and labeled with a "P," which designates it as a Prohibited Area. Flight of aircraft is prohibited within this airspace.

33. A. - The solid magenta lines of the outer shelf of the Class C airspace are marked with the fraction 40/12, meaning the ceiling is 4,000 feet MSL and the floor is 1,200 feet MSL.

34. A. - The ICAO phonetic alphabet (Alpha, Bravo, Charlie, etc.) is used to prevent confusion between letters that sound similar, ensuring that call signs, waypoints, and other critical information are communicated accurately.

35. C. - As the bank angle increases in a level turn, the wings must generate more lift to counteract both weight and centrifugal force. This increased lift requirement results in a higher load factor on the aircraft structure.

36. C. - 14 CFR §107.7 requires a remote pilot to make their certificate, as well as any other required documents like registration, available for inspection upon request from the Administrator (FAA), NTSB, or any federal, state, or local law enforcement officer.

37. A. - Autokinesis is a common night illusion where a static point of light in a dark environment appears to move after a few seconds of staring at it. Pilots can prevent this by

using a systematic scan and not fixating on a single light.

38. B. - A standard briefing is a complete, comprehensive briefing for a planned flight. An abbreviated briefing is shortened and is used when a pilot needs to update information from a previous briefing or just needs one or two specific items.

39. C. - 14 CFR §107.39 generally prohibits flight over people. Exceptions include people directly involved in the flight operation (like a VO) or people protected by a structure or stationary vehicle that can provide reasonable protection from a falling sUAS. Operations under the specific categories for flight over people

40. B. - The information box for the VORTAC, located west of Harry Reid Intl' Airport, clearly indicates its frequency is 116.9 MHz.

41. A. - The airport data block for Henderson Exec (HND) lists "ATIS 120.775," which is the frequency for its Automated Terminal Information Service.

42. A. - The proper method for stating an aircraft registration is to use the ICAO phonetic alphabet for letters and to state each number individually.

43. C. - Excessive weight is detrimental to performance. An overloaded aircraft will have a higher takeoff speed, a longer takeoff run, and a reduced rate and angle of climb.

44. C. - Even though Class G is uncontrolled, Part 107 imposes its own standard weather minimums for all sUAS operations regardless of airspace class (unless a waiver is obtained). These minimums are 3 statute miles of visibility and maintaining a distance of 500 feet below and 2,000 feet horizontally from any clouds.

45. B. - The PAVE checklist prompts the pilot to consider the four fundamental risk elements of any flight: Pilot-in-command (health, currency, stress), Aircraft (airworthiness, performance), enVironment (weather, terrain, airspace), and External pressures (e.g., client demands, schedule).

46. B. - The mature stage is the most dangerous phase of a thunderstorm. It is characterized by the presence of both strong updrafts and downdrafts as precipitation begins to fall, creating extreme turbulence and wind shear.

47. B. - A heavier weight requires the propulsion system to produce more thrust to maintain flight, which consumes power more quickly and thus decreases endurance. The increased weight and inertia also make the aircraft less responsive to control inputs, reducing its maneuverability.

48. C. - Alert Areas are depicted on charts to inform pilots of areas that may contain a high volume of pilot training or other unusual aerial activities. Pilots are not prohibited from entering but should be extra vigilant, as all parties are responsible for collision avoidance.

49. C. - Hyperventilation is an over-breathing condition that expels too much carbon

dioxide. The proper treatment is to restore the body's CO2 level by consciously slowing the breathing rate. Breathing into a paper bag can also help, but controlling the breathing rate is the primary solution.

50. A. - The "WS" code in a TAF indicates a forecast for non-convective low-level wind shear. "WS020" means the shear is expected at 2,000 feet AGL, and "/31045KT" specifies the wind at that altitude will be from 310 degrees at 45 knots.

51. C. - Mandatory instruction signs have a red background with white text. They denote an entrance to a runway, a critical area, or a prohibited area, and they must not be crossed without ATC clearance at a controlled airport.

52. B. - To deviate from certain operational rules of Part 107, a remote pilot must apply for and receive a Certificate of Waiver from the FAA. The application must demonstrate that the proposed operation can be conducted safely.

53. A. - NSA are established to increase the security and safety of ground facilities. Pilots are requested to voluntarily avoid these areas, and flight may be temporarily prohibited by NOTAM.

54. B. - The false horizon illusion occurs when a pilot mistakes a sloped cloud formation, obscured horizon, or ground lights for the actual horizon. This can lead to the pilot placing the aircraft in a dangerous attitude.

55. B. - Military Training Routes (MTRs) with four-digit identifiers, such as VR1218 and VR1265, are designed to be flown at or below 1,500 feet AGL, posing a potential conflict for low-altitude sUAS operations.

56. C. - The large blue numbers on a sectional chart represent the Maximum Elevation Figure (MEF) for that quadrant. The 68 indicates that the highest known terrain or obstacle in that area is 6,800 feet MSL, rounded up to the next hundred feet.

57. B. - Stalling speed increases in proportion to the square root of the load factor. The square root of 3 is approximately 1.732. Therefore, the stalling speed will be about 1.73 times higher than in 1G flight.

58. B. - Temporary Flight Restrictions are regulatory and apply to all aircraft, including sUAS. The only way to operate within a TFR is to have a specific authorization or waiver from the FAA that grants permission for that specific event.

59. C. - The "F" in the IMSAFE checklist stands for Fatigue. It prompts the pilot to assess whether they are adequately rested, as fatigue is a major contributor to aviation accidents.

60. B. - A temperature inversion is a condition where a layer of warmer air sits on top of a layer of cooler air, reversing the normal decrease in temperature with altitude. This creates very stable conditions that can trap pollutants and restrict visibility.

PRACTICE TEST 3: ANSWER SHEET

1. Ⓐ Ⓑ Ⓒ
2. Ⓐ Ⓑ Ⓒ
3. Ⓐ Ⓑ Ⓒ
4. Ⓐ Ⓑ Ⓒ
5. Ⓐ Ⓑ Ⓒ
6. Ⓐ Ⓑ Ⓒ
7. Ⓐ Ⓑ Ⓒ
8. Ⓐ Ⓑ Ⓒ
9. Ⓐ Ⓑ Ⓒ
10. Ⓐ Ⓑ Ⓒ
11. Ⓐ Ⓑ Ⓒ
12. Ⓐ Ⓑ Ⓒ
13. Ⓐ Ⓑ Ⓒ
14. Ⓐ Ⓑ Ⓒ
15. Ⓐ Ⓑ Ⓒ
16. Ⓐ Ⓑ Ⓒ
17. Ⓐ Ⓑ Ⓒ
18. Ⓐ Ⓑ Ⓒ
19. Ⓐ Ⓑ Ⓒ
20. Ⓐ Ⓑ Ⓒ
21. Ⓐ Ⓑ Ⓒ
22. Ⓐ Ⓑ Ⓒ
23. Ⓐ Ⓑ Ⓒ
24. Ⓐ Ⓑ Ⓒ
25. Ⓐ Ⓑ Ⓒ
26. Ⓐ Ⓑ Ⓒ
27. Ⓐ Ⓑ Ⓒ
28. Ⓐ Ⓑ Ⓒ
29. Ⓐ Ⓑ Ⓒ
30. Ⓐ Ⓑ Ⓒ
31. Ⓐ Ⓑ Ⓒ
32. Ⓐ Ⓑ Ⓒ
33. Ⓐ Ⓑ Ⓒ
34. Ⓐ Ⓑ Ⓒ
35. Ⓐ Ⓑ Ⓒ
36. Ⓐ Ⓑ Ⓒ
37. Ⓐ Ⓑ Ⓒ
38. Ⓐ Ⓑ Ⓒ
39. Ⓐ Ⓑ Ⓒ
40. Ⓐ Ⓑ Ⓒ
41. Ⓐ Ⓑ Ⓒ
42. Ⓐ Ⓑ Ⓒ
43. Ⓐ Ⓑ Ⓒ
44. Ⓐ Ⓑ Ⓒ
45. Ⓐ Ⓑ Ⓒ
46. Ⓐ Ⓑ Ⓒ
47. Ⓐ Ⓑ Ⓒ
48. Ⓐ Ⓑ Ⓒ
49. Ⓐ Ⓑ Ⓒ
50. Ⓐ Ⓑ Ⓒ
51. Ⓐ Ⓑ Ⓒ
52. Ⓐ Ⓑ Ⓒ
53. Ⓐ Ⓑ Ⓒ
54. Ⓐ Ⓑ Ⓒ
55. Ⓐ Ⓑ Ⓒ
56. Ⓐ Ⓑ Ⓒ
57. Ⓐ Ⓑ Ⓒ
58. Ⓐ Ⓑ Ⓒ
59. Ⓐ Ⓑ Ⓒ
60. Ⓐ Ⓑ Ⓒ

PRACTICE TEST 3: QUESTIONS

1. A remote pilot is hired to inspect a bridge. The operation requires flying over a river that is adjacent to a congested urban area. Which hazardous attitude might lead the pilot to fly directly over the congested area instead of the river to get the job done faster?

   A. Macho.
   B. Invulnerability.
   C. Impulsivity.

2. To operate a small unmanned aircraft in Class C airspace, what is the required procedure?

   A. The remote pilot must have prior authorization from Air Traffic Control.
   B. The remote pilot must monitor the appropriate ATC frequency.
   C. The remote pilot must contact ATC immediately after takeoff.

3. Which weather phenomenon is always associated with the passage of a front?

   A. A change in wind direction and/or speed.
   B. The formation of cumulonimbus clouds.
   C. A significant drop in humidity.

4. If a remote pilot changes their permanent mailing address, they must notify the FAA of the change within how many days?

   A. 10 days.
   B. 30 days.
   C. 90 days.

5. A remote pilot is operating at a non-towered airport and needs to monitor manned aircraft communications. Which frequency should they use?

   A. The Automatic Terminal Information Service (ATIS) frequency.
   B. The Common Traffic Advisory Frequency (CTAF).
   C. The local approach control frequency.

6. What is the first step in the risk management process?

   A. Identify hazards present in the operational environment.
   B. Assess the severity of potential outcomes.

C. Develop mitigation strategies.

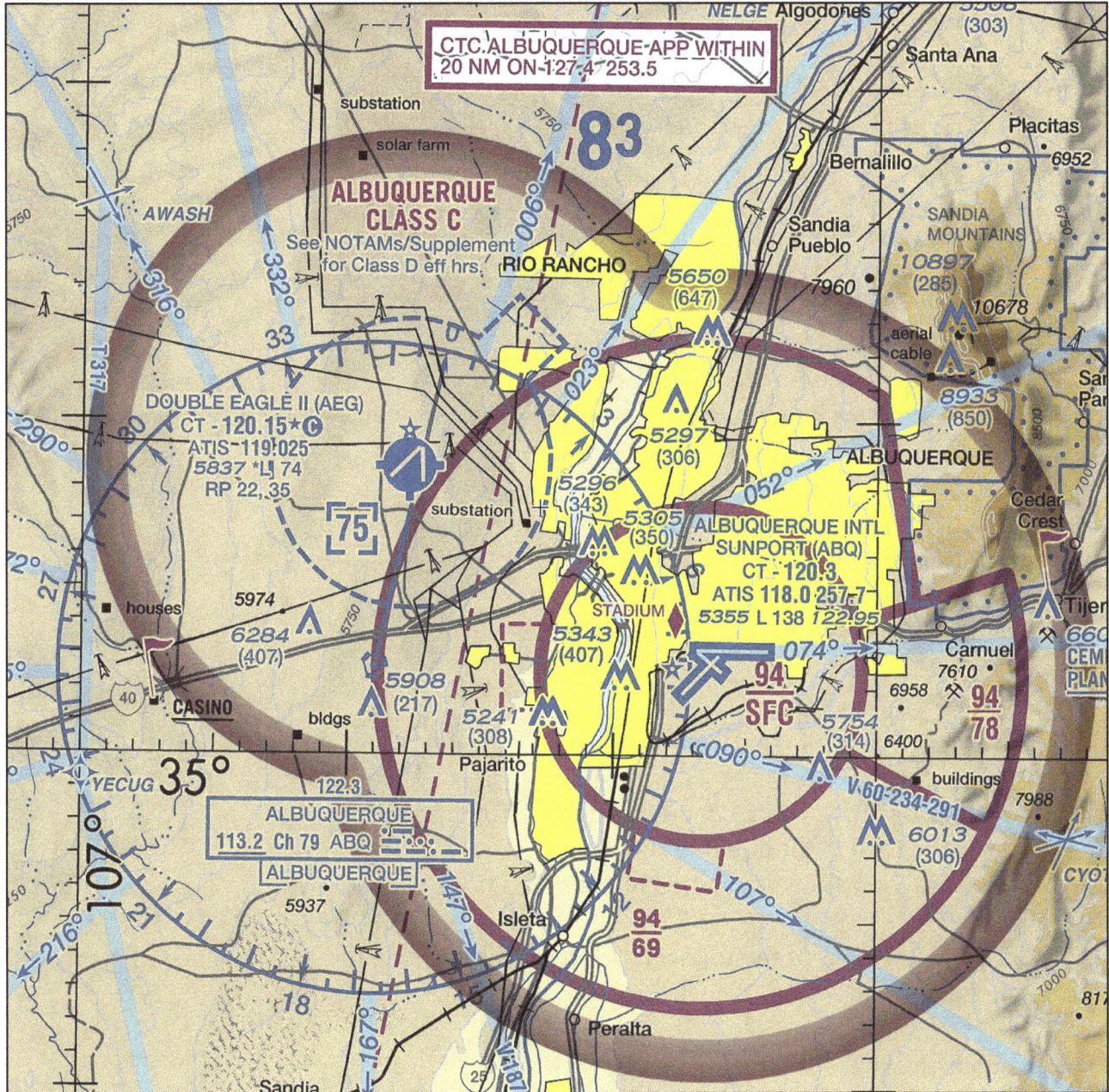

Figure 3-20.

7. Refer to Figure 3-20 above. What is the floor of the Class C airspace directly overlying Albuquerque Intl Sunport (ABQ)?

   A. The surface.
   B. 5,355 feet MSL.
   C. 9,400 feet MSL.

8. Refer to Figure 3-20 above. What is the highest elevation of the Sandia Mountains depicted on the chart?

   A. 10,897 feet MSL.
   B. 8,933 feet MSL.
   C. 10,678 feet MSL.

9. A remote pilot is planning a flight at 9 AM local time in an area where the end of morning civil twilight is at 6:30 AM. Does this operation require the sUAS to be equipped with anti-collision lighting?

   A. No, the flight is conducted during daylight hours.
   B. Yes, all flights within 3 hours of sunrise require anti-collision lights.
   C. Only if the visibility is less than 5 statute miles.

10. Which type of air mass is characterized by being cool and dry?

   A. Maritime Tropical.
   B. Continental Polar.
   C. Maritime Polar.

11. What is the purpose of a preflight inspection?

   A. To verify the sUAS is in a condition for safe operation.
   B. To log the total flight hours of the aircraft.
   C. To ensure the battery is charged to exactly 100%.

12. An increase in which of the following factors will decrease the performance of a small unmanned aircraft?

   A. Air density.
   B. Headwind.
   C. Humidity.

13. A remote pilot experiences a complete loss of the control link to their sUAS. The aircraft does not respond to any control inputs and does not execute its pre-programmed lost link procedure. This event is known as a

   A. flyaway.
   B. lost link.

C. system malfunction.

Figure 3-21.

14. Refer to Figure 3-21 above. What are the floor and ceiling of the outer shelf of the Green Bay Class C airspace?

   A. The floor is the surface, and the ceiling is 4,700 feet MSL.
   B. The floor is 1,900 feet MSL, and the ceiling is 4,700 feet MSL.
   C. The floor is 1,900 feet AGL, and the ceiling is 4,700 feet AGL.

15. Refer to Figure 3-21 above. What is the height above ground level (AGL) of the prominent stack located southeast of the Green Bay / Austin Straubel Intl (GRB) airport?

A. 2,049 feet AGL.
B. 1,149 feet AGL.
C. 900 feet AGL.

16. What is the minimum distance a small unmanned aircraft must maintain from clouds?

    A. 500 feet above and 1,000 feet horizontally.
    B. 1,000 feet below and 2,000 feet horizontally.
    C. 500 feet below and 2,000 feet horizontally.

17. Who is responsible for ensuring that all persons participating in an sUAS operation are briefed on emergency procedures?

    A. The Visual Observer.
    B. The owner of the sUAS.
    C. The Remote PIC.

18. A remote pilot is convicted of a drug-related offense. For how long can they be denied an application for a remote pilot certificate?

    A. Up to 1 year after the date of final conviction.
    B. Up to 6 months after the date of final conviction.
    C. For an indefinite period, subject to FAA review.

19. What is the typical upper limit of Class B airspace?

    A. 4,000 feet MSL.
    B. 10,000 feet MSL.
    C. 18,000 feet MSL.

20. To see an object more clearly at night, the remote pilot should use the technique of off-center viewing. This involves

    A. looking 5 to 10 degrees to the side of the object.
    B. looking directly at the object for at least 10 seconds.
    C. rapidly scanning the entire sky around the object.

21. In a METAR, what does the code "BR" signify?

    A. Broken clouds.
    B. Rain.

C. Mist.

22. When an sUAS is put into a steep turn, what is the direct effect on its stalling speed?

    A. It decreases due to the increased airspeed.
    B. It remains the same regardless of bank angle.
    C. It increases due to the higher load factor.

23. What is the primary responsibility of the Remote PIC during a crew briefing?

    A. To verify the identity of all crewmembers.
    B. To ensure all participants understand their roles, responsibilities, and the emergency procedures for the operation.
    C. To collect payment from the client before the operation begins.

24. What is the most significant hazard associated with a temperature inversion?

    A. Extreme turbulence and wind shear.
    B. The trapping of pollutants, leading to very poor visibility.
    C. The rapid formation of cumulonimbus clouds.

25. An sUAS is being used to inspect a roof. The building is located within the surface area of Class D airspace. What is required to conduct this operation legally?

    A. A Certificate of Waiver for operations over structures.
    B. Authorization from Air Traffic Control (ATC).
    C. Permission from the building owner only.

26. A remote pilot feels anxious and is breathing rapidly while trying to handle an unexpected situation during a flight. This condition is known as

    A. hypoxia.
    B. hyperventilation.
    C. dehydration.

27. What is the purpose of a runway holding position sign?

    A. To indicate the remaining distance of the runway in thousands of feet.
    B. To denote the entrance to a runway from a taxiway.
    C. To identify the location of a specific taxiway.

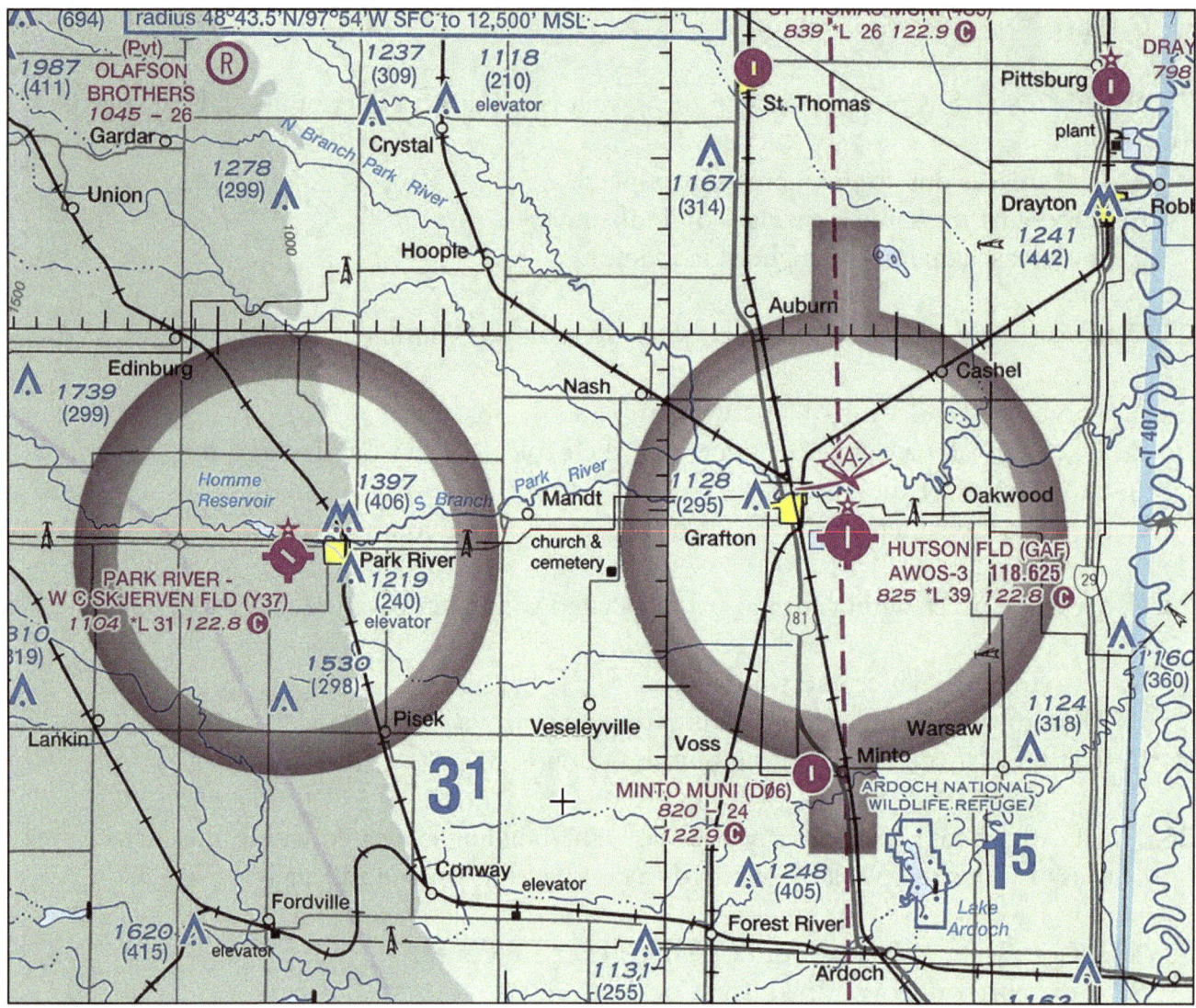

Figure 3-22.

28. Refer to Figure 3-22 above. When operating an sUAS inside the faded magenta circle near Hutson Fld (GAF), what is the maximum altitude you can fly in Class G airspace before entering controlled airspace?

   A. 699 feet AGL.
   B. 1,199 feet AGL.
   C. 400 feet AGL.

29. Refer to Figure 3-22 above. What is the length of the longest runway at Park River - W C Skjerven Fld (Y37)?

   A. 3,100 feet.
   B. 1,104 feet.

184 | REMOTE PILOT FAA PART 107 STUDY GUIDE

C. 2,800 feet.

30. What does the "A" in the IMSAFE checklist stand for?

    A. Attitude.
    B. Altitude.
    C. Alcohol.

31. A remote pilot is operating an sUAS that weighs 45 pounds. During a 30-degree banked turn, what approximate weight must the aircraft's structure support?

    A. 45 pounds.
    B. 52 pounds.
    C. 60 pounds.

32. Which of the following is a characteristic of a cold front?

    A. A gradual slope with widespread, light precipitation.
    B. Often associated with a narrow band of towering cumulus clouds and showery precipitation.
    C. Typically brings a rise in temperature and pressure after passage.

33. A remote pilot is planning an operation in a remote, uncontrolled area. The nearest airport is 50 miles away. What is the pilot's responsibility regarding airspace?

    A. No specific action is required as the flight is in Class G airspace.
    B. The pilot must file a flight plan with the nearest FSS.
    C. The pilot must still consult aeronautical charts to identify any special use airspace, such as MOAs or Restricted Areas, that may be in the vicinity.

34. The term "angle of attack" is defined as the angle between the

    A. aircraft's longitudinal axis and the horizon.
    B. wing chord line and the relative wind.
    C. direction of flight and the ground.

35. A remote pilot is asked to perform a flight that would require flying at night and over people. The pilot does not have a waiver for either operation. Which hazardous attitude would be represented by the pilot thinking, "It's a quick flight, it won't be a problem"?

    A. Anti-authority.

B. Resignation.
C. Invulnerability.

36. What is the primary function of the rudder on a fixed-wing unmanned aircraft?

   A. To control roll.
   B. To control pitch.
   C. To control yaw.

37. A remote pilot is operating in a rural area and notices a manned agricultural aircraft (crop duster) operating at a very low altitude. What action should the remote pilot take?

   A. Continue the operation, assuming the crop duster will see and avoid the sUAS.
   B. Immediately maneuver the sUAS to a safe location, land if necessary, and yield the right-of-way.
   C. Climb the sUAS to 400 feet AGL to stay above the crop duster.

38. What is the purpose of the "Remarks" section in a METAR?

   A. To provide the forecast for the next 2 hours.
   B. To provide operationally significant weather information that is not included in the main body of the report.
   C. To list the names of the weather observers on duty.

39. A remote pilot is required to report a safety-of-flight incident involving a small unmanned aircraft to the FAA if it results in

   A. any injury to a person.
   B. a serious injury to a person or any loss of consciousness.
   C. damage to the sUAS that requires minor repairs.

40. How is Class C airspace depicted on a Sectional Aeronautical Chart?

   A. A solid blue line.
   B. A dashed blue line.
   C. A solid magenta line.

41. A remote pilot is experiencing a high level of stress due to personal issues. What is the most prudent course of action regarding flight operations?

   A. Proceed with the flight, as personal stress does not affect piloting skills.

B. Ask a Visual Observer to handle all communications to reduce workload.
C. Acknowledge the stress as a potential hazard and refrain from flying until fit to do so.

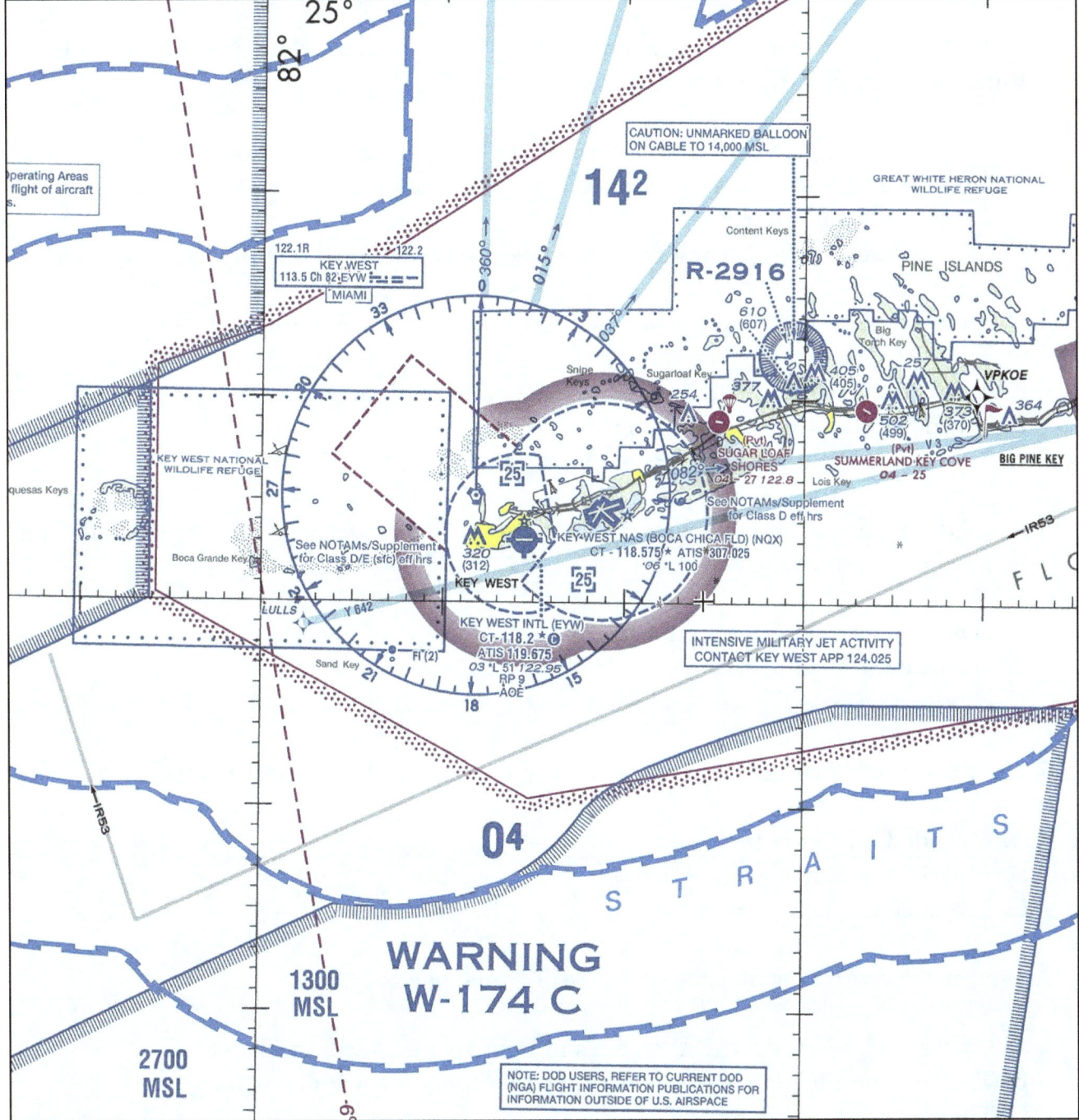

Figure 3-23.

42. Refer to Figure 3-23 above. What specific hazard is noted within the Restricted Area R-2916?

A. Intensive military jet activity.
B. A parachute jump zone.
C. An unmarked balloon on a cable extending up to 14,000 feet MSL.

43. Refer to Figure 3-23 above. What does the large area labeled "WARNING W-174 C" south of the Florida Keys signify?

    A. An area with a high concentration of unmarked hazards on the surface.
    B. An area over international waters containing activity that may be hazardous to nonparticipating aircraft.
    C. A Prohibited Area where all flight is forbidden for national security.

44. What is the primary reason for the "see and avoid" requirement for sUAS operations?

    A. To prevent collisions with other aircraft, people, and property.
    B. To ensure the sUAS does not get lost.
    C. To allow the remote pilot to maintain a stable video feed.

45. The DECIDE model is a tool for effective Aeronautical Decision-Making (ADM). The first step in this model is

    A. detect that a change has occurred.
    B. estimate the need to counter or react to the change.
    C. choose a desirable outcome for the flight.

46. How is Class E airspace that begins at 700 feet AGL depicted on a sectional chart?

    A. A shaded blue vignette.
    B. A dashed magenta line.
    C. A shaded magenta vignette.

47. Who may perform maintenance on a small unmanned aircraft?

    A. Only an FAA-certificated Airframe and Powerplant (A&P) mechanic.
    B. The Remote PIC or a person working under their direct supervision.
    C. The owner of the aircraft only.

48. A remote pilot is flying on a clear but hazy day. What effect can haze have on visual perception?

    A. It makes objects appear farther away than they actually are.

B. It makes objects appear closer than they actually are.
C. It has no effect on the perception of distance.

49. What is the purpose of an Automatic Terminal Information Service (ATIS) broadcast at a towered airport?

    A. To provide a continuous broadcast of non-control information, such as weather, runways in use, and pertinent NOTAMs.
    B. To provide air traffic control clearances for arriving and departing aircraft.
    C. To allow pilots to communicate with each other without involving ATC.

50. During preflight planning for a flight over a forested area, the remote pilot programs the lost link procedure to have the sUAS return to the takeoff point at an altitude of 150 feet AGL. What is a potential hazard with this plan?

    A. The altitude is too high and may interfere with manned aircraft.
    B. The pre-set altitude may not be sufficient to clear tall trees or terrain between the sUAS and the home point.
    C. The sUAS battery may not be sufficient for a return flight at that altitude.

51. What is the maximum allowable blood alcohol content (BAC) for any person acting as a crewmember for an sUAS?

    A. 0.08 percent.
    B. 0.04 percent.
    C. Any detectable amount.

52. Effective crew communication is a cornerstone of Crew Resource Management (CRM). What is the best way to ensure instructions are understood?

    A. Use standard aviation terminology and ask for confirmation or a read-back.
    B. Speak loudly and quickly.
    C. Use hand signals as the primary means of communication.

53. A remote pilot is operating in Class G airspace. The sectional chart indicates the floor of the overlying Class E airspace is at 1,200 feet AGL. What is the highest the sUAS can be flown without ATC authorization?

    A. 1,200 feet AGL.
    B. 700 feet AGL.
    C. 400 feet AGL.

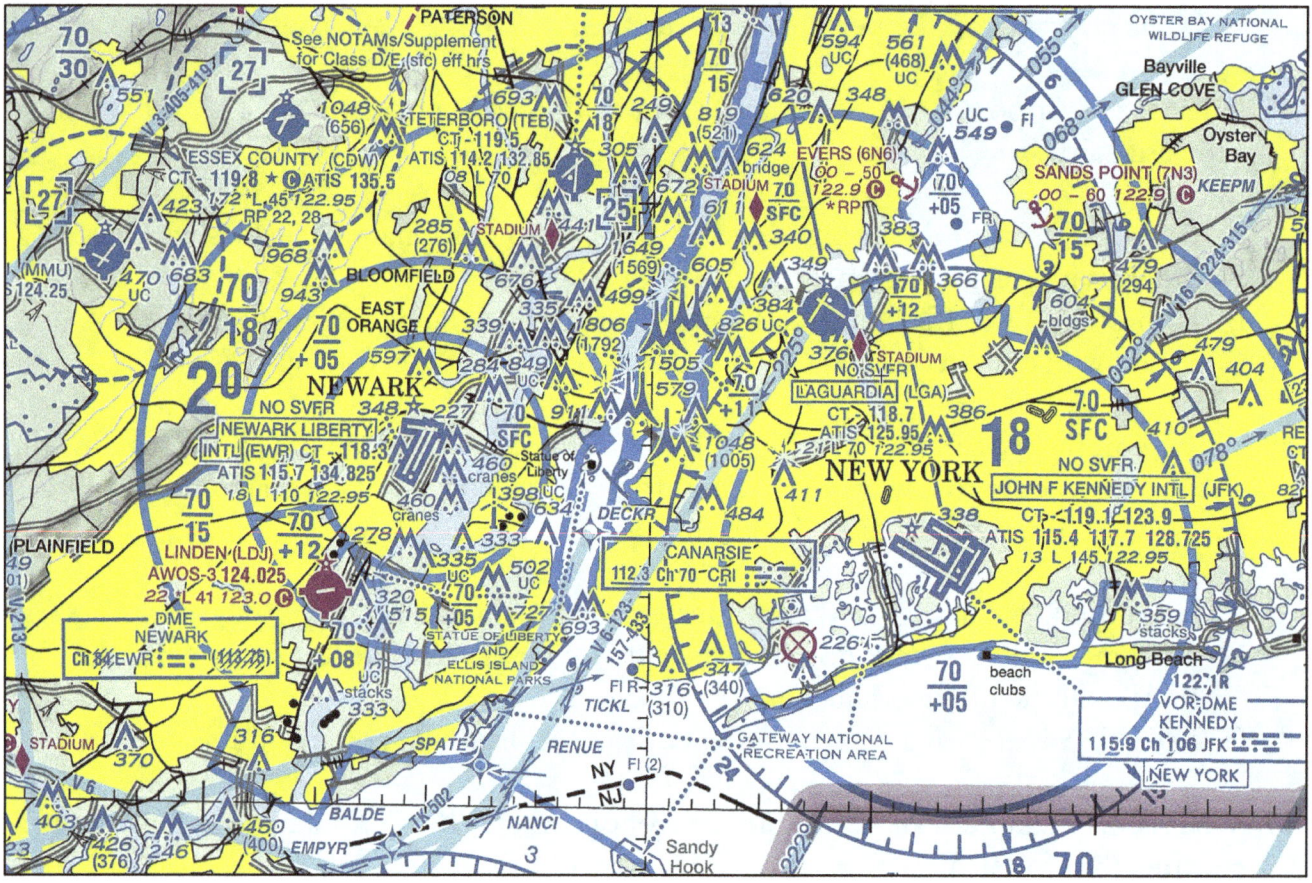

Figure 3-24.

54. Refer to Figure 3-24 above. What is the ATIS frequency for LaGuardia (LGA) airport?

   A. 118.7 MHz.
   B. 122.95 MHz.
   C. 125.95 MHz.

55. Refer to Figure 3-24 above. What is the length of the longest runway at Newark Liberty Intl (EWR)?

   A. 11,000 feet.
   B. 7,000 feet.
   C. 1,800 feet.

56. A remote pilot has been working long hours and has not had adequate sleep. This condition is known as

   A. acute fatigue.

B. chronic stress.
C. hypoxia.

57. Is it permissible under Part 107 to transport another person's property for compensation from a moving watercraft?

   A. Yes, as long as the operation is over a sparsely populated area.
   B. Yes, but only during daylight hours.
   C. No, operation from a moving vehicle while transporting property for compensation or hire is prohibited.

58. Operating a small unmanned aircraft in a manner that endangers the life or property of another is a violation of which specific regulation?

   A. 14 CFR §107.23 (Hazardous operation).
   B. 14 CFR §107.19 (Remote PIC).
   C. 14 CFR §107.31 (VLOS).

59. To ensure proper dark adaptation for a night flight, a pilot should avoid bright white light for at least

   A. 10 minutes.
   B. 30 minutes.
   C. 60 minutes.

60. The final authority as to the operation of the small unmanned aircraft rests with the

   A. Owner of the sUAS.
   B. Visual Observer.
   C. Remote PIC.

PRACTICE TEST 3: ANSWER KEY

1. C. - Impulsivity is the attitude of needing to do something—anything—immediately. This attitude can lead a pilot to rush and take the most direct route without properly considering the risks of flying over a congested area.
2. A. - 14 CFR §107.41 requires a remote pilot to obtain authorization from Air Traffic Control (ATC) before operating an sUAS in Class C airspace.
3. A. - A front is the boundary between two different air masses. As a front passes, the wind will shift, as the new air mass brings its own wind characteristics to the area.
4. B. - According to 14 CFR §107.77, a remote pilot must notify the FAA within 30 days of any change to their permanent mailing address.
5. B. - The CTAF is the designated frequency for pilots to self-announce their positions and intentions at airports without an operating control tower. Monitoring this frequency is crucial for situational awareness.
6. A. - The risk management process is a systematic approach that begins with identifying potential hazards. Without first identifying what could go wrong, it is impossible to assess the risk or develop effective ways to mitigate it.
7. A. - The inner core of the Class C airspace is marked with the fraction 94/SFC. The "SFC" indicates that the floor of the airspace in this area is the surface.
8. A. - The chart shows a spot elevation of 10,897 within the Sandia Mountains, which represents the highest point of the terrain in that specific location in feet above Mean Sea Level (MSL).
9. A. - The requirement for anti-collision lighting applies to operations during civil twilight and at night. Since the planned flight at 9 AM is well after the beginning of daylight (sunrise), anti-collision lighting is not required by regulation.
10. B. - Air masses take on the characteristics of their source region. A continental polar air mass originates over a large landmass in a polar region, making it cool and dry.
11. A. - The Remote PIC is required by 14 CFR §107.49 to conduct a preflight inspection to determine that the entire system (aircraft, control station, and data link) is safe for the intended flight.
12. C. - An increase in humidity means the air contains more water vapor, which is less dense than dry air. This less dense air (higher density altitude) reduces propeller efficiency and overall aircraft performance.
13. A. - A "flyaway" is an event where the sUAS becomes uncontrollable and does not operate in the expected manner, such as following its lost link programming. This is a

serious emergency situation that requires immediate notification to crewmembers.

14. B. - The solid magenta lines of the outer shelf of the Class C airspace are marked with the fraction 47/19. This indicates the ceiling is at 4,700 feet MSL and the floor is at 1,900 feet MSL.

15. B. - The obstacle symbol for the stack shows two numbers: 2049 and (1149). The number in parentheses, (1149), represents the height of the obstacle in feet AGL.

16. C. - 14 CFR §107.51 requires that the sUAS be operated no less than 500 feet below clouds and 2,000 feet horizontally from them.

17. C. - According to 14 CFR §107.49, prior to flight, the Remote PIC must ensure that all persons directly participating in the operation are informed about operating conditions, emergency procedures, and their specific roles and responsibilities.

18. A. - 14 CFR §107.57 states that a conviction for the violation of any federal or state statute relating to drugs is grounds for the denial of an application for a remote pilot certificate for a period of up to 1 year after the date of final conviction.

19. B. - Class B airspace is generally established from the surface to 10,000 feet Mean Sea Level (MSL) around the nation's busiest airports. Its configuration is individually tailored and often resembles an upside-down wedding cake.

20. A. - This technique focuses the object's image on the peripheral part of the retina, where the light-sensitive rods are most concentrated, rather than on the fovea, which is cone-dense and creates a night blind spot.

21. C. - The code "BR" is derived from the French word "brume" and is used in METARs to indicate mist, which is an obscuration where visibility is 5/8 statute mile or greater but less than 7 statute miles.

22. C. - A steep turn increases the load factor on the aircraft. Because stalling speed increases in proportion to the square root of the load factor, a higher load factor results in a higher stalling speed.

23. B. - The Remote PIC is responsible for conducting a preflight briefing to ensure every member of the crew is fully aware of the operational plan, contingency plans, and their specific duties to ensure a safe and coordinated flight.

24. B. - In a temperature inversion, a layer of warm air traps cooler air beneath it. This prevents vertical air movement, which can trap smoke, haze, and other pollutants, often resulting in significantly reduced surface visibility.

25. B. - Any operation within the lateral boundaries of Class D airspace, regardless of altitude, requires prior authorization from Air Traffic Control. This is typically obtained through the LAANC system.

26. B. - Hyperventilation is an abnormal increase in the rate and depth of breathing, often caused by stress or anxiety. It leads to an excessive loss of carbon dioxide from the blood and can cause dizziness and other impairing symptoms.

27. B. - A runway holding position sign, with its red background and white characters, is the airport equivalent of a stop sign. It marks the location where an aircraft on a taxiway must stop until it receives clearance to enter or cross the runway.

28. A. - Inside the faded magenta circle, Class E airspace begins at 700 feet AGL. Class G airspace extends from the surface up to, but not including, the floor of the overlying controlled airspace. Therefore, the top of Class G is 699 feet AGL.

29. A. - The airport data block for Park River (Y37) reads "1104 *L 31 122.8 C". The number "31" after the runway lighting symbol (*L) indicates the length of the longest runway in hundreds of feet (31 x 100 = 3,100 feet).

30. C. - The IMSAFE checklist is a personal health assessment tool. The "A" stands for Alcohol, reminding the pilot to consider the regulations (8 hours bottle-to-throttle) and the effects of any recent alcohol consumption.

31. B. - In a 30-degree bank, the load factor is approximately 1.154 Gs. To find the total load on the structure, multiply the aircraft's weight by the load factor: 45 lbs * 1.154 ≈ 52 pounds.

32. B. - A cold front is the leading edge of a dense, cold air mass that plows under warmer air, forcing it to rise rapidly. This rapid lifting often creates vertically developed clouds (cumulus and cumulonimbus) with showers and thunderstorms.

33. C. - Even in remote Class G airspace, special use airspace can exist. The Remote PIC is responsible for checking sectional charts to ensure the planned flight path does not conflict with any Restricted Areas, MOAs, or other designated airspace.

34. B. - The angle of attack is a critical aerodynamic angle formed by the chord line of the airfoil (an imaginary line from the leading to the trailing edge) and the direction of the oncoming air, or relative wind.

35. C. - The invulnerability attitude is the belief that "it won't happen to me." This can lead a pilot to believe they can safely ignore regulations because they don't think an accident or violation will occur on their flight.

36. C. - The rudder is the primary flight control surface that controls the aircraft's movement around its vertical axis, which is known as yaw.

37. B. - Manned aircraft, especially those in low-level operations like agricultural flights, may not see a small UAS. The Remote PIC must yield the right-of-way to all manned aircraft and take proactive measures to avoid any potential conflict.

38. B. - The remarks (RMK) section contains important information that elaborates on or supplements the coded data in the METAR, such as the beginning and ending times of precipitation, or the type of automated station.

39. B. - According to 14 CFR §107.9, an accident report is required if any person suffers a serious injury (as defined by the FAA) or any loss of consciousness. Minor injuries do not trigger the reporting requirement.

40. C. - Class C airspace is depicted by solid magenta lines on sectional charts. The airspace is typically shown with two circles, a core surface area and an outer shelf area with defined altitudes.

41. C. - Stress is a significant physiological factor that can impair judgment, decision-making, and overall performance. A pilot experiencing high stress should recognize this as a risk and ground themselves until the stress is managed.

42. C. - A caution box within the boundaries of R-2916 states "CAUTION: UNMARKED BALLOON ON CABLE TO 14,000 MSL," identifying a significant hazard to air traffic.

43. B. - A Warning Area (W-Area) is airspace of defined dimensions, extending from 3 nautical miles outward from the coast of the U.S., that contains activity that may be hazardous to nonparticipating aircraft.

44. A. - The "see and avoid" principle is a fundamental safety rule in aviation. For sUAS, it requires the Remote PIC and any visual observers to maintain constant awareness of the airspace to prevent the sUAS from colliding with other aircraft or creating a hazard to people or property on the ground.

45. A. - The DECIDE model begins with "Detect." A pilot must first recognize that a change has occurred in the flight environment (e.g., weather change, system malfunction) before they can proceed with the other steps of the decision-making process.

46. C. - The floor of Class E airspace at 700 feet AGL is depicted by a broad, shaded magenta line or vignette. The airspace inside this shaded area is Class E from 700 feet AGL upwards, while the airspace outside is Class G up to 1,200 feet AGL.

47. B. - Part 107 does not require maintenance to be performed by a certified mechanic. The Remote PIC is responsible for ensuring the sUAS is in a condition for safe operation, and they may perform or supervise the maintenance themselves.

48. A. - Haze creates an illusion of distance. Because objects are less clear through the haze, the brain interprets them as being farther away than their actual distance, which can be hazardous when judging separation from other aircraft or obstacles.

49. A. - ATIS is a pre-recorded broadcast designed to relieve frequency congestion by providing essential but routine information to pilots, allowing them to be prepared before

contacting the control tower.

50. B. - A critical part of risk management is ensuring that emergency procedures are safe. A pre-set return-to-home altitude must be high enough to clear all obstacles along any potential return path.

51. B. - 14 CFR §91.17 specifies that no person may act as a crewmember of a civil aircraft while having a blood alcohol concentration of 0.04 percent or greater. This rule is applicable to all sUAS crewmembers.

52. A. - Using clear, standard phraseology and ensuring that the message was received and understood (e.g., via a read-back) prevents misunderstandings and is a key practice for effective CRM.

53. C. - The maximum altitude rule of 400 feet AGL under Part 107 applies regardless of the overlying airspace floor, unless operating near a structure. The pilot must adhere to the 400-foot limit.

54. C. - The airport data block for LaGuardia (LGA) clearly lists "ATIS 125.95," which is the frequency for its Automated Terminal Information Service.

55. A. - The airport data for Newark Liberty Intl (EWR) includes "L 110". The number "110" indicates the length of the longest runway in hundreds of feet (110 x 100 = 11,000 feet).

56. A. - Acute fatigue is short-term tiredness resulting from strenuous activity, excitement, or lack of sleep. It is a normal part of everyday life but can be a significant hazard in aviation if not properly managed with rest.

57. C. - While 14 CFR §107.25 allows for operations from a moving vehicle over a sparsely populated area, it explicitly prohibits such operations when the aircraft is transporting another person's property for compensation or hire. This part of the rule cannot be waived.

58. A. - 14 CFR §107.23(a) explicitly states that no person may operate an sUAS in a careless or reckless manner so as to endanger the life or property of another.

59. B. - The rods in the human eye, which are responsible for night vision, can take up to 30 minutes to fully adapt to darkness. Exposure to a bright light during this period can ruin that adaptation, requiring the process to start over.

60. C. - 14 CFR §107.19 establishes that the Remote PIC is directly responsible for, and is the final authority as to, the operation of the sUAS. This is a foundational principle of Part 107.

APPENDIX

CERTIFICATION KNOWLEDGE TEST, ELIGIBILITY, AND TEST CENTER

Your Guide to the Drone Pilot Exam

To earn a Remote Pilot Certificate with a small UAS rating, you may need to pass an initial aeronautical knowledge test. This exam is a key step for any applicant who doesn't already meet the specific requirements outlined in 14 CFR part 107 for existing pilots.

The exam consists of **60 multiple-choice questions**. You will have **two hours** to complete the entire exam.

What to Expect on the Exam

The **60-question** test covers five core topics, with some areas making up a larger portion of the exam than others.

UAS Topics	Percentage of Items on Test
I Regulations	15-25%
II. Airspace & Requirements	15-25%
III. Weather	11-16%
IV. Loading & Performance	7-11%
V. Operations	35-45%

English Language Proficiency

You must have the ability to read, write, speak, and understand **English**. This will be evaluated throughout the application and testing process. An exception may be granted if an applicant cannot meet one of these standards due to a medical issue, such as a hearing impairment.

Test Eligibility Requirements

Before you can take the exam, you'll need to meet a few requirements:
1. Must be at least **16 years old**.
2. Obtain an **FAA Tracking Number** (FTN) by creating a free account on the Integrated Airman Certification and Rating Application (IACRA) website: https://iacra.faa.gov/
3. Present proper identification at the testing center, which must include your photo, signature, and date of birth. If your ID shows a P.O. box, you'll also need to provide proof of a current physical address.

Passing Scores and Retake Policy

A score of 70% or higher is required to pass the exam.

If you don't pass on your first attempt, you can take the test again, but you must wait 14 calendar days. When you go to retake the exam, you must bring your previous test report that shows the failing score. You do not need an instructor's endorsement to retest.

How to Schedule Your Exam

All official FAA knowledge tests are administered by a company called PSI at their authorized testing centers.

To find a location, schedule a date, and pay the test fee, visit the PSI scheduling website: https://faa.psiexams.com/faa/login. You can register online or use the site to find the customer service number to register by phone. Be sure to review the center's cancellation policy if you think your plans might change.

TEST-TAKING STRATEGIES

Make Predictions

Your mind is often sharpest right after reading a question. Use this focus to your advantage by **predicting the answer before** looking at the choices.

This technique is especially useful for questions that test factual knowledge. By forming an answer in your mind first, you prevent yourself from being swayed or confused by cleverly designed incorrect answers (distractors). Scan the options to see if your prediction is there. If it is, you can be highly confident in your choice.

Pro Tip: Even if you find your prediction, always read every answer choice thoroughly to ensure you haven't missed a better option.

Answer the Right Question

Test creators are experts at writing plausible-sounding wrong answers. Don't select an option just because it's a true statement; it **must answer the specific question being asked**.

A common trap is an answer choice that is factually correct on its own but irrelevant to the question. After you've made a selection, quickly reread the question to confirm your choice directly addresses it. Pay close attention to the end of the question, as test authors sometimes add a word or phrase that completely redirects the focus.

Use the Process of Elimination

When faced with a complex question, your first step is to ensure you understand what it's asking. If needed, **rephrase the question in your own words** to simplify it.

Once you're clear on the goal, immediately eliminate any answer choices you know are incorrect. Even knocking out one option greatly improves your odds of selecting the correct one.

Tackle Difficult Questions

No matter how much you prepare, you'll likely encounter a few questions that stump you. When this happens, don't **waste precious time**.

Quickly use the process of elimination to discard any obviously wrong answers. Then, carefully evaluate each remaining option on its own merits. Ask yourself, "Could this possibly be the correct answer?" This focused approach can help you spot details you initially missed. Make your best educated guess and confidently move on.

Decipher Confusing Choices

Be wary of automatically selecting an answer simply because it's the easiest to understand. Test-makers sometimes design questions where the **correct answer is complex or confusing**, while an incorrect option seems appealingly simple.

When you encounter a confusing answer choice, give it extra attention. Try to rephrase it or break it down. If you can confidently eliminate all other options, the confusing one is likely correct.

Analyze Difficult Words

Don't fall into the trap of choosing an answer just because it contains the only word you recognize. Instead, **try to dissect complex words** by looking for familiar prefixes, suffixes, and root words.

Pay close attention to two types of words:
- **Qualifiers:** Words like may, can, often, and rarely allow for exceptions, making a statement more likely to be true.
- **Absolutes:** Words like always, never, exactly, and only leave no room for exceptions. These often appear in incorrect answer choices.

Spot "Switchback" and Negative Words

Always watch out for words that alter the meaning of a sentence.

Switchback Words: Words like **but**, **although**, and **however** can change the direction of a thought and are often used to throw you off.

Negative Words: Words like **not** and **except** completely reverse the logic of a question. Missing the word "not" in "Which of the following is not a cause...?" will lead you to the wrong answer.

A great strategy is to **circle or underline these critical words** in your test booklet to ensure you don't miss them.

TEST DAY RULES AND MATERIALS

Test Software

Before your exam officially begins, you'll have the chance to go through a short tutorial. This practice session lets you get used to the testing software. You'll learn how to navigate the program, select answers, mark questions to review later, and keep track on your time.

Materials

What the Testing Center Provides
You won't be expected to have all the necessary reference materials memorized. The test proctor will provide you with the official **Airman Knowledge Testing Supplement book**. This book contains all the figures, charts, and graphs you'll need to answer certain questions. They will also typically provide scratch paper for calculations.

What You Can Bring
You are allowed to bring certain tools with you. These items include:
- Scales, straightedges, protractors, and plotters
- Navigation computers (E6-B or mechanical)
- Blank log sheets and holding pattern entry aids

Any instructions, formulas, or diagrams that are permanently inscribed on these tools by the manufacturer are acceptable.

A Note on Calculators
The rules for calculators are very specific.
- **Simple calculators** that only perform basic arithmetic are generally allowed.
- Calculators with simple memory functions (like square root or percentage keys) may be permitted, but you **must prove to the proctor that the memory can be and has been cleared** before and after the test.
- Calculators with permanent memory, pre-programmed data, or the ability to store and retrieve text are **strictly forbidden**.

What to Leave at Home
You cannot bring any personal written materials into the exam. This includes handwritten notes, printed documents, instruction manuals for your tools, or dictionaries. Any device capable of storing and retrieving pre-written programs or test-related information is also prohibited.

CERTIFICATION PROCESS AFTER PASSING YOUR EXAM

Certification Process After Your Exam

Once you pass your Unmanned Aircraft General (UAG) knowledge test, the testing center will provide you with a printed copy of your **Airman Knowledge Test Report** (AKTR). This official document displays your score and is the key to the next steps in your certification. Keep the original copy of this report in a safe place.

Your passing test results are valid for 24 calendar months. You must complete your application for the Remote Pilot Certificate within this two-year window.
If you happen to lose your AKTR, the replacement process depends on when you took the test:
- **For tests taken on or after January 13, 2020:** You can reprint your test report directly from the testing provider's website: https://faa.psiexams.com/faa/login
- **For tests taken before January 13, 2020:** You must request a replacement from the FAA Airmen Certification Branch. More information on this older process can be found on the FAA's website.

Understanding Your Test Report Codes

If you happen to miss any questions on the exam, your AKTR will include specific codes that correspond to the subject areas you need to review. This is an excellent tool for identifying and strengthening any weak spots in your knowledge.
The code **UA.I.B.K10**, for example, can be broken down like this:
- **UA:** Stands for Unmanned Aircraft Systems (the overall subject).
- **I:** Represents the Area of Operation (in this case, Regulations).
- **B:** Indicates the specific Task (Operating Rules).
- **K10:** Points to the exact Knowledge Element (VLOS aircraft operations).

How to Apply for Your Remote Pilot Certificate

The application process differs depending on whether you are a new applicant or already hold a Part 61 pilot certificate. Below are the steps for each path.

Path 1: For New Applicants
If you **do not** hold a **Part 61 pilot certificate** (or your flight review is not current), this is your process. After passing the UAG knowledge test, your identity is verified at the testing center, so you do not need to meet with an FAA representative.

1. **Submit Application:** Go to the IACRA website and submit your application online.
2. **Receive Temporary Certificate:** You will receive an email notification from the FAA with instructions to print and sign your temporary Remote Pilot Certificate.
3. **Receive Permanent Certificate:** Your permanent, plastic certificate will be sent to you by mail.

Path 2: For Current Part 61 Certificate Holders

If you are a pilot with a current flight review, you have a different path. Instead of the UAG knowledge test, you must complete the "Part 107 Small UAS Initial (ALC-451)" online course on the FAA Safety Team (FAASTeam) website.

Online Application (Recommended)
1. **Submit Application:** Go to the IACRA website and submit your application online.
2. **Validate Identity:** You must meet with an FAA-authorized individual (such as a CFI, DPE, or FSDO representative) to validate your identity and your application. You will need to present your IACRA application ID, your identification, your online course completion certificate, your pilot certificate, and proof of your current flight review.
3. **Receive Temporary Certificate:** The representative will help process your application. You will then receive an email notification to print and sign your temporary certificate through IACRA.
4. **Receive Permanent Certificate:** Your permanent certificate will be sent to you by mail.

Paper Application
1. **Complete Form:** Fill out FAA Form 8710-13.
2. **Validate Identity:** Meet with an FAA-authorized individual to validate your identity and documents, just as you would with the online process.
3. **Receive Temporary Certificate:** The representative will issue your temporary certificate in person.
4. **Receive Permanent Certificate:** Your permanent certificate will be sent to you by mail.

ABBREVIATIONS AND ACRONYMS

Abbreviation / Acronym	Definition
14 CFR	Title 14 of the Code of Federal Regulations
AC	Advisory Circular
ACR	Airman Certification Representative
ACS	Airman Certification Standards
ADM	Aeronautical Decision-Making
AELS	Aviation English Language Standard
AFS	Flight Standards Service
AGL	Above Ground Level
AIM	Aeronautical Information Manual
AIRMET	Airmen's Meteorological Information
AKTC	Airman Knowledge Testing Center
AKTR	Airman Knowledge Test Report
ASOS	Automated Surface Observation System
ATC	Air Traffic Control
ATIS	Automatic Terminal Information Service
AWOS	Automated Weather Observing System
BVLOS	Beyond Visual Line-of-Sight
CFI	Certificated Flight Instructor
CFR	Code of Federal Regulations
COA	Certificate of Waiver or Authorization
CRM	Crew Resource Management
CS	Control Station
CTAF	Common Traffic Advisory Frequency
DOT	Department of Transportation
FAA	Federal Aviation Administration
FDC	Flight Data Center
FSDO	Flight Standards District Office
FSS	Flight Service Station
FTN	FAA Tracking Number
GPS	Global Positioning System
IACRA	Integrated Airman Certification and Rating Application
IFR	Instrument Flight Rules
METAR	Aviation Routine Weather Report (Meteorological Aerodrome Report)
MOA	Military Operations Area
MSL	Mean Sea Level

MTR	Military Training Routes
NAS	National Airspace System
NM	Nautical Miles
NOTAM	Notice to Air Missions
NTSB	National Transportation Safety Board
NWS	National Weather Service
ODA	Organization Designation Authorization
PIC	Pilot-in-Command
POH	Pilot's Operating Handbook
RPE	Remote Pilot Examiner
SAFO	Safety Alert for Operators
SIDA	Security Identification Display Area
SIGMET	Significant Meteorological Information
SM	Statute Miles
SMS	Safety Management System
sUAS	Small Unmanned Aircraft System
TAF	Terminal Aerodrome Forecast
TFR	Temporary Flight Restrictions
TRSA	Terminal Radar Service Area
UA	Unmanned Aircraft
UAG	Unmanned Aircraft General (Knowledge Test)
UAS	Unmanned Aircraft System
UNICOM	Aeronautical Advisory Communication Station
UTC	Coordinated Universal Time
VLOS	Visual Line-of-Sight
VO	Visual Observer

www.ingramcontent.com/pod-product-compliance
Lightning Source LLC
Chambersburg PA
CBHW082208070526

44585CB00020B/2325